BILLY GRAHAM

ANGELS

HOW TO BE
BORN AGAIN

THOMAS NELSON
Since 1798

NASHVILLE   DALLAS   MEXICO CITY   RIO DE JANEIRO

OTHER BOOKS BY BILLY GRAHAM

Death and the Life After

The Holy Spirit

Hope for the Troubled Heart

How to Be Born Again

The Journey

Peace with God

The Secret of Happiness

Unto the Hills

ANGELS

BILLY GRAHAM

THOMAS NELSON
Since 1798

NASHVILLE   DALLAS   MEXICO CITY   RIO DE JANEIRO

ANGELS: GOD'S SECRET AGENTS

Published in Nashville, Tennessee, by Thomas Nelson. Thomas Nelson is a registered trademark of Thomas Nelson, Inc.

Thomas Nelson, Inc. titles may be purchased in bulk for educational, business, fund-raising, or sales promotional use. For more information, please e-mail SpecialMarkets@ThomasNelson.com.

ISBN 978-0-8499-4683-7

Library of Congress Cataloging-in-Publication Data

Graham, Billy, 1918–
    Angels: God's Secret Agents.
    ISBN 978-0-8499-4214-3 (TP)
    ISBN 978-0-8499-1167-2 (HC)
    ISBN 978-0-8499-1059-3 (TP)
    1. Angels. I. title.
    BT966.2.G7 1994 235'.3   94-31578

Printed in the United States of America

11 12 13 14 HCI 5 4 3 2 1

The angels are the dispensers and administrators of the divine beneficence toward us; they regard our safety, undertake our defense, direct our ways, and exercise a constant solicitude that no evil befall us.

JOHN CALVIN
Institutes of the Christian Religion, I

CONTENTS

PUBLISHER'S PREFACE

If ever there was a time when people needed the special power and blessings of heaven in their lives, that time is now. We live in troubled times. Political, social, and economic issues loom so large in our daily lives, we often seem to be in danger of losing any sense of happiness or peace. And many people have lost touch with basic values and beliefs. For many people, life is so difficult and serious that they simply don't pause to discover the inner strength that comes through the supernatural. That is why this book was written and why it is being released in this special new edition.

When this momentous work was first published in 1975, there was almost nothing in print on the subject of angels. True, there were many works on the occult, on mysticism, and even on devil worship. In the age of Charles Manson, many people were coming to believe in the reality of evil in the world. But the same people who were fascinated by movies such as *The Exorcist* or *Rosemary's Baby* apparently associated the whole subject of angels with fairy tales and fables. Even people with strong religious convictions weren't sure if angels even existed.

But many things have changed since 1975. For one thing, new beliefs and new ideas about spirituality have become all too common. The New Age movement has introduced a whole host of strange and disturbing beliefs about God and His creation. In early 1994 the *New York Times* best-seller list included eight separate books on the subject of angels. These works ranged from collections of poetry and fantasy to how-to courses on contacting the spirits. Most of them seemed to be written for the growing number of people who now believe in the dynamic forces of the spirit world but who have very little knowledge of what the Bible teaches on these subjects. At a time when many people have lost touch with their Christian heritage, there is a great risk of falling for ideas that sound exotic and appealing but that are actually misleading and extremely dangerous.

Yes, there are angels in our very midst—but not all supernatural forces are good, and not all angels are from God. Paul warns that "Satan transforms himself into an angel of light" and deceives many people—including many spiritual leaders. He writes, "Therefore it is no great thing if his ministers also transform themselves into ministers of righteousness, whose end will be according to their works" (2 Corinthians 11:14, 15 NKJV).

So the problem for people today is not simply believing that angels exist, but being able to distinguish between angels and demons. In bringing out this beautiful new edition of Billy Graham's classic book, we are excited to introduce a new generation to this timely message. You will discover how personal faith in Jesus Christ will allow you to experience the dynamic presence of angels in your daily life, along with unprecedented peace, fulfillment, and power. We trust that Dr. Graham's personal insights into this fascinating subject will help each reader achieve a new level of happiness and a dynamic, new hope for the future.

Preface to the
Second Edition

When I decided to preach a sermon on angels, I found practically nothing in my library. Upon investigation I soon discovered that little had been written on the subject in this century. This seemed a strange and ominous omission. Bookstores and libraries have shelves of books on demons, the occult, and the devil. Why was the devil getting so much more attention from writers than angels? Some people seem to put the devil on a par with God. Actually, Satan is a fallen angel.

Even when people in our modern age have had their attention drawn to the subject of angels from time to time, those ideas have often been fanciful or unbiblical. As I write this preface to the second edition, a popular television program tells the story of an "angel" who has been sent to earth in the form of a man to help people who are facing problems. The popularity of the program suggests many people find it great entertainment—but I cannot help but feel it also reinforces the idea in many minds that angels are just a product of our imagination, like Santa Claus or magical elves. But the Bible stresses their reality and underlines their constant—if unseen—ministry on behalf of God's people. In a materialistic world that nevertheless is riddled with evil and suffering, we need to discover afresh the Bible's teaching about angels.

The English painter Sir Edward Coley Burne-Jones wrote to Oscar Wilde that "the more materialistic science becomes, the more angels shall I paint: their wings are my protest in favor of the immortality of the soul."

Angels have a much more important place in the Bible than the devil and his demons. Therefore, I undertook a biblical study of the subject of angels. Not only has it been one of the most fascinating studies of my life, but I believe the subject is more relevant today than perhaps at any time in history.

The Bible teaches that angels intervene in the affairs of nations. God often uses them to execute judgment on nations. They guide, comfort, and provide for the people of God in the midst of suffering and persecution. Martin Luther once said in *Table Talk*, "An angel is a spiritual creature without a body created by God for the service of christendom and the church."

As an evangelist, I have often felt too far spent to minister from the pulpit to men and women who have filled stadiums to hear a message from the Lord. Yet again and again my weakness has vanished and my strength has been renewed. I have been filled with God's power not only in my soul but physically. On many occasions, God has become especially real, and has sent His unseen angelic visitors to touch my body to let me be His messenger for heaven, speaking as a dying man to dying men.

In the midst of a world that seems destined to live in a perpetual state of crisis, the subject of angels will be of great comfort and inspiration to believers in God—and a challenge to unbelievers to believe.

French philosopher and mathematician Blaise Pascal once said, "Certain authors, when they speak of their work say, 'my book,' 'my commentary,' 'my history.' They would be better to say 'our book,' 'our commentary,' 'our history,' since their writings generally contain more of other people's good things than their own."

This is our book, and I wish to thank all who have helped me with this intriguing and sometimes complicated subject.

In its writing, editing, and counseling, I am indebted to—Ralph Williams, who helped with research for my original writing of the manuscript; Dr. Harold Lindsell, former editor of *Christianity Today*, who went through the original manuscript and offered many helpful suggestions; and Mr. Paul Fromer, professor at Wheaton College, who helped with content, style, and organization.

To my faithful staff at Montreat who typed, retyped, and read the manuscript and called to my attention many areas of possible improvement—Karlene Aceto, Elsie Brookshire, Lucille Lytle, Stephanie Wills and Sally Wilson.

To Calvin Thielman, pastor of Montreat Presbyterian Church, and Dr. John Akers for their suggestions.

To my wife, Ruth, who was an encouragement and a help from start to finish.

Especially, to our heavenly Father who helped me see this neglected and important subject.

Through the months I have gathered ideas and even quotations from sources long-since forgotten. To everyone whose books and articles I have read, to every man or woman with whom I have talked or prayed about the subject of angels, I express my gratitude. Each has contributed to this book. I regret it is not possible to list each one by name.

This new edition of the book is largely as it was written in 1975. I have added some new material and expanded certain points.

It is still my prayer that God will use this book to bring comfort to the sick and the dying, to bring encouragement to those who are under the pressures of everyday living, and to bring guidance to those who are frustrated by the events of our generation.

Billy Graham
Montreat, North Carolina

1

ARE ANGELS
GOD'S SECRET AGENTS?

M y wife, who was born and raised in China, recalls that in her childhood days tigers lived in the mountains. One day a poor woman went up to the foothills to cut grass. To her back was tied a baby, and a little child walked beside her. In her hand she carried a sharp sickle to cut grass. Just as she reached the top of a hill, she heard a roar. Frightened almost speechless, she looked around to see a mother tigress springing at her, followed by two cubs.

This illiterate Chinese mother had never attended school or entered a church. She had never seen a Bible. But a year or two earlier a missionary had told her about Jesus, "who is able to help you when you are in trouble." As the claws of the tigress tore her arm and shoulder, the woman cried out in a frenzy, "O Jesus, help me!" The ferocious beast, instead of attacking again to get an easy meal, suddenly turned and ran away.

The Bible says, "He will give his angels charge of you, to guard you in all your ways" (Psalm 91:11 RSV). Had God sent an angel to help this poor ignorant Chinese woman? Are there supernatural beings today who are able to influence the affairs of men and nations?

In *A Slow and Certain Light*, Elizabeth Elliot told about her father's experiences with angelic helpers:

> My father, when he was a small boy, was climbing on an upper story of a house that was being built. He walked to the end of a board that was not nailed at the other end, and it slowly began to tip. He knew that he was doomed, but inexplicably the board began to tip the other way, as though a hand had pushed it down again. He always wondered if it was an angel's hand.

HELP FROM ANGELS

A celebrated Philadelphia neurologist had gone to bed after an exceptionally tiring day. Suddenly he was awakened by someone knocking on his door. Opening it he found a little girl, poorly dressed and deeply upset. She told him her mother was very sick and asked him if he would please come with her. It was a bitterly cold, snowy night, but though he was bone tired, the doctor dressed and followed the girl.

As *Reader's Digest* reports the story, he found the mother desperately ill with pneumonia. After arranging for medical care, he complimented the sick woman on the intelligence and persistence of her little daughter. The woman looked at him strangely and then said, "My daughter died a month ago." She added, "Her shoes and coat are in the clothes closet there." Amazed and perplexed, the doctor went to the closet and opened the door. There hung the very coat worn by the little girl who had brought him to tend to her mother. It was warm and dry and could not possibly have been out in the wintry night.

Could the doctor have been called in the hour of desperate need by an angel who appeared as this woman's young daughter? Was this the work of God's angels on behalf of the sick woman?

The Reverend John G. Paton, pioneer missionary in the New Hebrides Islands, told a thrilling story involving the protective care of angels. Hostile natives surrounded his mission headquarters one night, intent on burning the Patons out and killing them. John Paton and his wife prayed all during that terror-filled night that God would deliver them. When daylight came they were amazed to see that, unaccountably, the attackers had left. They thanked God for delivering them.

A year later, the chief of the tribe was converted to Jesus Christ, and Mr. Paton, remembering what had happened, asked the chief what had kept him and his men from burning down the house and killing them. The chief replied in surprise, "Who were all those men you had with you there?" The missionary answered, "There were no men there; just my wife and I." The chief argued that they had seen many men standing guard—hundreds of big men in shining garments with drawn swords in their hands. They seemed to circle the mission station so that the natives were afraid to attack.

Only then did Mr. Paton realize that God had sent His angels to protect them. The chief agreed that there was no other explanation. Could it be that God had sent a legion of angels to protect His servants, whose lives were being endangered?

A Persian colporteur was accosted by a man who asked him if he had a right to sell Bibles. "Why, yes," he answered, "we are allowed to sell these books anywhere in the country!" The man looked puzzled and asked, "How is it, then, that you are always surrounded by soldiers? I planned three times to attack you, and each time, seeing the soldiers, I left you alone. Now I no longer want to harm you." Were these soldiers heavenly beings?

During World War II, Captain Eddie Rickenbacker and the rest of the crew of the B-17 in which he was flying ran out of fuel and "ditched" in the Pacific Ocean. For weeks nothing was heard of him. The newspapers reported his disappearance, and across the country thousands of people prayed. Mayor LaGuardia asked the whole city of New York to pray for him. Then he returned. The Sunday papers headlined the news, and in an article, Captain Rickenbacker himself told what had happened. "And this part I would hesitate to tell," he wrote, "except that there were six witnesses who saw it with me. A gull came out of nowhere, and lighted on my head—I reached up my hand very gently—I killed him and then we divided him equally among us. We ate every bit, even the little bones. Nothing ever tasted so good." This gull saved the lives of Rickenbacker and his companions. Years later I asked him to tell me the story personally, because it was through this experience that he came to know Christ. He said, "I have no explanation except that God sent one of His angels to rescue us."

During my ministry I have heard or read literally thousands of stories. Could it be that these were all hallucinations or accidents or fate or luck? Or were real angels sent from God to perform certain tasks?

THE CURRENT CULT OF THE DEMONIC

Just a few years ago such ideas would have been scorned by most educated people. Science was king, and science was tuned in to believe only what could be seen or measured. The idea of supernatural beings was thought to be nonsense, the ravings of the lunatic fringe.

All this has changed. Think, for example, of the morbid fascination modern society has for the occult. Walk into a bookstore; visit any newsstand at a modern airport; go to a university library. You will be confronted by shelves and tables packed with books about the devil, Satan worship, and demon possession. A number of Hollywood films, television programs and as many as one in four hard-rock pop songs are devoted to, or thematically make reference to, the devil. Years ago the Rolling Stones sang their "Sympathy for the Devil" to the top of the popularity chart; another group answered back with a symphony to the devil.

The Exorcist proved to be one of the biggest money-makers of any film in history. Arthur Lyons gave his book a title that is frighteningly accurate: *The Second Coming: Satanism in America.* This theme, which intellectuals would have derided a generation ago, is now being dealt with seriously by such people as noted author John Updike and Harvard professor Harvey Cox. Some polls indicate that 70 percent of Americans believe in a personal devil. Some years ago Walter Cronkite announced a poll over his CBS network news showing that the number of Americans who believe in a personal devil has increased 12 percent. This was in the mid-1970s. What would the figure be today? It is ironic that a generation ago, scientists, psychologists, sociologists, and even some theologians were predicting that by the late 1970s there would be a sharp decline in belief in the supernatural. The reverse is true!

Some years ago, in a medium-sized metropolitan area, I turned out of curiosity to the entertainment pages of the local newspaper and studied them carefully. I was unprepared for the shock I received as I read the descriptions of the themes and content of the feature motion pictures being shown in the theaters in that area. They focused on sadism, murder, demon possession and demonism, devil worship and horror, not to mention those that depicted erotic sex. It seemed that each advertisement tried to outdo the others in the degree of shock, horror and mind-bending emotional devastation. The picture hasn't changed. If anything, the movies are even worse today!

Even in the Christian world the presses have turned out a rash of books on the devil by both Catholic and Protestant writers. I myself have thought about writing a book on the devil and his demons.

THE REALITY AND POWER OF SATAN

The Bible does teach that Satan is a real being who is at work in the world together with his emissaries, the demons. In the New

Testament they intensified their activities and bent every effort to defeat the work of Jesus Christ, God's Son. The apparent increase in satanic activity against people on this planet today may indicate that the second coming of Jesus Christ is close at hand. Certainly, the activity of Satan is evident on every side. We can see it in the wars and other crises that affect all people daily. We can also see it in the attacks of Satan against individual members of the body of Christ.

Some years ago I had dinner with several senators and congressmen in a dining room in the Capitol building. We began discussing the rising interest in the occult with special reference to *The Exorcist*. One of the senators, who had recently passed through a deep religious experience, said that due to his past experience with the occult, whenever he knew of a theater that was showing *The Exorcist* he would drive a block around it. He was afraid even to go near it. He said, "I know that both angels and demons are for real."

Several years ago the late Pope Paul said he was sure that the evil forces attacking every level of society had behind them the work of a personal devil with a whole kingdom of demons at his command. The Roman Catholic Church has been rethinking its position on the reality of the spirit world; and interest in this subject has revived among both theological liberals and evangelicals in Protestant churches everywhere.

UNIDENTIFIED FLYING OBJECTS

The renewed interest in the occult and satanism is not the only evidence of the new openness to the supernatural. It also was

revealed in the widespread revival of speculation about the so-
called "unidentified flying objects"—UFOs—some years ago. Even
some of today's popular movies center on visitors from outer space.

Some reputable scientists deny and others assert that UFOs do
appear to people from time to time. Some scientists have reached
the place where they think they can prove that these are possibly
visitors from outer space. Some Christian writers have speculated
that UFOs could very well be a part of God's angelic host who
preside over the physical affairs of universal creation. While we
cannot assert such a view with certainty, many people are now
seeking some type of supernatural explanation for these phenomena. Nothing can hide the fact, however, that these unexplained
events are occurring with greater frequency around the entire
world and in unexpected places.

Some years ago, Japan witnessed a typical example of unexplained objects that appeared in the night skies. On January 15,
1975, a squadron of UFO-like objects, resembling a celestial string
of pearls, soared silently through the evening skies over half the
length of Japan. As government officials, police, and thousands of
curious citizens stared at the sky in wonder, from fifteen to twenty
glowing objects, cruising in straight formation, flew over Japan
inside a strange misty cloud. Further, they were sighted and
reported in cities seven hundred miles apart in less than an hour.

Hundreds of frantic telephone calls jammed switchboards of
police stations and government installations as the spectacular formation sped south. "All the callers reported seeing a huge cloud
passing over the city."

They said they saw strange objects inside the cloud moving in a straight line, recalled Duty Officer Takeo Ohira. Were they planes? "No," said Hiroshi Mayazawa, "because no planes or natural phenomena appeared on my radar. It was an exceptionally clear night. To me the whole thing is a mystery."

Professor Masatoshi Kitamura watched the dazzling display in the night sky from the control room of Tokyo's Meteorological Bureau station near the airport. He said, "I was mystified. Nothing showed up on my radar. I reported my sighting to the airport control tower, and they told me nothing showed on their radar either."

OTHER EXPLANATIONS

Erich von Daniken's *Chariots of the Gods?*, published many years ago, was reissued in paperback by Berkeley in 1984. It theorizes that in prehistory astronauts from distant stars visited earth in spaceships. From these visits grew man's idea of gods and many of his conceptions of them. Immanuel Velikovsky, in his equally popular *Worlds in Collision* and *Ages in Chaos* put forward the notion that the turbulent history of the Middle East in the second millennium B.C. can be traced to a violent scattering of the solar system that caused ruin on earth. The knowledge of the intense suffering of those times was soon repressed but lies buried in man's racial memory, explaining his modern self-destructive behavior.

Men would dismiss these grandiose cosmologies lightly if it were not that they, along with a number of other theories, have been put forward with such frequency and serious import that no one can shrug them off. They are being studied seriously at many of our universities. As a theme for talk shows, hardly anything or anyone can top concerns like this.

Some sincere Christians, whose views are anchored in a strong commitment to Scripture, contend that these UFOs are angels. But are they? These people point to certain passages in Isaiah, Ezekiel, Zechariah, and the book of Revelation, and draw parallels to the reports of observers of alleged UFO appearances. They take the detailed descriptions, for example, of a highly credible airline crew and lay them alongside Ezekiel 10, and put forward a strong case. In Ezekiel 10 we read, "Each of the four cherubim had a wheel beside him—'The Whirl-Wheels,' as I heard them called, for each one had a second wheel crosswise within, sparkled like chrysolite, giving off a greenish-yellow glow. Because of the construction of these wheels, the cherubim could go straight forward in each of four directions; they did not turn when they changed direction but could go in any of the four ways their faces looked. . . And when they rose into the air the wheels rose with them, and stayed beside them as they flew. When the cherubim stood still, so did the wheels, for the spirit of the cherubim was in the wheels" (verses 9-13, 16-17 TLB).

Any attempt to connect such passages with the visits of angels may, at best, be speculation. Nor should we become too preoccupied or overly fascinated with trying to identify contemporary theories and speculations about UFOs or similar phenomena with biblical passages. Secular speculations often, in fact, run counter to the Bible's teaching concerning the origin of life on this planet. What is interesting, however, is that such theories are now being given serious attention even by people who make no claim to believe in the God of the Bible.

A further evidence of the renewed interest in the supernatural is the widespread fascination with extrasensory perception—ESP. The subjective science of parapsychology is now one of the fastest-growing fields of academic research in our universities today.

At Duke University, Dr. Joseph B. Rhine took up the study of extrasensory perception in the 1930s and championed it to the point where a department of parapsychology was established at the university. He became its pioneering professor. Today scientists are probing every conceivable frontier for ESP possibilities. Its line-up of protagonists reads like a Who's Who. Not only is serious intellectual and scientific study being carried on, but the subject is immensely popular because many of its aggressive proponents profess to be nonreligious. It has gained even more widespread respectability in communist societies (such as in the Soviet Union) than here in the United States. It plays a role of a "substitute religion" in some cases, although it has been used primarily as a technique to influence people.

Notice also the reaction on network talk shows. When a celebrity steps through the grand entrance and strolls to the guest chair, he is asked, "Do you believe in ESP?" To say, "No," in the middle 1980s would be as unfashionable as to have said, "Yes," a generation ago.

WHY I WROTE THIS BOOK

But why write a book on angels? Isn't talking about angels merely adding to the speculation about supernatural phenomena? What possible value is there in such a discussion? Didn't the fascination with angels vanish with the Middle Ages?

Because all the powers of the evil world system seem to be preying on the minds of people already disturbed and frustrated in our generation, I believe the time has come to focus on the positives of the Christian faith. John the apostle said, "Greater is he that is in you, than he that is in the world" (1 John 4:4). Satan is indeed capable of doing supernatural things—but he acts only by the permissive will of God; he is on a leash. It is God who is all powerful. It is God who is omnipotent. God has provided Christians with both offensive and defensive weapons. We are not to be fearful; we are not to be distressed; we are not to be deceived; nor are we to be intimidated. Rather, we are to be on our guard, calm and alert, "lest Satan should get an advantage of us, for we are not ignorant of his devices" (2 Corinthians 2:11).

One of Satan's sly devices is to divert our minds from the help God offers us in our struggles against the forces of evil. However, the Bible testifies that God has provided assistance for us in our spiritual conflicts. We are not alone in this world! The Bible teaches us that God's Holy Spirit has been given to empower us and guide us. In addition, the Bible—in nearly three hundred different places—also teaches that God has countless angels at His command. Furthermore, God has commissioned these angels to aid His children in their struggles against Satan. The Bible does not give as much information about them as we might like, but what it does say should be a source of comfort and strength for us in every circumstance.

I am convinced that these heavenly beings exist and that they provide unseen aid on our behalf. I do not believe in angels because someone has told me about a dramatic visitation from an angel, impressive as such rare testimonies may be. I do not believe in angels because UFOs are astonishingly angel-like in some of their reported appearances. I do not believe in angels because ESP experts are making the realm of the spirit world seem more and more plausible. I do not believe in angels because of the sudden worldwide emphasis on the reality of Satan and demons. I do not believe in angels because I have ever seen one—because I haven't.

I believe in angels because the Bible says there are angels; and I believe the Bible to be the true Word of God.

I also believe in angels because I have sensed their presence in my life on special occasions.

So what I have to say in the chapters that follow will not be an accumulation of my ideas about the spirit world, nor even a reflection of my own spiritual experiences in the spirit realm. I propose to put forward, at least in part, what I understand the Bible to say about angels. Naturally, this will not be an exhaustive study of the subject. I hope, however, that it will arouse your curiosity sufficiently for you to dig out from the Bible all that you can find on this subject after you have read this book. More than that, it is my prayer that you will discover the reality of God's love and care for you as evidenced in the ministry of His angels on your behalf, and that you would go forth in faith each day trusting God's constant watch-care over you.

Spiritual forces and resources are available to all Christians. Because our resources are unlimited, Christians will be winners. Millions of angels are at God's command and at our service. The hosts of heaven stand at attention as we make our way from earth to glory, and Satan's BB guns are no match for God's heavy artillery. So don't be afraid. God is for you. He has committed His angels to wage war in this conflict of the ages—and they will win the victory. The apostle Paul has said in Colossians 2:15, "And having spoiled principalities and powers, he made a show of them openly, triumphing over them." Victory over the flesh, the world, and the devil is ours now! The angels are here to help, and they are prepared for any emergency.

As you read this book, therefore, I pray that God will open your eyes to the resources He has provided for all who turn to Him for strength. I pray also that God will use it to show you your constant need of Him, and how He has sent His Son, Jesus Christ, into the world to deliver you from both the guilt and power of sin.

The British express train raced through the night, its powerful headlight piercing the darkness. Queen Victoria was a passenger on the train.

Suddenly the engineer saw a startling sight. Revealed in the beam of the engine's light was a strange figure in a black cloak standing in the middle of the tracks and waving its arms. The engineer grabbed for the brake and brought the train to a grinding halt.

He and his fellow trainmen clambered down to see what had stopped them. But they could find no trace of the strange figure. On a hunch the engineer walked a few yards further up the tracks. Suddenly he stopped and stared into the fog in horror. The bridge had been washed out in the middle and ahead of them it had toppled into a swollen stream. If the engineer had not heeded the ghostly figure, his train would have plummeted down the stream.

While the bridge and the tracks were being repaired, the crew made a more intensive search for the strange flagman. But not until they got to London did they solve the mystery.

At the base of the engine's headlamp, the engineer discovered a huge dead moth. He looked at it a moment, then on impulse wet its wings and pasted it to the glass of the lamp.

Climbing back into his cab, he switched on the light and saw the "flagman" in the beam. He knew the answer now: the moth had flown into the beam seconds before the train was due to reach the washed-out bridge. In the fog, it appeared to be a phantom figure waving its arms.

When Queen Victoria was told of the strange happening, she said, "I'm sure it was no accident. It was God's way of protecting us."

No, the figure the engineer saw in the headlight's beam was not an angel, yet God, quite possibly through the ministry of His unseen angels, had placed the moth on the headlight lens exactly when and where it was needed. Truly "he will command his angels concerning you to guard you in all your ways" (Psalm 91:11 NIV).

2

ANGELS ARE FOR REAL

Speculation about the nature of angels has been around since long before Queen Victoria's time, and it continues down to the present time. Yet through revelation in the Bible God has told us a great deal about them. For this reason, theologians through the ages have universally agreed about the importance of "angel-ology" (the orderly statement of biblical truth about angels). They judged it worthy of treatment in any book of systematic theology. They wrote at length, distinguishing between good angels and satanology (the study of fallen and thus evil angels). But today we have neglected the theme of good angels, although many are giving the devil and all of his demons rapt attention, even worshiping them.

Angels belong to a uniquely different dimension of creation that we, limited to the natural order, can scarcely comprehend. In this angelic domain the limitations are different from those God has imposed on our natural order. He has given angels higher knowledge, power, and mobility than humans. Have you ever seen or met one of these superior beings called angels? Probably not, for both the Bible and human experience tell us visible appearances by angels are very rare—but that in no way makes angels any less real or powerful. They are God's messengers whose chief business is to carry out His orders in the world. He has given them an ambassadorial charge. He has designated and empowered them as holy deputies to perform works of righteousness. In this way they assist Him as their creator while He sovereignly controls the universe. So He has given them the capacity to bring His holy enterprises to a successful conclusion.

ANGELS ARE CREATED BEINGS

Don't believe everything you hear (and read!) about angels! Some would have us believe that they are only spiritual will-o'-the-wisps. Some view them as only celestial beings with beautiful wings and bowed heads. Others would have us think of them as effeminate weirdos.

The Bible states that angels, like men, were created by God. At one time no angels existed; indeed there was nothing but the Triune God: Father, Son, and Holy Spirit. Paul, in Colossians 1:16, says, "For by him were all things created, that are in heaven, and that are in earth, visible and invisible." Angels indeed are among the invisible things made by God, for "all things were created by him, and for him." This creator, Jesus, "is before all things, and by him all things consist" (Colossians 1:17), so that even angels would cease to exist if Jesus, who is Almighty God, did not sustain them by His power.

It seems that angels have the ability to change their appearance and shuttle in a flash from the capital glory of heaven to earth and back again. Although some interpreters have said that the phrase "sons of God" in Genesis 6:2 refers to angels, the Bible frequently makes it clear that angels are nonmaterial; Hebrews 1:14 calls them ministering "spirits." Intrinsically, they do not possess physical bodies, although they may take on physical bodies when God appoints them to special tasks. Furthermore, God has given them no ability to reproduce, and they neither marry nor are given in marriage (Mark 12:25).

The empire of angels is as vast as God's creation. If you believe the Bible, you will believe in their ministry. They crisscross the Old and New Testaments, being mentioned directly or indirectly nearly three hundred times. Some biblical scholars believe that angels can be numbered potentially in the millions since Hebrews 12:22 speaks of "an innumerable [myriads—a great but indefinite number] company of angels." As to their number, David recorded twenty thousand coursing through the skyways of the stars. Even with his limited vision, he impressively notes, "The chariots of God are twenty thousand, even thousands of angels" (Psalm 68:17). Matthew Henry says of this passage, "Angels are 'the chariots of God,' his chariots of war, which he makes use of against his enemies, his chariots of conveyance, which he sends for his friends, as he did for Elijah . . . , his chariots of state, in the midst of which he shows his glory and power. They are vastly numerous: 'Twenty thousands,' even thousands multiplied."

Ten thousand angels came down on Mount Sinai to confirm the presence of God as He gave the Law to Moses (Deuteronomy 33:2). An earthquake shook the mountain. Moses was held in speech-bound wonder at this mighty cataclysm attended by the visitation of heavenly beings. Furthermore, in the New Testament John tells us of having seen ten thousand times ten thousand angels ministering to the Lamb of God in the throne room of the universe (Revelation 5:11). The book of Revelation also says that armies of angels will appear with Jesus at the Battle of Armageddon when God's foes gather for their final defeat. Paul says in 2 Thessalonians, "The Lord Jesus shall be revealed from heaven with his mighty angels" (1:7).

Think of it! Multitudes of angels, indescribably mighty, performing the commands of heaven! More amazingly, even one angel is indescribably mighty, as though an extension of the arm of God. Singly or corporately, angels are for real. They are better organized than were the armies of Alexander the Great, Napoleon, or Eisenhower. From earliest antiquity, when the angels guarding the gates of Eden sealed its entrance, angels have manifested their presence in the world. God placed angelic sentinels called cherubim at the east of the Garden of Eden. They were commissioned not only to bar man's return into Eden, but with "a flaming sword flashing back and forth to guard the way to the tree of life" (Genesis 3:24 NIV) lest Adam by eating of its fruit should live forever. If Adam had lived in his sin forever—this earth would long ago have been hell. Thus, in one sense, death is a blessing to the human race.

ANGELS SERVE GOD AND REGENERATE MEN

Witness the unprecedented and unrepeated pageantry at Mount Sinai. When God moves toward man, it is an event of the first magnitude and can include the visitation of angelic hosts. In the billowing clouds that covered Sinai, an angelic trumpeter announced the presence of God. The whole mountain seemed to pulsate with life. Consternation gripped the people below. The earth seemed convulsed with a nameless fear. As God came to the mountaintop, He was accompanied by thousands of angels. Moses, the silent, lone witness, must have been overcome with even a limited vision of the forces of God. It staggers the imagination to wonder what kind of a headline would be prompted in the daily press for even a man-sided view of such a heavenly visitation. "And so terrible was the sight, that Moses said, I exceedingly fear and quake" (Hebrews 12:21).

The appearance of God was glorious. He shone like the sun when it goes to its strength. In his commentary, Matthew Henry says, "Even Seir and Paran, two mountains at some distance, were illuminated by the divine glory which appeared on Mount Sinai, and reflected some of the rays of it, so bright was the appearance, and so much taken notice to set forth the wonders of the divine providence (Habakkuk 3:3, 4; Psalm 18:7–9). The Jerusalem Targum has a strange gloss [note of explanation] upon this, that, 'when God came down to give the law, he offered it on Mount Seir to the Edomites, but they refused it, because they found in it, *Thou shalt not kill*. Then he offered it on Mount Paran to the Ishmaelites, but they also refused it, because they found in it, *Thou shalt not steal*;

and then he came to Mount Sinai and offered it to Israel, and they said *All that the Lord shall say we will do.*'" This account by the Jerusalem Targum is, of course, fictional, but it throws an interesting light on how some Jews later regarded this extraordinary and spectacular event.

BELIEF IN ANGELS: A GENERAL PHENOMENON

The history of virtually all nations and cultures reveals at least some belief in angelic beings. Ancient Egyptians made the tombs of their dead more impregnable and lavish than their homes because they felt angels would visit there in succeeding ages. Islamic scholars have proposed that at least two angels are assigned to each person: one angel records the good deeds and the other the bad. In fact, long before Islam arose, and even apart from contact with Scripture, some religions taught the existence of angels. But no matter what the traditions, our frame of reference must be the Scripture as our supreme authority on this subject.

Today some hard-nosed scientists lend credence to the scientific probability of angels when they admit the likelihood of unseen and invisible intelligence. Increasingly, our world is being made acutely aware of the existence of occult and demonic powers. People pay attention as never before to sensational headlines promoting films and books concerning the occult. News accounts of strange happenings around the world fascinate readers and TV viewers everywhere. Ought not Christians, grasping the eternal dimension of life, become conscious of the sinless angelic powers who are for real, and who associate with God Himself and administer His works in our behalf? After all, references to the holy angels in the Bible far outnumber references to Satan and his subordinate demons.

COSMIC POWERS

If the activities of the devil and his demons seem to be intensifying in these days, as I believe they are, should not the incredibly greater supernatural powers of God's holy angels be even more indelibly impressed on the minds of people of faith? Certainly the eye of faith sees many evidences of the supernatural display of God's power and glory. God is still in business too.

Christians must never fail to sense the operation of angelic glory. It forever eclipses the world of demonic powers, as the sun does the candle's light.

If you are a believer, expect powerful angels to accompany you in your life experiences. And let those events dramatically illustrate the friendly presence of "the holy ones," as Daniel calls them.

Angels speak. They appear and reappear. They are emotional creatures. While angels may become visible by choice, our eyes are not constructed to see them ordinarily any more than we can see the dimensions of a nuclear field, the structure of atoms, or the electricity that flows through copper wiring. Our ability to sense reality is limited: The deer of the forest far surpass our human capacity in their keenness of smell. Bats possess a phenomenally sensitive built-in radar system. Some animals can see things in the dark that escape our attention. Swallows and geese possess sophisticated guidance systems that appear to border on the supernatural. So why should we think it strange if men fail to perceive the evidences of angelic presence? Could it be that God granted Balaam and his ass a new optical capacity to view the angel? (See Numbers 22:23, 31.) Without this special sense, they might have thought him to be only a figment of their imagination.

Reports continually flow to my attention from many places around the world telling of visitors of the angelic order appearing, ministering, fellowshiping, and disappearing. They warn of God's impending judgment; they spell out the tenderness of His love; they meet a desperate need; then they are gone. Of one thing we can be sure: angels never draw attention to themselves but ascribe glory to God and press His message upon the hearers as a delivering and sustaining word of the highest order.

Demonic activity and Satan worship are on the increase in all parts of the world. The devil is alive and more at work than at any other time. The Bible says that since he realizes his time is short, his activity will increase. Through his demonic influences he does succeed in turning many away from true faith; but we can still say that his evil activities are countered for the people of God by His ministering spirits, the holy ones of the angelic order. They are vigorous in delivering the heirs of salvation from the stratagems of evil men. They cannot fail.

Believers, look up—take courage. The angels are nearer than you think. For after all (as we have already noted), God has given "his angels charge of you, to guard you in all your ways. On their hands they will bear you up, lest you dash your foot against a stone" (Psalm 91:11–12 RSV).

3

ANGELS—VISIBLE OR INVISIBLE?

The spirit world and its activities are big news today. And the idea of the supernatural is not only seriously regarded, but is accepted as a fact. Many of the most recent books on the subject border on the sensational, or are purely speculative, or have been dreamed up in somebody's imagination. But those who take the Bible at full value cannot discount the subject of angels as speculation or hollow conjecture. After all, the Scriptures mention their existence almost three hundred times.

HAVE YOU EVER SEEN AN ANGEL?

I have already said that the angels are created spirit beings who can become visible when necessary. They can appear and disappear.

They think, feel, will, and display emotions. But some people have questions about them that ought not concern us. The old debate about how many angels can dance on the head of a pin is foolish. And to ask how many angels can be crowded into a telephone booth or into a Volkswagen hardly merits our attention. On the other hand, we should know what the Bible teaches about them as oracles of God who give divine or authoritative decisions and bring messages from God to men. To fulfill this function, angels have not infrequently assumed visible, human form. The writer to the Hebrews asks, "Are they [angels] not all ministering spirits?" (1:14). Now, have you ever seen a pure spirit? I can't say that I have. Yet I do know that down through the ages God has chosen to manifest His own spiritual presence in different ways. At the baptism of Jesus, God the Holy Spirit was present in the form of a dove. So God has chosen also to manifest His presence through His angels, who are lesser beings to whom He has given the power to assume forms that occasionally make them visible to men.

ARE ANGELS TO BE WORSHIPED?

It is no mere accident that angels are usually invisible. Though God in His infinite wisdom does not, as a rule, permit angels to take on physical dimensions, people tend to venerate them in a fashion that borders on worship. We are warned against worshiping the creature rather than the Creator (Romans 1:24–25). It is no less than heretical, and indeed is a breach of the first commandment, to worship any manifestation of angelic presence, patron, or blesser.

Paul has pointed out that while unusual manifestations may be deeply significant, Jesus Christ the incarnate God, the second person of the Trinity, who is creator of all things and by whom all things exist, is worthy of our worship (Colossians 2:18). We are not to pray to angels. Nor are we to engage in "a voluntary humility and worshiping" of them. Only the Triune God is to be the object of our worship and of our prayers.

Moreover, we should not confuse angels, whether visible or invisible, with the Holy Spirit, the third person of the Trinity and Himself God. Angels do not indwell men; the Holy Spirit seals them and indwells them when he has regenerated them. The Holy Spirit is all-knowing, all-present, and all-powerful. Angels are mightier than men, but they are not gods and they do not possess the attributes of the Godhead.

Not angels, but the Holy Spirit convicts men of sin, righteousness, and judgment (John 16:7). He reveals and interprets Jesus Christ to men, while angels remain messengers of God who serve men as ministering spirits (Hebrews 1:14). So far as I know, no Scripture says that the Holy Spirit ever manifested Himself in human form to men. Jesus did this in the incarnation. The glorious Holy Spirit can be everywhere at the same time, but no angel can be in more than one place at any given moment. We know the Holy Spirit as spirit, not flesh, but we can know angels not as spirits alone but sometimes also in visible form.

At the same time, both angels and the Holy Spirit are at work in our world to accomplish God's perfect will. Frankly, we may not always know the agent or means God is using—the Holy Spirit or the angels—when we discern God's hand at work. We can be sure, however, that there is no contradiction or competition between

God the Holy Spirit and God's command of the angelic hosts. God Himself is in control to accomplish His will—and in that we can rejoice!

God uses angels to work out the destinies of men and nations. He has altered the courses of the busy political and social arenas of our society and directed the destinies of men by angelic visitation many times over. We must be aware that angels keep in close and vital contact with all that is happening on the earth. Their knowledge of earthly matters exceeds that of men. We must attest to their invisible presence and unceasing labors. Let us believe that they are here among us. They may not laugh or cry with us, but we do know they delight with us over every victory in our evangelistic endeavors. Jesus taught that "there is joy in the presence of the angels of God when one sinner repents" (Luke 15:10 TLB).

ANGELS VISIBLE? INVISIBLE?

In Daniel 6:22 we read, "My God hath sent his angel, and hath shut the lions' mouths." In the den, Daniel's sight evidently perceived the angelic presence, and the lions' strength more than met its match in the power of the angel. In most instances, angels, when appearing visibly, are so glorious and impressively beautiful as to stun and amaze men who witness their presence.

Can you imagine a being, white and dazzling as lightning? General William Booth, founder of the Salvation Army, described a vision of angelic beings, stating that every angel was surrounded with an aura of rainbow light so brilliant that were it not withheld, no human being could stand the sight of it.

Who can measure the brilliance of the lightning flash that illuminates the countryside for miles around? The angel who rolled away the stone from the tomb of Jesus was not only dressed in white, but shone as a flash of lightning with dazzling brilliance (Matthew 28:30). The keepers of the tomb shook and became as dead men. Incidentally, that stone weighed several times more than a single man could move, yet the physical power of the angel was not taxed in rolling it aside.

Abraham, Lot, Jacob and others had no difficulty recognizing angels when God allowed them to manifest themselves in physical form. Note, for example, Jacob's instant recognition of angels in Genesis 32:1, 2. "And Jacob went on his way, and the angels of God met him. And when Jacob saw them, he said, This is God's host: and he called the name of that place Mahanaim."

Further, both Daniel and John described the glories of the angels (Daniel 10:6 and Revelation 10:1) visibly descending from heaven with immeasurable beauty and brilliance, shining like the sun. Who has not thrilled to read the account of the three Hebrew children, Shadrach, Meshach, and Abednego? They refused to fall in line with the music of obeisance and worship the king of Babylon. They learned that the angel presence can be observed on occasion by people in the unbelieving world on the outside. After they had refused to bow, the angel preserved them from being burned alive or even having the smell of smoke on their garments from the seven-times-hotter fire. The angel came to them in the midst of the flame without harm and was seen by the king who said, "I see four men . . . in the midst of the fire" (Daniel 3:25).

On the other hand, the Bible indicates angels are more often invisible to human eyes. Whether visible or invisible, however, God causes His angels to go before us, to be with us, and to follow after us.

All of this can be fully understood only by believers who know that angelic presences are in control of the battlefield about us, so that we may stand with complete confidence in the midst of the fight. "If God be for us who can be against us?" (Romans 8:31).

WHAT DO YOU SEE WHEN YOU SEE AN ANGEL?

God is forever imaginative, colorful, and glorious in what He designs. Some of the descriptions of angels, including the one of Lucifer in Ezekiel 28, indicate that they are exotic to the human eye and mind. Apparently angels have a beauty and variety that surpass anything known to men. Scripture does not tell us what elements make up angels. Nor can modern science, which is only beginning to explore the realm of the unseen, tell us about the constitution or even the work of angels.

The Bible seems to indicate that angels do not age, and never says that one was sick. Except for those who fell with Lucifer, the ravages of sin that have brought destruction, sickness, and chaos to our earth have not affected them. The holy angels will never die.

The Bible also teaches that angels are sexless. Jesus said that in heaven men "neither marry, nor are given in marriage, but are as the angels of God in heaven" (Matthew 22:30). This may indicate that angels enjoy relationships that are far more thrilling and exciting than sex. The joy of sex in this life may be only a foretaste of something that believers will enjoy in heaven which is far beyond anything man has ever known.

How are we to understand "theophanies"? (This is a theological term for the visible appearances of Jesus Christ in other forms prior to His incarnation.) Some passages in the Old Testament tell us that the second person of the Trinity appeared and was called either "the Lord" or "the angel of the Lord." Nowhere is it clearer than in Genesis 18 where three men appear before Abraham. Their leader is clearly identified with the Lord, whereas the other two are merely angels. There are no grounds for questioning the very early and traditional Christian interpretation that in these cases there is a preincarnation manifestation of the second person of the Trinity, whether He is called "the Lord" or "the Angel of the Lord" (*Zondervan Pictorial Encyclopedia of the Bible*).

We must remember, then, that in some cases in the Old Testament God Himself appeared in human form as an angel. This reinforces the idea of the relationship between God and His angels. Nevertheless, in almost all of the cases where angelic personages appear, they are God's created angelic beings and not God Himself.

Yes, angels are real. They are not the product of our imagination, but were made by God Himself. Think of it! Whether we see them or not, God has created a vast host of angels to help accomplish His work in this world. When we know God personally through faith in His Son, Jesus Christ, we can have confidence that the angels of God will watch over us and assist us because we belong to Him.

4

ANGELS—HOW THEY
DIFFER FROM MAN

The Bible tells us that God has made man "a little lower than the angels." Yet it also says angels are "ministering spirits, sent forth to minister for them who shall be heirs of salvation" (Hebrews 2:5–7; 1:13–14). This sounds like a contradiction: man lower—but eventually higher through redemption. How can we explain this?

First we must remember that this Scripture is speaking both of Jesus Christ and men. Jesus did "stoop" when He became man. And as a man He was a little lower than the angels in His humanity—although without losing in any sense His divine nature. But it also speaks about men other than Jesus. God has made men head over all the creatures of our earthly world, but they are lower than angels with respect to their bodies and to their place while here on earth. In his *Institutes*, John Calvin said, "The angels are the dispensers and administrators of the Divine beneficence toward us; they regard our safety, undertake our defense, direct our ways, and exercise a constant solicitude that no evil befall us."

God commands angels to help men since they will be made higher than the angels at the resurrection. So says Jesus in Luke 20:36. God will alter the temporary lower position of man when the kingdom of God has come in its fullness.

Now let us examine in detail how God says angels differ from men. Although angels are glorious beings, the Scriptures make it clear that they differ from regenerated men in significant ways. How can the angels who have never sinned fully understand what it means to be delivered from sin? How can they understand how precious Jesus is to those for whom His death on Calvary brings light, life, and immortality? Is it not stranger still that angels themselves will be judged by believers who were once sinners? Such judgment, however, apparently applies only to those fallen angels who followed Lucifer.

Thus Paul writes in 1 Corinthians 6:3, "Know ye not that we shall judge angels?" But even the holy angels have limitations, though the Bible speaks of them as being superior to men in many ways.

IS GOD "FATHER" TO ANGELS?

God is not called "Father" by the holy angels because, not having sinned, they need not be redeemed. All the fallen angels cannot call God "Father" because they cannot be redeemed. The latter case is one of the mysteries of Scripture: God made provision for the salvation of fallen men, but He made no provision for the salvation of fallen angels. Why? Perhaps because, unlike Adam and Eve, who were enticed toward sin by sinners, the angels fell when there were no sinners, so no one could entice them to sin. Thus, their sinful state cannot be altered; their sin cannot be forgiven; their salvation cannot be achieved.

The wicked angels would never want to call God "Father," though they may call Lucifer "father," as many Satan worshipers do. They are in revolt against God and will never voluntarily accept His sovereign lordship, except in that Day of Judgment when every knee will bow and every tongue confess that Jesus Christ is Lord (Philippians 2:9–10). Yet even holy angels who might like to call God "Father" could do so only in the looser sense of that word. As Creator, God is the Father of all created beings; since angels are created beings, they might think of Him this way. But the term is normally reserved in Scripture for lost men who have been redeemed. So in a real sense, even ordinary men cannot call God "Father" except as their Creator God—until they are born again.

ANGELS ARE NOT HEIRS OF GOD

Christians are joint heirs with Jesus Christ through redemption (Romans 8:17), which is made theirs by faith in Him based on His death at Calvary. Angels who are not joint heirs must stand aside when the believers are introduced to their boundless, eternal riches. The holy angels, however, who are ministering spirits, have never lost their original glory and spiritual relationship with God. This assures them of their exalted place in the royal order of God's creation. By contrast, Jesus identified Himself with fallen men in the incarnation when He was "made a little lower than the angels for the suffering of death" (Hebrews 2:9). That He chose to taste the death we deserve also shows that the holy angels do not share our sinfulness—nor our need of redemption.

ANGELS CANNOT TESTIFY OF

SALVATION BY GRACE THROUGH FAITH

Who can comprehend the overwhelming thrill of fellowship with God and the joy of salvation that even angels do not know? When the local church assembles as a group of Christian believers, it represents in the human sphere the highest order of the love of God. No love could go deeper, rise higher, or extend farther than the amazing love that moved Him to give His only begotten Son. The angels are aware of that joy (Luke 15:10), and when a person accepts God's gift of eternal life through Jesus Christ, angels set all the bells of heaven to ringing with their rejoicing before the Lamb of God.

Yet although the angels rejoice when people are saved and glorify God who has saved them, they cannot do one thing: testify personally to something they have not experienced. They can only point to the experiences of the redeemed and rejoice that God has saved them. This means that throughout eternity we humans alone will give our personal witness to the salvation that God achieved by grace and that we received through faith in

Jesus Christ. The man who has never married cannot fully appreciate the wonders of that relationship. The person who has never lost a father or mother cannot understand what the loss means. So angels, great as they are, cannot testify to salvation the same way as those who have experienced it.

ANGELS HAVE NO EXPERIENTIAL KNOWLEDGE
OF THE INDWELLING GOD

Nothing in the Bible indicates that the Holy Spirit indwells angels as He does redeemed people. Since He seals believers when they accept Christ, such sealing would be unnecessary for the angels who never fell and who therefore need no salvation.

But there is a second reason for this difference. Redeemed men on earth have not yet been glorified. Once God has declared them just and given them life, He embarks on a process of making them inwardly holy while they live here below. At death, He makes them perfect. So the Holy Spirit takes His abode in the hearts of all believers while they are still on earth, to perform His unique ministry, one that angels cannot perform. God the Father sent Jesus the Son to die; Jesus performed His unique ministry as His part of God's saving process. Likewise, the Holy Spirit has a role, one different from the Son's. Sent by the Father and the Son, He not only guides and directs believers, but also performs a work of grace in their hearts, conforming them to the image of God to make them holy like Christ. Angels cannot provide this sanctifying power.

Furthermore, angels themselves do not need the ministry of

the Holy Spirit the way believers do. The angels have already been endowed with authority by virtue of their relationship to God through creation and continuing obedience. They are unspoiled by sin. People, however, are not yet perfect and therefore need what the Holy Spirit alone can give. Someday we will be as perfect as angels are now.

ANGELS DO NOT MARRY OR PROCREATE

I have already said that angels do not marry. In Matthew 22:30, Jesus points out that "in the resurrection they [men] neither marry, nor are given in marriage, but are as the angels of God in heaven." Because of this we can make a deduction: the number of angels remains constant. For the obedient angels do not die. The fallen angels will suffer the final judgment at the time God finishes dealing with them. While we cannot be certain, some scholars estimate that as many as one-third of the angels cast their lot with Satan when he mysteriously rebelled against his Creator. In any event, the book of Hebrews says the angels constitute an "innumerable company," vast hosts that stagger our imagination. A third of them would likely be counted in the hundreds of thousands—ones who are now desperate demons.

Just as angels differ from people with respect to marriage, so they differ in other important ways. Nothing in Scripture says that angels must eat to stay alive. But the Bible says that on certain occasions angels in human form did indeed eat. David refers to the manna eaten by the children of Israel in the wilderness as the bread of angels. In Psalm 78:25, Asaph says, "Man did eat angels' food." We can hardly disregard what happened to Elijah after he won a great victory over the priests of Baal on Mount Carmel. Because Jezebel threatened his life, he needed help from God. So God's angel came to the tired, discouraged prophet and set before him food and drink. When he had eaten twice he was sent on his journey; the food he had eaten was enough to keep him for forty days and forty nights (1 Kings 19:5). Not without reason some have concluded that Elijah indeed ate angels' food.

When Abraham was encamped in the plains of Mamre, three angels visited him, of whom one may have been the Lord Jesus (Genesis 18:1–2). These heavenly beings ate and drank what he provided for them by way of customary entertainment. Shortly thereafter, when God decided to destroy Sodom and Gomorrah, two angelic beings came to save backslidden Lot and his family. Lot made them a feast, and there again they ate food, including unleavened bread (Genesis 19).

It is interesting that after His resurrection, Jesus ate with His disciples. Luke's account says that the disciples "gave him a piece of a broiled fish, and of an honeycomb. And he took it, and did eat before them" (Luke 24:42–43).

THE KNOWLEDGE OF ANGELS

Angels excel humankind in their knowledge. When King David was being urged to bring Absalom back to Jerusalem, Joab asked a woman of Tekoah to talk to the king. She said: "My lord is wise, according to the wisdom of an angel of God, to know all things that are in the earth" (2 Samuel 14:20). And angels possess knowledge that men do not have. But however vast is their knowledge, we can be sure they are not omniscient. They do not know everything. They are not like God. Jesus bore testimony to the limited knowledge of the angels when He was speaking of His second coming. In Mark 13:32, He said, "But of that day and that hour knoweth no man, no, not the angels which are in heaven."

Angels probably know things about us that we do not know about ourselves. And because they are ministering spirits, they will always use this knowledge for our good and not for evil purposes. In a day when few men can be trusted with secret information, it is comforting to know that angels will not divulge their great knowledge to hurt us. Rather, they will use it for our good.

THE POWER OF ANGELS

Angels enjoy far greater power than men, but they are not omnipotent or "all powerful." In 2 Thessalonians 1:7, Paul refers to the "mighty angels of God." From the word translated "mighty" here we get the English word *dynamite*. In material power, angels are God's dynamite! In 1 Peter we read, "Angels who are greater in might and power [than men] do not bring a reviling judgment against them before the Lord" (2 Peter 2:11 NASB). Peter's testimony here reinforces Paul's. We should also note that it took only one angel to slay the firstborn of Egypt in Moses' day, and one to shut the lions' mouths for Daniel.

In Psalm 103:20, David speaks about [God's] "angels that excel in strength." Nowhere in Scripture is that strength manifested more dramatically than in the climax of this age. Following the

Battle of Armageddon, Scripture pictures what will happen to Satan: He is to be bound and cast into a bottomless pit. But what power, apart from God Himself, can do this to Satan, whose power we all know about and whose evil designs we have experienced? The Bible says that one angel will come from heaven. He will have a great chain in his hand. He will lay hold of Satan and bind him with that chain. And then he will cast him into the pit. How great is the power of one of God's mighty angels.

DO ANGELS SING?

There has been much conjecture about angel choirs. We at least assume that angels can and do sing, even if the Scriptures do not pointedly say so. In *Hamlet*, William Shakespeare seemed to underscore the possibility that angels sing when he stated, "Now cracks a noble heart, Good night, sweet prince: / and flights of angels sing thee to thy rest."

Some Bible students insist that angels do not sing. This seems inconceivable. Angels possess the ultimate capacity to offer praise, and their music from time immemorial has been the primary vehicle of praise to our all-glorious God. Music is the universal language. It is likely that John saw a massive heavenly choir (Revelation 5:11–12) of many millions who expressed their praise of the heavenly Lamb through magnificent music. I believe angel choirs will sing in eternity to the glory of God and the supreme delight of the redeemed.

While it is partly speculative, I believe that angels have the capacity to employ heavenly celestial music. Many dying believers have testified that they have heard the music of heaven. Most of my close friends tease me because I cannot carry a tune. When I am singing beside people in a congregation, I usually throw them off-key. But from years of listening I recognize good music when I hear it—even if I can't produce it myself. And there have been times when I have seriously tried to understand and appreciate music I did not like, whether it was a difficult opera or rock. I think that before we can understand the music of heaven, we will have to go beyond our earthly concept of music. I think most earthly music will seem to us to have been in the "minor key" in comparison to what we are going to hear in heaven.

The Bible tells us of many who sang: Moses (Exodus 15:1), Miriam (Exodus 15:20–21), David (Psalms), and many others. Thousands of worshipers at the temple continually sang, praising the Lord (2 Chronicles 5:12). Thousands of singers preceded the ark of the covenant (1 Chronicles 15:27–28). We all think of Psalms as the hymnbook of the Bible.

New Testament believers also sang with rapturous joy. Though the Bible does not say it, it implies that angels, who are of a higher creative order, are tuned to sing with no discordant note to God and the Lamb. Paul reminds us that there is a language of man and a language of angels (1 Corinthians 13:1). Angels have a celestial language and make music that is worthy of the God who made them. I believe in heaven we will be taught the language and music of the celestial world. The wonderful hymn "Holy, Holy Is What the Angels Sing" by Johnson Oatman, Jr., and J. Sweney expresses this thought in verse 4:

So, altho' I'm not an angel,
yet I know that over there
I will join the blessed chorus
that the angels cannot share;
I will sing about my Saviour,
who upon dark Calvary
Freely pardoned my transgressions,
died to set a sinner free.

ANGELS WORSHIP BEFORE THE THRONE

Unquestionably angels ascribe honor and glory to the Lamb of God. But angels do not spend all their time in heaven. They are not omnipresent (everywhere present at the same time), so they can be in only one place at a given time. Yet, as God's messengers, they are busy around the world carrying out God's orders. Is it not, therefore, obvious that when they are engaged in their ministry here they cannot stand before God's throne? But when angels do stand before the throne of God, indeed they worship and adore their Creator.

We can look for that future day when angels will have finished their earthly ministry. Then they will gather with all the redeemed before the throne of God in heaven. There they will offer their praise and sing their songs. In that day the angels who veiled their faces and stood mute when Jesus hung on the cross will then ascribe glory to the Lamb whose work is finished and whose kingdom has come. The angels may also stop to listen as the redeemed children of God express their own thanksgiving for salvation. It may well be true as the hymn writer has said in verse 3 of, "Holy, Holy Is What the Angels Sing:"

> Then the angels stand and listen,
> for they cannot join that song,
> Like the sound of many waters,
> by that happy, blood-washed throng.

But the children of God will also stop to listen to the angels. They have their own reasons for singing, ones that differ from ours. They have given themselves to the service of God Almighty. They have had a part in bringing in the kingdom of God. They have helped the children of God in difficult circumstances. So theirs shall be a shout and a song of victory. The cause they represent has been victorious; the fight they fought is finished; the enemy they met has been conquered; their wicked companion angels who fell shall vex them no more. The angels sing a different song. But they sing; my, how they sing! And I believe that angels and those of us who have been redeemed will compete with each other for the endless ages of eternity to see who can best ascribe glory and praise to our wonderful God!

Do you have that hope of eternity in your heart right now? Do you know—beyond doubt—that some day you will join the angels in heaven in singing praises to God? If not, make your commitment to Christ today. Without Christ you are separated from God and without hope of eternal life. You need to have your sins forgiven, and you need to be renewed and cleansed by the power of God. And this can happen if you will give your life to Christ and trust Him as your personal Lord and Savior. Christ came to take away your sins by His death on the cross. You deserved to die—but He died in your place! "For Christ died for sins once for all, the righteous for the unrighteous, to bring you to God" (1 Peter 3:18 NIV). Right now by a simple prayer of faith you can know that some day you will join with the angels and with millions of believers from across the ages in singing praises to God in heaven. Take that step of faith today.

5

ANGELIC ORGANIZATION

We cannot study the subject of angels in the Bible without becoming aware of ranks among angelic beings. The evidence shows that they are organized in terms of authority and glory.

Though some see the ranking of celestial powers as conjectural, it seems to follow this pattern: archangels, angels, seraphim, cherubim, principalities, authorities, powers, thrones, might, and dominion (Colossians 1:16; Romans 8:38).

Medieval theologians divided angelic beings into ten grades. Some people, however, have asked whether some of these grades—the principalities, authorities, powers, thrones, might, and dominion—could not refer to human institutions and human beings. To answer, we must understand Colossians 1:16. Paul is speaking about creation of things both seen and unseen. On this verse Matthew Henry says that Christ "made all things out of nothing, the highest angel in heaven as well as men upon earth. He made the world, the upper and lower world, with all the inhabitants of both. . . . He [Paul] speaks here as if there were several orders of angels: 'Whether thrones, or dominions, or principalities, or powers,' which must signify either different degrees of excellence or different offices and employments." Perhaps any list that ranks angelic beings will err, but we can be sure they differ in power, some having authority others do not possess. While I do not wish to be dogmatic, I think there are different ranks of angels and that the list given in Colossians does refer to these celestial personalities. Let's look at four of them:

ARCHANGEL

While Scripture designates only Michael as an archangel (Jude 9), we have biblical grounds for believing that before his fall Lucifer was also an archangel, equal or perhaps superior to Michael. The prefix "arch" suggests a chief, principal, or great angel. Thus, Michael is now the angel above all angels, recognized in rank to be the first prince of heaven. He is, as it were, the prime minister in God's administration of the universe, and is the "angel administrator" of God for judgment. He must stand alone, because the Bible never speaks of archangels, only *the* archangel. His name means "who is like unto the Lord."

In the Old Testament, Michael seems to be identified primarily with Israel as a nation. Thus, God speaks of Michael as prince of His chosen people, "the great prince which standeth for the children of thy people" (Daniel 12:1). He especially protects and defends God's people whoever they are.

Further, in Daniel he is referred to as "Michael, your prince" (Daniel 10:21). He is God's messenger of law and judgment. In this capacity he appears in Revelation 12:7–12 leading the armies that battle Satan, the great dragon, and all of his demons. Michael with his angels will be locked in the titanic struggle of the universe at the last conflict of the age, which will mark the defeat of Satan and all forces of darkness. Scripture tells us in advance that Michael will finally be victorious in the battle. Hell will tremble; heaven will rejoice and celebrate!

Bible students have speculated that Michael cast Lucifer and his fallen angels out of heaven, and that Michael enters into conflict with Satan and the evil angels today to destroy their power and to give to God's people the prospect of their ultimate victory.

Michael, the archangel, will shout as he accompanies Jesus at His second coming. Not only does he proclaim the matchless and exciting news that Jesus Christ returns, but he speaks the word of life to all who are dead in Christ and who await their resurrection. "For the Lord himself shall descend from heaven with a shout, with the voice of the archangel . . . and the dead in Christ shall rise first" (1 Thessalonians 4:16).

THE ANGEL GABRIEL

Gabriel is one of the most prominent angels mentioned in Scripture.

Gabriel, in Hebrew, means "God's hero," or "the mighty one," or

"God is great." Scripture frequently refers to him as "the messenger of Jehovah" or "the Lord's messenger." However, contrary to popular opinion and to the poet John Milton, it never calls him an archangel. Yet it refers to his work more often than to Michael's.

Ministry of Gabriel

Gabriel is primarily God's messenger of mercy and promise. He appears four times in the Bible, always bearing good news (Daniel 8:16; 9:21; Luke 1:19, 26). We may question whether he blows a silver trumpet, since this idea arises from folk music and finds only indirect support in Scripture. But the announcements of Gabriel in unfolding the plans, purposes, and verdicts of God are of monumental importance.

In Scripture we gain our first glimpse of Gabriel in Daniel 8:15–16. There he announces the vision of God for the "end time." God has charged him to convey the message from the "situation room" of heaven that reveals God's plan in history. In verse 17 Gabriel says, "Understand, . . . the vision belongs to (events that shall occur in) the time of the end" (AMP).

Daniel, while in prayer, records Gabriel's second appearance to him: "While I was speaking in prayer, the man Gabriel, whom I had seen in the former vision, being caused to fly swiftly, came near to me and touched me about the time of the evening sacrifice" (Daniel 9:21 AMP). To Daniel he said, "Understand the vision" (9:23), and then revealed to him the magnificent sequence of events at the end time. Gabriel, sketching panoramically the procession of earthly kingdoms, assured Daniel that history would culminate in the return of Christ, "the prince of princes" (Daniel 8:25

AMP) and conqueror of the "king of fierce countenance" (Daniel 8:23 AMP). The prophetic announcement by Daniel in his prayer to God is twofold. He expressly refers to the more immediate judgment upon Israel (Daniel 9:16) and then to the awesome portent of "end-time judgment" and "tribulation," which shall be for "seven years" (Daniel 9:27). In a later chapter, "Angels in Prophecy," we will trace how the angels supervise the fearsome events of the end time.

Gabriel in the New Testament

Gabriel first appears in the New Testament in Luke 1. He identifies himself to Zacharias (verse 19), announces the birth of John the Baptist, and describes his life and ministry as the forerunner of Jesus.

But in his most important appearance, Gabriel informs the Virgin Mary about Jesus, the incarnate God! What a message to deliver to the world through a teenage girl! What a wonderfully holy girl she must have been, to be visited by the mighty Gabriel. He declares:

> Fear not, Mary: for thou hast found favour with God. And, behold, thou shalt conceive in thy womb, and bring forth a son, and shalt call his name Jesus. . . . And he shall reign over the house of Jacob for ever; and of his kingdom there shall be no end. (Luke 1:30–33)

Throughout all time, this divine declaration of Gabriel shall be the Magna Charta of the incarnation and the foundation stone of the world to come: God became flesh to redeem us.

SERAPHIM

It would appear from the Bible that celestial and extraterrestrial beings differ in rank and authority. The seraphim and cherubim follow in order after the archangel and angels. These may possibly define the angelic authority to which Peter refers when he speaks of Jesus, "who is gone into heaven, and is on the right hand of God; angels and authorities and powers being made subject unto him" (1 Peter 3:22).

The word *seraphim* may come from the Hebrew root meaning "love" (though some think the word means "burning ones" or "nobles"). We find the seraphim only in Isaiah 6:1–6. It is an awe-inspiring sight as the worshiping prophet beholds the six-winged seraphim above the throne of the Lord. We can assume that there were several seraphim, since Isaiah speaks about "each one" and "one cried unto another."

The ministry of the seraphim is to praise the name and character of God in heaven. Their ministry relates directly to God and His heavenly throne, because they are positioned above the throne—unlike the cherubim, who are beside it. Students of the Bible have not always agreed on the duties of the seraphim, but we know one thing: they are constantly glorifying God. We also learn from Isaiah 6:7 that God can use them to cleanse and purify His servants.

They were indescribably beautiful. "With two [wings] he covered his face, and with two he covered his feet, and with two he did fly" (implying that some angelic beings fly). The Scriptures do not, however, support the common belief that all angels have wings. The traditional concept of angels with wings is drawn from their ability to move instantaneously and with unlimited speed from place to place, and wings were thought to permit such limitless movement. But here in Isaiah 6 only two of the seraphim's wings were employed for flying.

The glory of the seraphim reminds us of Ezekiel's description of the four living creatures. He did not call them seraphim, but they too performed their service for God. Like seraphim they acted as both agents and spokesmen of God. In both cases, the glory displayed was a witness to God, though only the seraphim, of course, hovered over the heavenly throne as functionaries and attendants, with a chief duty of praising God. In all these manifestations, we see God willing that men should know of His glory. He determines to maintain an adequate witness to that glory in both terrestrial and celestial realms.

CHERUBIM

Cherubim are real, and they are powerful. But the cherubim in the Bible were often symbolic of heavenly things. "At God's direction they were incorporated into the design of the Ark of the Covenant and the Tabernacle. Solomon's temple utilized them in its decoration" (*Zondervan Pictorial Encyclopedia*). They had wings, feet, and hands. Ezekiel 10 pictures the cherubim in detail as having not only wings and hands, but being "full of eyes," encompassed by "wheels within wheels."

But Ezekiel sounds a somber note in chapter 10 also, and the cherubim provide the clue. The prophet presents his vision that prophesies the destruction of Jerusalem. In Ezekiel 9:3, the Lord has descended from His throne above the cherubim to the threshold of the temple, while in 10:1 He returns again to take His seat above them. In the calm before the storm, we see the cherubim stationed on the south side of the sanctuary. Being stationed in position toward the city, they witness the beginning of the gradual withdrawal of God's glory from Jerusalem. The fluttering of their wings indicates immensely important events to follow (10:5). Then the cherubim rise up in preparation for the departure.

While Ezekiel 10 is difficult to understand, one point comes across clearly. The cherubim have to do with the glory of God. This chapter is one of the most mysterious and yet descriptive passages of the glory of God to be found in the Bible, and it involves angelic beings. It should be read carefully and prayerfully. The reader gets a sense of God's greatness and glory as in few other passages in the Bible.

While the seraphim and the cherubim belong to different orders and are surrounded by much mystery in Scripture, they share one thing. They constantly glorify God. We see the cherubim beside the throne of God. "Thou that dwellest between the cherubim, shine forth" (Psalm 80:1). He sitteth between the cherubim" (Psalm 99:1). God's glory will not be denied, and every heavenly being gives silent or vocal testimony to the splendor of God. In Genesis 3:24, we see cherubim guarding the tree of life in Eden. In the tabernacle in the wilderness, designs representing the guardian cherubim formed a part of the mercy seat and were made of gold (Exodus 25:18).

The cherubim did more than guard the most holy place from

those who had no right of access to God. They also assured the right of the high priest to enter the holy place with blood as the mediator with God on behalf of the people. He, and he alone, was permitted to enter into the inner sanctuary of the Lord. By right of redemption and in accordance with the position of believers, each true child of God now has direct access as a believer-priest to the presence of God through Jesus. Cherubim will not refuse the humblest Christian access to the throne. They assure us that we can come boldly—because of Christ's work on the cross! The veil in the temple has been rent. As Paul says, "Ye are no more strangers and foreigners, but fellow citizens with the saints, and of the household of God" (Ephesians 2:19). Further, Peter assures, "Ye are a chosen generation, a royal priesthood, an holy nation, a peculiar people; that ye should show forth the praises of him who hath called you out of darkness into his marvelous light" (1 Peter 2:9).

The inner sanctuary of God's throne is always open to those who have repented of sin and trusted Christ as Savior.

Many believe that the "living creatures" often mentioned in the book of Revelation are cherubim. But as glorious as the angelic and heavenly beings are, they become dim beside the inexpressible glory resident in our heavenly Lamb, the Lord of glory, to whom all powers in heaven and on earth bow in holy worship and breathless adoration.

6

LUCIFER AND
THE ANGELIC REBELLION

Few people realize the profound part angelic forces play in human events. It is Daniel who most dramatically reveals the constant and bitter conflict between the holy angels faithful to God and the angels of darkness allied with Satan (Daniel 10:11–14). This Satan, or the devil, was once called "Lucifer, the son of the morning." Along with Michael, he may have been one of the two archangels, but he was cast from heaven with his rebel forces, and continues to fight. Satan may appear to be winning the war because sometimes he wins important battles, but the final outcome is certain. One day he will be defeated and stripped of his powers eternally. God will shatter the powers of darkness.

Many people ask, "How could this conflict come about in

God's perfect universe?" The apostle Paul calls it "the mystery of iniquity" (2 Thessalonians 2:7). While we have not been given as much information as we might like, we do know one thing for certain: The angels who fell, fell because they had sinned against God. In 2 Peter 2:4 the Scripture says, "God spared not the angels that sinned but cast them down to hell, and delivered them into chains of darkness, to be reserved unto judgment." Perhaps the parallel passage in Jude 6 puts the onus of responsibility more directly on the shoulders of the angels themselves. "The angels," wrote Jude quite deliberately, "kept not their first estate, but left their own habitation."

Thus, the greatest catastrophe in the history of the universal creation was Lucifer's defiance of God and the consequent fall of perhaps one-third of the angels who joined him in his wickedness.

When did it happen? Sometime between the dawn of creation and the intrusion of Satan into the Garden of Eden. The poet Dante reckoned that the fall of the rebel angels took place within twenty seconds of their creation and originated in the pride that made Lucifer unwilling to await the time when he would have perfect knowledge. Others, like Milton, put the angelic creation and fall immediately prior to the temptation of Adam and Eve in the Garden of Eden.

The important question is not, "When were angels created?" but, "When did they fall?" It is difficult to suppose that their fall occurred before God placed Adam and Eve in the garden. We know for a fact that God rested on the seventh day, or at the end of all creation, and pronounced everything to be good. By implication, up to this time even the angelic creation was good. We might then ask, "How long were Adam and Eve in the garden before the angels fell and before Satan tempted the first man and woman?" This question must remain unanswered. All we can say positively is that Satan, who had fallen before he tempted Adam and Eve, was the agent and bears a greater guilt because there was no one to tempt him when he sinned; on the other hand, Adam and Eve were faced with a tempter.

Thus, we pick up the story where it began. It all started mysteriously with Lucifer. He was the most brilliant and most beautiful of all created beings in heaven. He was probably the ruling prince of the universe under God, against whom he rebelled. The result was insurrection and war in heaven! He began a war that has been raging in heaven from the moment he sinned and was brought to earth shortly after the dawn of human history. It sounds like a modern world crisis!

Isaiah 14:12–14 records the conflict's origin. Prior to his rebellion, Lucifer, an angel of light, is described in scintillating terms in Ezekiel 28:12–17 (NASB): "You had the seal of perfection, full of wisdom and perfect in beauty. . . . You were the anointed cherub who covers, and I placed you there. You were on the holy mountain of God. You walked in the midst of the stones of fire. You were blameless in your ways from the day you were created, until unrighteousness was found in you. . . . Your heart was lifted up because of your beauty; you corrupted your wisdom by reason of your splendor." When the angel Lucifer rebelled against God and His works, some have estimated that as many as one-third of the angelic hosts of the universe may have joined him in his rebellion. Thus, the war that started in heaven continues on earth and will see its climax at Armageddon with Christ and His angelic army victorious.

Leslie Miller, in his excellent little book *All About Angels*, points out that Scripture sometimes refers to angels as stars. This explains why prior to his fall Satan was called "the star of the morning." And to this description John adds a qualifying detail: "His tail swept a third of the stars out of the sky and flung them to the earth" (Revelation 12:4 NIV).

REBELLION IN HEAVEN

The apostle Paul understood and spoke of the war of rebellion in the heavens when he referred to the former Lucifer, now Satan, as "the prince of the power of the air, the spirit that now worketh in the children of disobedience" (Ephesians 2:2). He also says that in fighting the organized kingdom of satanic darkness, we struggle against "the world forces of this darkness . . . the spiritual forces of wickedness in the heavenly places" (Ephesians 6:12 NASB).

We can describe all unrighteousness and transgression against God as "self-will" against the will of God. This definition applies to human beings today as well as to angels.

LUCIFER'S FIVE "I WILLS"

Lucifer, the son of the morning, was created, as were all angels, for the purpose of glorifying God. However, instead of serving God and praising Him forever, Satan desired to rule over heaven and creation in the place of God. He wanted supreme authority!

Lucifer said (Isaiah 14), "I will ascend into heaven." "I will exalt my throne above the stars of God." "I will sit also upon the mount of the congregation." "I will ascend above the heights of the clouds." "I will be like the most high." I . . . I . . . I . . . I . . . I.

Lucifer was not satisfied with being subordinated to his creator. He wanted to usurp God's throne. He exulted at the thought of being the center of power throughout the universe—he wanted to be the Caesar, the Napoleon, the Hitler of the entire universe. The "I will" spirit is the spirit of rebellion. His was a bold act to dethrone the Lord Most High. Here was a wicked schemer who saw himself occupying the superlative position of power and glory. He wanted to be worshiped, not to worship.

Satan's desire to replace God as ruler of the universe may have been rooted in a basic sin that leads to the sin of pride I have already mentioned. Underneath Satan's pride lurked the deadliest of all sins, the sin of covetousness. He wanted what did not belong to him. Virtually every war ever fought began because of covetousness. The warfare in heaven and on earth between God and the devil certainly sprang from the same desire—the lust for what belonged to God alone.

Today, as always in the past, virtually no one can sin alone. The influences of sin are contagious. The Bible speaks of "the dragon . . . and his angels" (Revelation 12:7), indicating that along with Lucifer, myriads of angels also chose to deny the authority of God and subsequently lost their high position. They chose to participate in the "war program" of Lucifer. As a result of their fall, those angels have been "reserved unto judgment" (2 Peter 2:4) and have their part with Lucifer in the "everlasting fire, prepared for the devil and his angels" (Matthew 25:41). But until this happens, they constitute a mighty force—capable of wreaking havoc among individuals, families, and nations! Watch out for, they are dangerous, vicious and deadly. They want you under their control, and they will pay any price to get you!

Satan, the fallen prince of heaven, has made his decision to battle against God to the death. He is the master craftsman who has plotted destruction during all the ages since he first rebelled. His "I will" spirit has worked through his consuming hatred of God to write his tragic story in the annals of human history. In his warfare against God, Satan uses the human race, which God created and loved. So God's forces of good and Satan's forces of evil have been engaged in a deadly conflict from the dawn of our history. Unless world leaders and statesmen understand the true nature of this warfare, they will continue to be blind leaders of the blind. They can only patch a little here and patch a little there. We will find no final solution to the world's great problems until this spiritual warfare has been settled. And it will be settled in the last war of history—Armageddon. Then Christ and His angelic armies will be the victors!

PAST, PRESENT, AND FUTURE IN PERSPECTIVE

Lucifer became Satan, the devil, the author of sin; and it is sin that has always deceived, disturbed, betrayed, depraved, and destroyed all that it has touched.

Will there never be an end to this battle of the ages, this war against God lustfully conceived in Lucifer and perpetrated on earth?

Not only does the battle rage on earth, but it rages in heaven. "And there was war in heaven: Michael and his angels fought against the dragon; and the dragon fought and his angels . . . and the great dragon was cast out" (Revelation 12:7, 9).

Satan and his demons are known by the discord they promote, the wars they start, the hatred they engender, the murders they initiate, the opposition to God and His commandments. They are dedicated to the spirit of destruction. On the other hand the holy angels obey their Creator. No discordant note sounds among the angels of heaven. They are committed to fulfill the purpose for which all true children of God pray, "Thy kingdom come. Thy will be done . . . as it is in heaven" (Matthew 6:10).

The Bible refers to Lucifer and the fallen angels as those who sinned and did not keep their first position (Jude 6). They committed the sins of consummate pride and covetousness. The sin of pride particularly has caused the downfall of Lucifer in heaven; most certainly it can bring mortal man down too. We must be on guard against pride, or we are headed for a fall patterned after the fall of Lucifer and his angels, who turned into demons.

Could it be that God wanted to be sure that men would not question the existence of Satan and his demon-hosts? Perhaps He had this in mind when He inspired the writing of Ezekiel 28, which sets forth the typology of Satan in the earthly sense. This account by the prophet Ezekiel speaks of an earthly prince of the city of Tyre. He seems to be an earthly symbol of Satan. It is clear from the passage that the king of Tyre became a devil incarnate and an earthly illustration of the heavenly Lucifer who became the devil.

We live in a perpetual battlefield—the great war of the ages continues to rage. The lines of battle press in ever more tightly about God's own people. The wars among nations on earth are merely popgun affairs compared to the fierceness of battle in the spiritual, unseen world. This invisible spiritual conflict is waged around us incessantly and unremittingly. Where the Lord works, Satan's forces hinder; where angel beings carry out their divine directives, the devils rage. All this comes about because the powers of darkness press their counterattack to recapture the ground held for the glory of God.

Were it not for the angel hosts empowered by God to resist the demons of Satan, who could ever hope to press through the battlements of the fiendish demons of darkness to the Lord of eternal liberty and salvation? Paul speaks the truth when he says that the forts of darkness are impregnable. Yet they yield to the warfare of faith and light as angel hosts press the warfare to gain the victory for us (2 Corinthians 10:4–5).

SATAN ON THE ATTACK

Revelation 12:10 speaks of Satan as "the accuser of the brethren" and Ephesians 6:12 (NIV) describes the "rulers . . . authorities . . . the powers of this dark world . . . the spiritual forces of evil in the heavenly realms." Although Satan and his evil followers press their warfare in the heavens, it seems that their primary endeavor is to destroy faith in the world.

Isaiah 13:12–14 clearly points up Satan's objectives: he works to bring about the downfall of nations, to corrupt moral standards, and to waste human resources. Corrupting society's order, he wants to prevent the attainment of order and to shake the kingdoms of our God. He uses his destructive power to create havoc, fire, flood, earthquake, storm, pestilence, disease, and the devastation of peoples and nations. The description of Satan's great power ends with the words, "who opened not the house of his prisoners" (Isaiah 14:17). This undoubtedly refers to the prison house of Satan, Hades or the abode of the dead so clearly pictured in Luke 16:19–31.

Satan has great power. He is cunning and clever, having set himself against God and His people. He will do everything in his power to hold people captive in sin and to drag them down to the prison of eternal separation from God.

Since the fall of Lucifer, that angel of light and son of the morning, there has been no respite in the bitter battle of the ages. Night and day Lucifer, the master craftsman of the devices of darkness, labors to thwart God's plan of the ages. We can find inscribed on every page of human history the consequences of the evil brought to fruition by the powers of darkness with the devil in charge. Satan never yields an inch, nor does he ever pause in his opposition to the plan of God to redeem the "cosmos" from his control. He forever tries to discredit the truthfulness of the Word of God; he coaxes men to deny the authority of God; and he persuades the world to wallow in the deluding comforts of sin. "He was a murderer from the beginning, not holding to the truth, for there is no truth in him. When he lies, he speaks his native language, for he is a liar and the father of lies" (John 8:44 NIV). Sin is the frightful fact in our world. It writes its ruin in vice and lust, in the convulsions of war, in selfishness and sorrow, and in broken hearts and lost souls. It remains as the tragedy of the universe and the tool of Satan to blunt or destroy the works of God.

SATANIC INTRIGUE

God cannot tolerate sin forever if He is just. He will not permit the perversions of Lucifer to mock Him, for the inescapable answer to the evil of the world is found in the unalterable law of the Word of God that "the wages of sin is death; but the gift of God is eternal life through Jesus Christ our Lord" (Romans 6:23). Satan's attacks, which began at the dawn of history, will continue until God begins to bring down the curtain on this frightening drama at Armageddon.

Satan's ideology is based on the little word "if." Through all time he has sought to discredit God by making Him out a liar in the eyes of man. He never ceases trying to discredit the claims of the Word of God and to rob mankind of the strength and comfort of faith. The all-time tool of Lucifer is an "if," but God declares that there are no "ifs," "buts," or "ands" about His program for salvation. God's plan is unalterable; His antidote for the satanic "if" works and is unchangeable. God assures us that through the work of Christ and the labors of His angelic deputies, we can look for the triumphant and victorious warfare over the armies of Lucifer.

It is not surprising that the fallen Lucifer hatched his plot to usurp the preeminence of God in His creation. In the first conversation in the garden, the serpent embodying Lucifer asked, "Hath God said, Ye shall not eat of every tree of the garden?" (Genesis 3:1). To this question Eve replied, "But God did say, You must not eat fruit from the tree that is in the middle of the garden, and you must not touch it, or you will die" (Genesis 3:3 NIV).

Hear Lucifer reply, if you eat of the fruit of this tree "ye shall not surely die" (Genesis 3:4). He says in effect that God does not know what He is talking about.

Satan often works by interjecting a question to raise doubts. It is deadly to doubt God's Word! Satan's strategy is to persuade us to rationalize. Eve probably began to reason with the enemy: Is it possible that God would be so unjust and unkind as to forbid this seemingly innocent thing?—"It was pleasant to the eyes" (Genesis 3:6).

Eve foolishly parleyed with the tempter. In her own mind she began to doubt the truth and the wisdom of God. How easily Satan covers with a light color ideas that are dark. His intrigue comes to us colored in the light of our own desires. Time after time he injects his subtle "ifs." "This tree is to be desired to make one wise." Eve listened; she reasoned with herself, she took, she tasted. Satan never fails to appeal to the appetites of the flesh and to the seeming sensual satisfactions that come from the inventions of sin. Our senses are inlets through which Satan can work, prod, and inject his deadly "ifs."

The Genesis account states that Eve ate first and then gave some to Adam to eat. If they had fixed their minds on God and trusted His wisdom, recognizing the danger that lurked in the fruit He had forbidden, all history would have been radically different and had another ending. Had they only realized the consequences of disobedience, had they only seen the danger of the satanic "if," had they only envisioned the flaming sword barring them forever from the garden! Had they only realized the terrible consequences of a single "innocent" moment, they would not have had to stand over the silent, lifeless form of their son Abel. His tragic death was the fruit of the seductive power of sin in their own lives. Apart from it our world would have been paradise today!

Had Adam and Eve resisted the devil, he would have fled, forever defeated. But they fell, and thus death passed upon all men (Genesis 3:13). This is where death began! Sin works the same with all of us, whatever our condition, nature, or environment. We are depraved by nature because we inherited it from our parents (Romans 3:19). The stream has been polluted. We must bear the sentence of guilt and the stain of sin. Each must give account of himself to God.

Listen to Satan's "ifs" of death being injected into the minds of people today: "if" you live a good life, "if" you do what is right, "if" you go to church, "if" you work for the benefit of others—if, if, if. But the Bible teaches that these "ifs" are not enough to meet God's requirements for salvation. Our good works and intentions are not enough. Jesus said, "Ye must be born again" (John 3:7). Only when we turn to Christ in faith and trust, confessing our sins to Him and seeking His forgiveness, can we be assured of our salvation. Satan will do all in his power to make us trust ourselves instead of Christ. But only Christ can save us—and He will, if we will commit our lives to Him and trust His work on the cross for our salvation. "For God so loved the world that he gave his one and only Son, that whosoever believes in him shall not perish but have eternal life" (John 3:16 NIV).

These are Satan's approaches today. The hiss of the serpent is the "if" of death. The stench of death is everywhere today! As C. S. Lewis points out, "War does not increase death—death is total in every generation." But we can find eternal life when we believe in Jesus Christ.

Have you made your personal commitment to Christ, and are you trusting Him alone for your salvation? If you have never taken that step of faith, or if you are unsure about your relationship to Christ, turn to Him today and receive Him as your personal Lord and Savior. "To all who received him, to those who believed in his name, he gave the right to become children of God" (John 1:12 NIV). This can be your experience today if you will ask Christ to come into your heart by faith.

7

ANGELS AS
MESSENGERS OF GOD

Angels minister to us personally. Many accounts in Scripture confirm that we are the subjects of their individual concern. In his book *Table Talk*, Martin Luther said, "An angel is a spiritual creature created by God without a body, for the service of Christendom and the church."

We may not always be aware of the presence of angels. We can't always predict how they will appear. But angels have been said to be our neighbors. Often they may be our companions without our being aware of their presence. We know little of their constant ministry. The Bible assures us, however, that one day our eyes will be unscaled to see and know the full extent of the attention angels have given us (1 Corinthians 13:11–12).

Many experiences of God's people suggest that angels have been ministering to them. Others may not have known they were being helped, yet the visitation was real. The Bible tells us that God has ordered angels to minister to His people—those who have been redeemed by the power of Christ's blood.

DANIEL AND THE ANGEL

In the Old Testament, Daniel vividly describes the bitter conflict between the angelic forces of God and the opposing demons of darkness. Before the angel came to him, he had spent three weeks mourning (Daniel 10:3). He ate no bread, meat, or wine, nor did he anoint himself. As he stood by the Tigris River, a man appeared clothed in linen. His face looked like lightning and his eyes like flaming torches. His voice sounded like the roar of a crowd.

Daniel alone saw the vision. The men who were with him did not. Yet a great dread came upon them, and they ran away to hide. Left alone with the heavenly visitor, Daniel's strength departed from him, so great was the effect of this personage on him.

Daniel was held in the bonds of a great sleep, yet he heard the voice of the angel. A hand touched him, and the angel described an experience he himself had just had. The angel had started to come to Daniel from the moment he began to pray but enroute was waylaid by a demon prince who engaged him in conflict and delayed him. Then Michael came to help this subordinate angel, freeing him to fulfill his mission to Daniel.

The angel had a message. He was to show Daniel what God foresaw would befall the world—especially Israel in the latter days. Daniel then found himself weak and unable to speak, so the angel touched his lips and also restored his strength. Having finished his mission, the angel told Daniel he was returning to fight with the demon prince in the unending struggle of the forces of good versus the forces of evil. In all this Daniel was having no hallucination or dream. It was a genuine experience with a real person, and no one ever could have persuaded Daniel otherwise.

He had pleaded with God for the sons of Israel. His prayer session, accompanied by fasting, had lasted for three weeks. At that moment he received the news from the "angel visitor" sent from heaven that his prayer had been heard. This incident makes it clear that delays are not denials, and that God's permissive will is involved in all of life.

UNSEEN FORCES AT WORK

During several world crises I have had the privilege of talking with some heads of state or secretaries of state. During the 1967 War in the Middle East, for example, Secretary of State Dean Rusk, who was visiting my home town of Montreat, North Carolina, invited me to his room. While we were discussing the war that had just broken out, I told him I believed "supernatural forces are at work."

On the eve of one of his missions abroad during the Ford Administration, Secretary of State Kissinger briefed me on some of the staggering problems facing the world. I told him I believed the world was experiencing an unseen spiritual war in which the powers of darkness were attacking the forces of God. As we have moved through the turbulent events of the past decade, I have become more convinced than ever that the activities of the unseen demonic forces are increasing. A well-known television newscaster said to me in his office, "The world is out of control." It seems incredible that such a warfare is taking place—but the Bible says it is!

Dr. A. C. Gaebelein has called it "the conflict of the ages." It will be resolved only when Jesus Christ returns to earth. This is why the world is crying for "a leader." The Antichrist, who will be Satan's "front," will arrive on the scene for a brief time and seemingly be "The Answer." But after only a few months, the world will be thrown back into chaos and conflict. He will prove to be "The Lie" (2 Thessalonians 2:3–10). Then the One whom God chose and anointed before time began will return to earth with His mighty, holy angels. At the end of the age, He will throw the devil and his demons into the lake of fire. Thus, for the true believer the conflict now raging will end as God intends. Righteousness will prevail.

JACOB'S EXPERIENCE

The experience of Jacob with angels is a splendid illustration of their ministry for God to men. In some ways Jacob was a cheat. He had stolen the birthright from his brother. He lied to his father and deceived him when his sight was almost gone. He fled from his brother, who would have killed him. He married his Uncle Laban's two daughters, and when their father and brothers no longer looked on him with favor, he took his family and flocks back to Canaan.

Though Jacob was a cunning schemer and skilled in deception,

God was concerned for him as the one who was in "the line of promise." From him the twelve tribes of Israel were to come. While he was en route home, the Scripture tells us that "the angels of God met him." So overcome was he by what happened that he said, "This is God's army!" (Genesis 32:2 AB), and called the place Mahanaim, meaning "two camps." He called the angels "God's hosts." But the story does not end there. Having formerly cheated his brother Esau, he now feared him, not knowing whether he would be welcomed or killed. So Jacob prayed, admitting he was not worthy of the least of God's mercies. He asked to be delivered from the hand of his brother Esau.

The night before Jacob met Esau he was alone, his family and servants having gone ahead. Suddenly a man appeared and wrestled with him until daybreak, when he finally touched Jacob's thigh, "and the hollow of the thigh was out of joint." At this, Jacob realized the man was a heavenly visitor and would not let him go until the man had blessed him. When he had told the stranger his name, the man said, "Thy name shall be called no more Jacob, but Israel: for as a prince hast thou power with God and with men and hast prevailed." When Jacob asked the man to identify himself, he received no reply. But the man blessed him there. Jacob called the place Peniel, meaning "face of God," saying, "I have seen God face to face, and my life is preserved" (Genesis 32:24–30).

It may well be that the wrestler was Jesus, appearing fleetingly in human form. In the former part of the story, many angels were surrounding Jacob. Through the two experiences, God revealed His will for Jacob's life more fully and promised that he would be a prince. The next day he therefore went forward cheerfully to meet Esau; everything turned out well for him and his family. Centuries later Hosea testified to this incident, saying that the God of heaven had appeared to Jacob, ministering to him in the person of an angel (Hosea 12:3–6).

Moses and Abraham are perhaps the two greatest Old Testament characters; angels were involved in their lives on important occasions. We have already seen how angels ministered to Abraham. We must look at the experience of Moses at the burning bush (Exodus 3).

MOSES MEETS AN ANGEL

The background is important. For forty years Moses had lived amid the splendors of Egypt, coming to know its language, customs, and laws. He lived a life of luxury and occupied an important position in the social structure. Then, because of the misadventure of slaying an Egyptian, he fled to the desert. For forty years more he was tutored as a sheepherder in the "university of solitude." Scripture says little about that period, but it represented a great change in circumstances to go from the court of Pharaoh to a field of grazing sheep. It was not exactly an occupation that ranked high in the social order. He was an outcast, a lonely figure compared to his former life. And it took God forty years to bring him to the place where he was serviceable for the job God had in mind for him. So it was that at eighty years of age when the life work of most people has already been completed, Moses was ready for God's call.

One day as he was going about his duties, Moses saw a bush burning. It struck him as peculiar because the bush was not consumed. More than that, "the angel of the LORD appeared unto him in a flame of fire out of the midst of the bush." Since we have no reason to suppose that Moses had ever seen an angel before, this must have been an extraordinary visitation to him. Further, his curiosity was aroused. Then it was that God Himself spoke to Moses out of the bush.

Moses was profoundly moved. Having told him to remove his shoes because he was standing on holy ground, God identified Himself as the God of Abraham, Isaac and Jacob. At this Moses was awestruck and hid his face, fearing to look at God. God then disclosed to Moses His plan to release the Israelites from their captivity in Egypt, using Moses as their leader. When asked by Moses whom he should say had told him this when he approached the Israelites, God responded, "Say I AM hath sent me unto you."

Moses was not at all enthusiastic about what God told him to do. He began to offer what he thought were compelling reasons to be excused from that service. First, he said that the people of Israel would never believe him and therefore would not accept his leadership. In answer, God asked him what he had in his hand. Moses said, "a rod." "Cast it on the ground," God said, and suddenly it became a serpent. But when Moses picked it up, it again became a rod. Then at God's command he put his hand in his robe and, withdrawing it, found it leprous. But putting it back a second time and withdrawing it, he found it free of all disease. By such signs, God said, would He show the people Moses' divine commission.

Then Moses made another excuse: he said he couldn't talk, professing to be slow of speech. Perhaps this was the result of forty years in virtual silence on the backside of the desert, but God even refused this excuse, saying He would send Aaron to be his voice. And so Moses went from the desert to Egypt to begin the work of deliverance. But the incident is important in our study because it is tied closely to the angel of the Lord in the burning bush. This again shows that God used angels (or appeared as an angel) to make His will known and communicate His decisions to men.

The presence of angels became part of "the Exodus experience." Thus, in Numbers 20:16 the Bible says, "When we cried unto the LORD, he heard our voice, and sent an angel, and hath brought us forth out of Egypt." Isaiah says that "in all their affliction he was afflicted, and the angel of his presence saved them: in his love and in his pity he redeemed them; and he bare them, and carried them all the days of old" (63:9). It may well be that some of these instances involved angelic forms taken by Jesus Christ, the second person of the Trinity. We can only speculate. In that event, it makes alive the thrilling testimony of Paul who declared that "Jesus Christ [is] the same yesterday, and today, and forever" (Hebrews 13:8).

THE MYSTERY OF ANGELS

Therefore, just as Jesus is with us now through the Holy Spirit, revealing Himself and His will, so was He with His people in ages past, and so shall He be for all time to come, the angel of God's presence who leads us. To His "faithful" of past ages, God the Father revealed His presence through angels; through the angel of the Lord, God the Son, Jesus Christ, He revealed Himself and redeemed us by the Son's crucifixion, death, and resurrection. Here is mystery too deep for any of us to fathom fully.

Jewish scholars called the angel of the Lord by the name "Metatron, the angel of countenance," because He witnesses the countenance of God continuously and, therefore, works to extend the program of God for each of us.

God has given us the fullest revelation—Jesus Christ in the flesh—so He no longer needs to manifest Himself in the form of "the angel of the Lord" in this age of grace. Consequently, the angels who appear in the New Testament or even today are always "created spirits" and not God in that special angel form He used now and then in the Old Testament. The appearance of God the Son in physical form (a theophany) in the Old Testament is no longer necessary. Consider the presence of angels in the New Testament subsequent to the thrilling account of the birth of God the Son in the flesh through His incarnation at Bethlehem. The angels then were to minister the message of God and to establish the message of the gospel of Christ but never to supplant it or to detract from it.

ANGELS ARE MINISTERING SPIRITS

God uses both men and angels to declare His message to those who have been saved by grace. "Are they [angels] not all ministering spirits, sent forth to minister for them who shall be heirs of salvation?" (Hebrews 1:14). What a glorious honor it will be for angels to know us by name because of our faithful witness to others. Angels will share our rejoicing over those who repent (Luke 15:10), even though they cannot preach the gospel themselves.

In this regard, consider Philip the deacon, whom God was

using as a minister of revival in Samaria. An angel appeared with instructions for him to go to the desert (Acts 8:26), and by God's appointment he met the Ethiopian to whom he became the voice for God in preaching the word of truth.

Angels visited John too. As he looked out upon the lonely seas from the Isle of Patmos and wondered why he was isolated from all but heaven, the angel of the apocalypse came to announce the message that formed the book of Revelation with its prophecies of the end time (Revelation 1:1–3).

An angel ministered in a somewhat similar way in an incident in Daniel's life. Chapter 5 describes a great feast ordered by Belshazzar in Babylon. It had been prepared ostensibly to show the glory of the kingdom, but in reality Belshazzar meant it to parade his own personal greatness. It was a feast for the thousands of his kingdom's greatest nobles. But on this occasion they desecrated the sacred vessels taken from the temple at Jerusalem by using them for an ignoble purpose: they ate, drank and offered homage to idols of wood and stone, silver and gold. The god of materialism was in power. Suddenly the fingers of a man's hand appeared and traced on the wall a record of God's judgment on Babylon. "Mene, Mene, Tekel, Upharsin," the hand wrote—"You have been weighed in the balances and been found wanting. Your kingdom is finished" (verses 25–27). It was one of God's angels sent to announce the impending judgment. Not only were the days of King Belshazzar numbered, but God was finished with him.

Later Daniel prayed for the people, "And he [Gabriel] informed me, and talked with me, and said, O Daniel, I am now come forth to give thee skill and understanding. . . . therefore, understand the matter, and consider the vision" (Daniel 9:22–23). In answer to Daniel's prayer, God gave him a panoramic view of the future "history" of the human race. It is my belief that the world is now possibly reaching the climax of those great visions that God gave Daniel.

The scene in the time of Belshazzar seems almost contemporary, those times and conditions resembling so closely what we see and hear today. It may even be that God is writing another story of impending judgment through the crises of the hour. He is telling men everywhere that unless they repent of their sins, their days like Belshazzar's are numbered and they are finished.

Let us conclude this study of the personal ministry of angels by noting some further incidents when God used angels to declare His plan to men.

THE ANGEL GABRIEL

At the beginning of the New Testament, Zacharias the priest saw the angel of the Lord, receiving from him the message that proclaimed the birth of John, who was to prepare the way for the promised Messiah. The angel (Gabriel in this instance, a special angelic minister of promise) encouraged Zacharias to believe the miracle surrounding the birth of John.

Later Gabriel appeared to the Virgin Mary, announcing to her the divinely conceived plan of the incarnation by which God's Son, Jesus Christ, should be conceived miraculously in her womb by the power of the Holy Spirit. Whatever Mary's questions may have been, they were answered by the angel's witness, "The Holy

Ghost shall come upon thee, and the power of the Highest shall overshadow thee: therefore also that holy thing which shall be born of thee shall be called the Son of God" (Luke 1:35). Not only did Gabriel, the special angel of ministry and revelation, bring this message to Mary, but either he or another angel also confirmed to Joseph that he should take Mary as his wife, "For that which is conceived in her is of the Holy Ghost" (Matthew 1:20). He also told Joseph the plan of God that Jesus should "save his people from their sins" (Matthew 1:21).

The special angels of proclamation have faithfully bridged the centuries, carrying the message of God's will in times of oppression, discouragement, and waning endurance. God's restoring servants, His heavenly messengers, have encouraged, sustained, and lifted the spirits of many flagging saints; and they have changed many hopeless circumstances into bright prospects. Angels have ministered the message "All is well" to satisfy fully the physical, material, emotional, and spiritual needs of His people. They could testify, "The angel of the Lord came unto me."

8

ANGELS PROTECT AND DELIVER US

The enemies of Christ who attack us incessantly would often be thwarted if we could grasp God's assurance that His mighty angels are always nearby, ready to help. Tragically, most Christians have failed to accept this fact so frequently expressed in the Bible. I have noticed, though, that in my travels the closer I get to the frontiers of the Christian faith the more faith in angels I find among believers. Hundreds of stories document extraordinary divine intervention every year: God is using His angels as ministering spirits.

ANGELS ARE DIVINE PROTECTORS

God's angels often protect His servants from potential enemies. Consider 2 Kings 6:14–17. The king of Syria had dispatched his army to Dothan, learning that Elisha the prophet was there. Upon dressing in the morning, the prophet's helper exclaimed excitedly to Elisha that the surrounding countryside bristled with armies and implements of war. Elisha assured him, "Don't be afraid! . . . our army is bigger than theirs" (verse 16 TLB). Elisha then prayed that God would open the eyes of the young man to see the hosts of protective angels. As He did so, the young man "could see horses and chariots of fire everywhere on the hills surrounding the city." This passage has been one of the great assurances and comforts to me in my ministry.

The angels minister to God's servants in time of hardship and danger. We find another outstanding illustration of this in Acts 27:23–25. Paul, on his way to Rome, faced shipwreck with more than two hundred others on board. Speaking to the fear-ridden crew, he said, "Last night an angel of the God whose I am and whom I serve, stood beside me and said, 'Do not be afraid, Paul. You must stand trial before Caesar; and God has graciously given you the lives of all who sail with you'" (verses 23–24 NIV).

Some believe strongly that each Christian may have a guardian angel assigned to watch over him or her. This guardianship possibly begins in infancy, for Jesus said, "See that you do not look down on one of these little ones. For I tell you that their angels in heaven always see the face of my Father in heaven" (Matthew 18:10).

ANGELS AT WORK FOR US

The most important characteristic of angels is not that they have power to exercise control over our lives, or that they are beautiful, but that they work on our behalf. They are motivated by an inexhaustible love for God and are jealous to see that the will of God in Jesus Christ is fulfilled in us.

David says of angels, "He who dwelleth in the secret place of the Most High shall abide under the shadow of the Almighty. . . . For he shall give his angels charge over thee, to keep thee in all thy ways. They shall bear thee up . . . lest thou dash thy foot against a stone" (Psalm 91:1, 11–12).

My wife, Ruth, tells of a strange incident in a Christian book-room in Shanghai, China. She learned of it through her father, the late Dr. L. Nelson Bell, who served in the hospital in Tsing-kiangpu, Kiangsu province. It was at this store that Dr. Bell bought his gospel portions and tracts to distribute among his patients.

The incident occurred in 1942, after the Japanese had won control of certain areas of China. One morning around nine o'clock, a Japanese truck stopped outside the bookroom. It was carrying five marines and was half-filled with books. The Christian Chinese shop assistant, who was alone at the time, realized with dismay that they had come to seize the stock. By nature timid, he felt this was more than he could endure.

Jumping from the truck, the marines made for the shop door, but before they could enter, a neatly dressed Chinese gentleman entered the shop ahead of them. Though the shop assistant knew practically all the Chinese customers who traded there, this man was a complete stranger. For some unknown reason, the soldiers seemed unable to follow him, and loitered about, looking in at the four large windows, but not entering. For two hours they stood around, until after eleven, but never set foot inside the door. The stranger asked what the men wanted, and the Chinese shop assistant explained that the Japanese were seizing stocks from many of the book shops in the city, and now this store's turn had come. The two prayed together, the stranger encouraging him, and so the two hours passed. At last the soldiers climbed into their truck and drove away. The stranger also left, without making a single purchase or even inquiring about any items in the shop.

Later that day the shop owner, Mr. Christopher Willis (whose Chinese name was Lee), returned. The shop assistant said to him, "Mr. Lee, do you believe in angels?"

"I do," said Mr. Willis.

"So do I, Mr. Lee." Could the stranger have been one of God's protecting angels? Dr. Bell always thought so.

Corrie ten Boom wrote of a remarkable experience at the terrible Nazi Ravensbruck prison camp:

Together we entered the terrifying building. At a table were women who took away all our possessions. Everyone had to undress completely and then go to a room where her hair was checked.

I asked a woman who was busy checking the possessions of the new arrivals if I might use the toilet. She pointed to a door, and I discovered that the convenience was nothing more than a hole in the shower room floor. Betsie stayed close beside me all the time. Suddenly I had an inspiration, "Quick, take off your woolen underwear," I whispered to her. I rolled it up with mine and laid the bundle in a corner with my little Bible. The spot was alive with cockroaches, but I didn't worry about that. I felt wonderfully relieved and happy. "The Lord is busy answering our prayers,

Betsie," I whispered. "We shall not have to make the sacrifice of all our clothes."

We hurried back to the row of women waiting to be undressed. A little later, after we had had our showers and put on our shirts and shabby dresses, I hid the roll of underwear and my Bible under my dress. It did bulge out obviously through my dress; but I prayed, "Lord, cause now Thine angels to surround me; and let them not be transparent today, for the guards must not see me." I felt perfectly at ease. Calmly I passed the guards. Everyone was checked, from the front, the sides, the back. Not a bulge escaped the eyes of the guard. The woman just in front of me had hidden a woolen vest under her dress; it was taken from her. They let me pass, for they did not see me. Betsie, right behind me, was searched.

But outside awaited another danger. On each side of the door were women who looked everyone over for a second time. They felt over the body of each one who passed. I knew they would not see me, for the angels were still surrounding me. I was not even surprised when they passed me by; but within me rose the jubilant cry, "O Lord, if Thou dost so answer prayer, I can face even Ravensbruck unafraid."

DIVINE SURVEILLANCE

Every true believer in Christ should be encouraged and strengthened! Angels are watching; they mark our path. They superintend the events of our lives and protect the interests of the Lord God, always working to promote His plans and to bring about His highest will for us. Angels are interested spectators and mark all we do, "for we are made a spectacle unto the world, and to angels, and to men" (1 Corinthians 4:9). God assigns angelic powers to watch over us.

Hagar, Sarah's maid, had fled from the tents of Abraham. It is ironic that Abraham, after having scaled such glorious heights of faith, should have capitulated to his wife's conniving and scolding, and to the custom of that day, to father a child by Hagar. And it is ironic that Sarah his wife should have been so jealous that when their own son, Isaac, was born years later, she wanted to get rid of both Hagar and the earlier child, Ishmael. So Abraham's self-indulgence led to sorrow, and he thrust Hagar out of his home.

Nonetheless, God sent His angel to minister to Hagar. "And the angel of the LORD found her by a fountain of water in the wilderness, by the fountain in the way to Shur" (Genesis 16:7). The angel spoke as an oracle of God, turning her mind away from the injury of the past with a promise of what she might expect if she placed her faith in God. This God is the God not only of Israel but the God of the Arabs as well (for the Arabs come from the stock of Ishmael). The very name of her son, Ishmael, meaning "God hears," was a sustaining one. God promised that the seed of Ishmael would multiply, and that his destiny would be great on the earth as he now undertook the restless pilgrimage that was to characterize his descendants. The angel of the Lord revealed himself as the protector of Hagar and Ishmael. Hagar in awe exclaimed, "Thou God seest me" (Genesis 16:13), or as it may be better translated, "I have seen Thou who seest all and who sees me."

Psalm 34:7 underscores the teaching that angels protect and deliver us, "The angel of the LORD encampeth round about those who fear him, and delivereth them." We also find this idea reflected in one of Charles Wesley's songs:

> Angels, where ere we go,
> Attend our steps whate'er betide.
> With watchful care their charge attend,
> And evil turn aside.

MIRACULOUS DELIVERIES

The great majority of Christians can recall some incident in which their lives, in times of critical danger, have been miraculously preserved—an almost plane crash, a near car wreck, a fierce temptation. Though they may have seen no angels, their presence could explain why tragedy was averted. We should always be grateful for the goodness of God, who uses these wonderful friends called angels to protect us. Evidence from Scripture as well as personal experience confirms to us that individual guardian, guiding angels attend at least some of our ways and hover protectively over our lives.

The Scriptures are full of dramatic evidences of the protective care of angels in their earthly service to the people of God. Paul admonished Christians to put on all the armor of God that they may stand firmly in the face of evil (Ephesians 6:10–12). Our struggle is not against flesh and blood (physical powers alone), but against the spiritual (superhuman) forces of wickedness in heavenly spheres. Satan, the prince of the power of the air, promotes a "religion" but not true faith; he promotes false prophets. So the powers of light and darkness are locked in intense conflict. Thank

God for the angelic forces that fight off the works of darkness. Angels never minister selfishly; they serve so that all glory may be given to God as believers are strengthened. A classic example of the protective agency of angels is found in Acts 12:5–11.

As the scene opened, Peter lay bound in prison awaiting execution. James, the brother of John, had already been killed, and there was little reason to suppose that Peter would escape the executioner's ax either. The magistrates intended to put him to death as a favor to those who opposed the gospel and the works of God. Surely the believers had prayed for James, but God had chosen to deliver him through death. Now the church was praying for Peter.

As Peter lay sleeping, an angel appeared, not deterred by such things as doors or iron bars. The angel came into the prison cell, shook Peter awake, and told him to prepare to escape. As a light shone in the prison, Peter's chains fell off, and having dressed, he followed the angel out. Doors supernaturally opened because Peter could not pass through locked doors as the angel had. What a mighty deliverance God achieved through His angel!

ANGELIC INTERVENTION

Many experiences in both Old and New Testaments grew out of the imprisonment of God's saints, calling either for God to deliver directly, or to intervene through angels acting in His name. Many today who are captive in the chains of depression can take courage to believe in the prospect of deliverance. God has no favorites and declares that angels will minister to all the heirs of faith.

If we, the sons of God, would only realize how close His ministering angels are, what calm assurance we could have in facing the cataclysms of life. While we do not place our faith directly in angels, we should place it in the God who rules the angels; then we can have peace.

Hebrews 11 contains a long list of men and women of faith. For most of them, God performed miracles, delivering them from disease, calamity, accidents, and even death. Someone has called this chapter "God's Hall of Fame." Angels helped these great men and women to subdue kingdoms, obtain promises, stop the mouths of lions, quench the violence of fire, escape the edge of the sword, and when they were weak, stand with the help of angels to defeat entire armies.

But the tempo changes in verse 35, with the opening words, "And others were tortured, not accepting deliverance." Those now mentioned were of equal faith and courage: they had to endure the trial of cruel mockings and scourgings. They suffered bonds and imprisonment. They were stoned, they were sawn asunder, they were slain with the sword. They wandered about in goatskins, being destitute, afflicted, and tormented. Time after time they must have called on God to send His mighty angels to help. No delivering angel came. They suffered and endured almost as though there were no God.

GOD'S WINNERS

Why? We find a clue when our Lord faced Calvary as He prayed, "If it be possible let this cup pass from me" (Matthew 26:39); but then He added, "nevertheless not my will, but thine, be done"

(Luke 22:42). In the sufferings and death of these great saints not physically delivered, God had a mysterious plan and was performing His will. Knowing this, they suffered and died *by faith*. This latter part of Hebrews 11 indicates that those who received no visible help in answer to prayer will have a far greater heavenly reward because they endured by "faith" alone. But having died, they did enjoy the ministry of angels who then escorted their immortal souls to the throne of God. If the first part of Hebrews 11 is called "God's Hall of Fame," the second should be called "God's Winners of the Medal of Honor."

Once when I was going through a dark period I prayed and prayed, but the heavens seemed to be brass. I felt as though God had disappeared and that I was all alone with my trial and burden. It was a dark night for my soul. I wrote my mother about the experience and will never forget her reply: "Son, there are many times when God withdraws to test your faith. He wants you to trust Him in the darkness. Now, Son, reach up by faith in the fog and you will find that His hand will be there." In tears I knelt by my bed and experienced an overwhelming sense of God's presence. Whether or not we sense and feel the presence of the Holy Spirit or one of the holy angels, by faith we are certain God will never leave us nor forsake us.

9

ANGELS—GOD'S AGENTS
IN JUDGMENT

The Bible says that throughout history angels have worked to carry out God's judgments, directing the destinies of nations disobedient to God. For example, God used angels in scattering the people of Israel because of their sins. He also used angels in bringing judgment on Sodom and Gomorrah, and eventually on Babylon and Nineveh. Further, at "the end of the age" angels will execute judgment on those who have rejected God's love.

The writer of Hebrews speaks of angelic forces as executors of God's judgments: "Who maketh his angels spirits, and his ministers a flame of fire" (Hebrews 1:7). The flaming fire suggests how awful are the judgments of God and how burning is the power of the angels who carry out God's decisions. Angels administer judgment in accord with God's principles of righteousness.

Unknown to men, they have undoubtedly in the past helped destroy evil systems like Nazism, because those governments came to the place where God could no longer withhold His hand. These same angels will carry out fearful judgments in the future, some of which the book of Revelation vividly describes.

We often get false notions about angels from plays given by Sunday school children at Christmas. It is true that angels are ministering spirits sent to help the heirs of salvation. But just as they fulfill God's will in salvation for believers in Jesus Christ, so they are also "avengers" who use their great power to fulfill God's will in judgment. God has empowered them to separate the sheep from the goats, the wheat from the chaff, and one of them will blow the trumpet that announces impending judgment when God summons the nations to stand before Him in the last great judgment.

ANGELS WARN OF JUDGMENT

In the case of Sodom and Gomorrah, there was no way judgment could be averted. Their wickedness had become too great. God had judged them; they had to be destroyed. But before God sends judgment, He warns. In this case, He used angels to point out to Abraham the approaching doom of Sodom and Gomorrah for their wickedness (Genesis 18). Abraham, whose nephew Lot and his family lived among these wicked people, began to plead with God to spare the two cities. Abraham asked God if He would avert judgment if fifty righteous people lived in Sodom. God told Abraham He would not destroy the city if there were fifty such people. Then Abraham asked for a stay of execution if there were only forty-five righteous people. God agreed. Then Abraham asked for deliverance if there were thirty righteous people. God agreed. Abraham then asked for twenty; then for ten. God agreed to withhold judgment if as many as ten righteous people could be found in Sodom. But not even ten such people lived there. Notice that God answered Abraham every time he asked. And He did not leave off answering until Abraham left off asking.

After this, God ordered the angelic ministers of judgment to rain destruction on these two wicked cities and all their inhabitants. Prior to the destruction of the cities, however, two unidentified heavenly messengers visited Sodom to warn Lot and his family to flee from the wrath about to come. So evil were the inhabitants of Sodom that they wanted to molest the angels physically. The angels blinded them and prevented them from carrying out their iniquitous conduct. In his book *All About Angels*, C. Leslie Miller states, "It is significant that although Lot, Abraham's nephew, had drifted far from the holy standards of his uncle and had sought the companionship and material benefits of an unholy alliance, yet the angels of the Lord were there to spare his life and assist him in avoiding the consequences of his own poor judgment."

Thus, we see something of the mercy, grace, and love of God toward even those who profess His name and try sincerely to live a God-honoring life in the midst of the most difficult circumstances.

THE ANGEL WHO DESTROYED THE ASSYRIAN ARMY

In 2 Kings 19, Scripture dramatically underscores God's use of angels to execute His judgments. King Hezekiah had received a letter from the commander of the Assyrian forces and immediately sought God's counsel. God gave Isaiah the answer, saying that not one Assyrian arrow would be fired into the city. He promised to defend Jerusalem on that occasion for David's sake. Dramatically, that night, just one angel struck the Assyrian encampment and 185,000 soldiers were found dead on the field of battle the next morning (verse 35).

THE ANGEL WHO SMOTE HEROD AGRIPPA

We have already referred to the case of Herod. Dressed in his royal apparel, he appeared before the people to make a speech. When he finished the people shouted, "It is the voice of a god, and not of a man" (Acts 12:22). Instead of disclaiming any such thing, Herod delighted in the impact he had made. God's response to this idolatrous act was prompt and, for Herod, disastrous. "Because he gave not God the glory," he "was eaten of worms, and gave up the ghost" (verse 23). "The angel of the Lord smote him."

THE ANGEL WHO ALMOST DESTROYED JERUSALEM

Nowhere in the Old Testament is there a more significant use of angelic power in judgment against God's own people than when David defied God's command by numbering Israel. God sent a pestilence among the Israelites and 70,000 died. He also sent a single angel to destroy the city of Jerusalem. David "saw the angel of the LORD stand between the earth and the heaven, having a drawn sword in his hand stretched out over Jerusalem" (1 Chronicles 21:16).

When David pleaded for mercy, the angel told him to set up an altar on the threshing floor of Araunah the Jebusite. God then accepted David's sacrifice there and said to the destroying angel, "It is enough: stay now thine hand" (2 Samuel 24:16). The Scripture significantly says that the same angel had already slain the 70,000 men (verse 17). Indeed, angels are God's agents in judgment.

New Testament history also records incidents where avenging angels judged the unrighteous acts of men and nations.

THE ANGEL WHO DESTROYED THE EGYPTIAN FIRSTBORN

One fateful night in Egypt just before the Exodus, the destroying angel was about to sweep over the land with a visitation of death (Exodus 12:18–30). How deeply must anxiety have etched itself upon the hearts of the Israelites. Believing Jews had offered sacrifices and generously sprinkled the blood over the doorposts and lintels of their homes. Then in accord with God's time schedule, judgment fell on Egypt as the dark and awesome moment of midnight arrived. The destroying angel (1 Corinthians 10:10; Hebrews 11:28) was God's minister of judgment, leaving death in his wake. The firstborn of every unbelieving Egyptian or Israeli household died under the judgment of a holy God who, however, had respect for the blood.

Down through the centuries this heartrending account has been the theme of Jews and Christians alike: "When I see the blood, I will pass over you." It has been the text of thousands of sermons by rabbis and Christian clergymen. It was not the quality of life of the people in the blood-sprinkled houses that counted. It was their faith, apart from works, that they showed by sprinkling the blood.

God had respect for only one thing: the blood sprinkled by faith.

How fearful it is to have these mighty angels carry out the judgments of an all-powerful God.

THE ANGEL WHO STOPPED ABRAHAM

In Genesis 22, God, wanting to test the reality of Abraham's faith, told him to sacrifice his beloved "son of promise," Isaac. God said, "Abraham . . . take now thy son, thine only son Isaac, whom thou lovest, and get thee into the land of Moriah; and offer him there for a burnt offering upon one of the mountains which I will tell thee of" (verses 1–2). What great suffering must have haunted and hurt the heart of Abraham through the long night as he considered what this supreme sacrifice entailed. Nevertheless, with nothing to go on but God's Word, Abraham by sheer, naked faith took fire, wood, and his son, and set off to do God's bidding. The Bible records no greater act of faith.

Having prepared the altar, Abraham placed Isaac, bound hand and foot, on the altar; then, unsheathing his knife, he raised his face toward heaven in submission to the Father's will. As Abraham lifted the knife in the air to plunge it into the heart of Isaac, "the angel of the LORD called unto him out of heaven, and said, Abraham, Abraham. . . . Lay not thine hand upon the lad, neither do thou any thing unto him; for now I know that thou fearest God, seeing thou hast not withheld thy son, thine only son from me" (Genesis 22:11–12).

The double use of the name always implies the importance of the message about to be given. When he heard his name called, faithful Abraham responded immediately, and God rewarded him for his unqualified obedience. "Abraham lifted up his eyes, and looked, and, behold, behind him a ram caught in a thicket by his horns: and Abraham went and took the ram, and offered him up for a burnt offering in the stead of his son" (Genesis 22:13).

Many scholars believe, as I do, that the angel here is a "theophany," an appearance of the Lord Jesus Christ Himself. He assumed the role of an angel, and God showed the principle of substitutionary atonement: God had demanded of Abraham the death of his son. The demand for the burnt offering had to be met, and it was met. But in the place of Isaac, God, through an angel, accepted the animal substitute. That same principle applies to us. True judgment demands that we die. And the judgment must be executed. But Jesus Christ Himself was the substitute offering. He died so that we do not have to die. He took our place so that the words used here, "in the stead of," can be wonderfully applied to every person who trusts in Christ. He died "in the stead of" all who believe on Him.

How could God have asked for a human sacrifice? How could He have asked Abraham to slay Isaac when He had forbidden the killing of people (Genesis 9:6)? Is not this inconsistent with the nature of God? He gives us the answer to these questions about judgment by death in the Epistle to the Romans. "He that spared not his own Son, but delivered him up for us all, how shall he not with him also freely give us all things?" (Romans 8:32). God could ask Abraham to slay Isaac because He Himself was willing to let His own Son die. He was not asking Abraham to do anything more than He was willing to do with His only begotten Son.

Neither Abraham nor Isaac had to drink the cup God presented.

Isaac did not die and Abraham did not slay him. But when we come to another cup in the Garden of Gethsemane, the picture is startlingly different. Jesus has now come; as the guiltless one for the guilty, as the sinless one for sinners, He was willing to accept the condemnation of God for the world's guilt, identifying Himself with it through His own death on Calvary.

Neither man nor angel could ever understand what was implied in the "cup" Jesus took in the Garden of Gethsemane that was to lead to His awful suffering, condemnation, and death (Mark 14:36; Luke 22:42). In the Garden as He wrestled over the cup He was to drink, no ministering angel could spare Him from it or alleviate His suffering. It was His and His alone. It settled down on the Savior as a cup of judgment He accepted and took upon Himself as the righteous one bearing the guilt of the wicked. The angels would have helped Him in that hour, but Christ did not call for their help. This one who said no to angel help said, in effect, "I will die for the sins of men because I love them so much." And in dying He was forsaken by men, by angels, and by the Father who is of purer eyes than to look upon sin and who in His Son's atoning agony turned His face from Him. That is why Jesus cried from the cross, "My God, my God, why hast thou forsaken me?" (Matthew 27:46). He died alone. Angels were ready to rescue Him, but He refused.

ANGELS AND THOSE WHO REJECT JESUS

It is clear in Scripture that angels will be God's emissaries to carry out His judgment against those who deliberately reject Jesus Christ and the salvation God offers through Him. While all men are sinners by nature, choice, and practice, yet it is their deliberate rejection of Jesus Christ as Savior and Lord that causes the judgment of eternal separation from God.

God has assigned angels at the end of the age to separate the sheep from the goats, the wheat from the tares, the saved from the lost. We are not called upon to obey the voice of angels. But we are to heed and obey the Word of God and the voice of God that calls upon us to be reconciled to Him by faith in Jesus Christ. If not, we will have to pay the penalty of unforgiven sin. The angels will administer that penalty. They "shall cast them into the furnace of fire" (Matthew 13:50). I am constantly astounded that God's decrees and warnings are considered so lightly in our modern world—even among Christians.

ANGELS AND ETERNAL LIFE

Every son of Adam's race is confronted with two ways of life: one, to eternal life; the other, to eternal death. We have seen how angels execute God's judgment on those who reject Jesus; the angels cast them into the furnace of fire. But there is a totally different judgment: the good and wonderful judgment unto everlasting life. God gives the angels a place in this too. He commissions them to escort believers to heaven and to give them a royal welcome as they enter the eternal presence of God. Each of us who trusts Christ will witness the rejoicing of angelic hosts around the throne of God.

In the story of the rich man and Lazarus (Luke 16), Jesus told of a beggar who died in the faith. He had never owned many of this world's goods, but he was rich in faith that counts for eternity.

When he died he was "carried by the angels into Abraham's bosom." Here were angelic pallbearers who took his immortal spirit to the place of glory where he was to be eternally with God—the place the Bible calls "heaven."

Another beautiful account of this kind comes from the life of the martyr Stephen (Acts 6:8–7:60). The "council, looking stedfastly on him, saw his face as it had been the face of an angel." Then Stephen in a powerful sermon declared that even unbelievers "received the law by the disposition of angels, and have not kept it" (Acts 7:53). When he had finished his discourse, Stephen saw the glory of God and Jesus at the Father's right hand. Immediately his enemies stoned him to death and he was received into heaven. Even as the angels escorted Lazarus when he died, so we can assume that they escorted Stephen; and so they will escort us when by death we are summoned into the presence of Christ. We can well imagine what Stephen's abundant entrance to heaven was like as the anthems of the heavenly host were sung in rejoicing that the first Christian martyr had come home to receive a glorious welcome and to gain the crown of a martyr.

Do you fear the judgment of God? Or do you know that Christ has taken your judgment upon Himself by His death on the cross? When you know Christ, you need not fear God's judgment, for He has fully purchased your salvation. Don't delay your decision for Christ, but open your heart to Him and you too will know the joy of sharing in His fellowship throughout all eternity in heaven.

10

ANGELS AND THE GOSPEL

While God has delegated angels to make special pronounce-ments for Him, He has not given them the privilege of proclaim-ing the gospel message. Why this is so, Scripture does not say. Perhaps spirit-beings who have never experienced the effects of separation from fellowship with God because of sin would be unable to preach with understanding.

But notice what the writer says in "Holy, Holy Is What the Angels Sing":

> Holy, Holy is what the angels sing,
> And I expect to help them make the
> courts of heaven ring.
> And when I sing redemption's story,

They will fold their wings,
For angels never felt the joy that our
salvation brings.

Down through the ages man's heart has remained unchanged. Whatever the color of his skin, whatever his cultural or ethnic background, he needs the gospel of Christ. But who has God ordained to bring that gospel to fallen men? Fallen angels cannot do it; they cannot even be saved from their own sins. Yet unfallen angels cannot preach the gospel either. Presumably they do not hear the gospel the way we do; in their purity they have escaped the effects of sin and are unable to comprehend what it means to be lost.

Rather, God has commanded the church to preach. This great task is reserved for believers. God has no other means. Only man can speak salvation's experience to man.

God has, however, assigned angels to assist those who preach. Their assistance includes the use of miraculous and corroborating signs. Missionaries of the eighteenth and nineteenth centuries have reported many wonderful incidents where angels seemed to help them proclaim the gospel. My wife, whose parents were missionaries to China, can remember many instances in her life where angels must have intervened in the ministry of her father and his fellow missionaries.

At any rate, you and I have the privilege of conveying a message to men from God in heaven, a message that angels cannot speak. Think of that! The story is told of a question asked of God: "In the event that men fail to preach the gospel as You have commanded, what other plan have You in mind?" "I have no other plan," He said.

No angel can be an evangelist. No angel can pastor a church, although angels watch over particular churches. No angel can do counseling. No angel can enjoy sonship in Jesus or be partaker of the divine nature or become a joint heir with Jesus in His kingdom. You and I are a unique and royal priesthood in the universe, and we have privileges that even angels cannot experience.

THE ANGEL AND ZACHARIAS

The birth of John the Baptist was dynamically connected with the "evangel" (a term meaning the gospel, the good news of God's salvation in Jesus Christ). His parents, Zacharias and Elizabeth, were both old, Elizabeth being beyond the age to bear children. She and her husband were descendants of Aaron and thus connected with the priesthood. Both walked blameless before the Lord and kept His commandments. They illustrate how God works through godly parents; not infrequently we find that some of His greatest servants have enjoyed the benefits of a godly home. John and Charles Wesley, founders of the Methodist Church, came from a godly home and were profoundly influenced by their mother. Adoniram Judson, the great missionary to Burma, came from a minister's home. Jonathan Edwards, pastor, evangelist, and educator in early America, was from a line of godly forebears.

When the angel appeared to Zacharias to announce the good news that Elizabeth would, despite her age, give birth to a son, his words were immersed in the evangel. He predicted John's ministry:

"Many of the children of Israel shall he turn to the Lord their God" (Luke 1:16). Thus, we learn that no one should presume that any person is saved, not even one born to a believing home, who has believing forebears, and grows up in a believing church. Moreover, John was "to make ready a people prepared for the Lord" (verse 17).

How great the message of the angel was and how seriously Zacharias regarded it can be seen from events some months later. Zacharias lost his ability to speak following the angel's visit; he did not regain it until the birth of John. But at that time his tongue was loosed and he was filled with the Holy Spirit. His thinking—during the long months while Elizabeth awaited the birth of the baby—now burst out in his first words, which reflect the angel's visit and concern for the evangel. Zacharias said, "Blessed be the Lord God of Israel; for he hath visited and redeemed his people, and hath raised up an horn of salvation for us in the house of his servant David." A moment later he added, "And thou, child [that is, John], shalt . . . give knowledge of salvation unto his people by the remission of their sins, through the tender mercy of our God; whereby the dayspring from on high hath visited us, to give light to them that sit in darkness and in the shadow of death, to guide our feet into the way of peace" (Luke 1:76–79).

Now that was really a message! And all of it rises from the visit of the angel, who told Zacharias about God's intention for John. But notice especially that the angel came, not simply to announce the birth of John, but to make it clear that John was to live his life as the forerunner of the Messiah and as one who would bring the knowledge of salvation and the remission of sins to his fellow Israelites.

THE ANGEL AND THE EVANGEL
IN THE BIRTH OF JESUS

The announcement to Mary that she was to be the mother of Jesus was made by no ordinary angel. It was Gabriel, one of three angels whose names have been given us in Scripture, who made the announcement. And it was connected with the evangel. This was true both of the words Gabriel spoke and the words Mary spoke while she was pregnant and looking toward the birth of her son. The angel told Mary that Jesus would be the Son of the Highest, that He would inherit the throne of His father David, would reign over the house of Jacob forever, and would be an everlasting kingdom. This was something far different from anything promised anyone else in Scripture. It was not promised to Abraham, or David, or Solomon. Only Jesus' name is connected with these promises, and all of them are inextricably connected with both personal and national salvation.

After Mary became pregnant, she visited Elizabeth and sang one of the sweetest songs known to literature. In it she makes evident that she has grasped what the angel told her. And what he told her she describes as salvation and the remission of sins: "My spirit hath rejoiced in God my Saviour" (Luke 1:47). Here was the news that Mary herself needed a Savior and had found Him. The very baby who was encased in her womb would one day offer Himself as a propitiation for her and for all people. And that baby in her womb was God Almighty who had humbled Himself to dwell among us in the flesh.

Indeed, she cries out that God's "mercy is on them that fear him from generation to generation." What is this but the glorious evangel, gospel, that God was in Christ reconciling the world to Himself? And this was the message Gabriel brought to Mary. He could not preach it himself, but he could bear witness to the gospel that was to be preached by Jesus Christ and His followers through all ages.

THE ANGEL, THE EVANGEL, AND JOSEPH

Joseph, the husband of Mary, was caught up in a seemingly abysmal situation. He was legally engaged to a girl who was pregnant. He knew he was not the father because they had not yet consummated their forthcoming marriage. Yet Mary was apparently guilty of adultery under Jewish law, unless Joseph was willing to believe her story that the Holy Spirit had come upon her, and that she had never engaged in sexual relations with a man. As the innocent party, Joseph was thinking seriously of putting Mary away according to the custom of that day. The Scripture says that "while he thought on these things" (Matthew 1:20), an angel appeared to him in a dream and told him the true story of the incarnation and the role of Mary. Responding, Joseph believed the angel. But the announcement contained more than the simple fact that Mary was innocent of any transgression and that Joseph was the chosen vessel of God in affording her protection in this extraordinary event.

The angel also told Joseph something that was to witness to the gospel. Though the angel could not preach to Joseph, he struck at the root of the matter when he proclaimed, "He shall save his people from their sins" (Matthew 1:21). Here was the gospel in all of its beauty, simplicity, and purity. According to the witness of the angel, sins can be forgiven. There is someone who can forgive sins. This is Jesus the Christ. The Savior has a people about whom He is concerned and guarantees that their sins will be forgiven. In the midst of the wonder of the incarnation, we should not overlook the fact that the angel was here bearing witness to the "evangel," the gospel. Jesus was not coming simply as God. He was coming as Redeemer and Savior to make men right with His Father and to assure them of the gift of everlasting life.

GABRIEL, THE EVANGEL, AND DANIEL

Long before the days of Zacharias, Elizabeth, Mary, Joseph, and John the Baptist, the angel Gabriel had borne witness of the evangel to the prophet Daniel. He had done this in connection with the prophecy of the seventy weeks. Daniel was deep in prayer, confessing both his sin and that of his people. While he was praying, Gabriel appeared to him. Notice again that Gabriel did not preach the word of salvation, but he bore eloquent testimony to it. He said that the seventy weeks were designed "to finish the transgression, to make an end of sins, and to make reconciliation for iniquity" (Daniel 9:24). Then he foretold the cutting off of the Messiah, an event that Isaiah 53 had prophesied and depicted so dramatically.

The Jews had had difficulty understanding the notion of a suffering Messiah, rather picturing Him as one who would come in power and glory to overthrow their enemies and to reign triumphantly over them. But Gabriel told Daniel that sin is a reality and must be paid for. The Messiah will do this by being cut off;

that is, He will die for the sins of men. Then the power of sin to separate us from God will end, and men will be reconciled to Him. We see that though Gabriel could not preach, he could prophesy! And how beautifully the prophecies of the Old Testament are linked together with the fulfillment in the New Testament. How gracious God was to use His angels as agents to make it plain to all they visited in all ages that their business was to witness to the evangel.

THE ANGEL, THE EVANGEL, AND THE SHEPHERDS

Does it not seem mysterious that God brought the first message of the birth of Jesus to ordinary people rather than to princes and kings? In this instance, God spoke through His holy angel to the shepherds who were keeping sheep in the fields. This was a lowly occupation, so shepherds were not well educated. But Mary in her song, the Magnificat, tells us the true story: "He hath put down the mighty from their seats, and exalted them of low degree. He hath filled the hungry with good things, and the rich he hath sent empty away" (Luke 1:52–53). What a word for our generation!

What was the message of the angel to the shepherds? First, he told them not to be afraid. Over and over again the presence of angels was frightening to those to whom they came. But unless they came in judgment, the angels spoke a word of reassurance. They calmed the people to whom they came. This tells us that the appearance of angels is awe-inspiring, something about them awakening fear in the human heart. They represent a presence that has greatness and sends a chill down the spine. But when the angel had quieted the fears of the shepherds, he brought this message, one forever to be connected with the evangel:

> For behold I bring you good tidings of great joy, which shall be to all people. For unto you is born this day in the city of David a Saviour, which is Christ the Lord.
>
> (Luke 2:10–11)

I could preach a dozen sermons on those two verses, for they contain many important theological themes. But note once more that the angel does not preach the gospel. Rather, he witnesses to it and demonstrates again the overwhelming concern angels have for it.

What did the angel say? First, he brought good tidings, not bad ones. The shepherds already knew the bad news—the human race had sinned and was lost. But the angel had come to tell them that God was doing something about their lostness. And he pointed out that the good news was not simply for the people of one nation, but for the whole world. Isaiah said, "The God of the whole earth shall he be called" (Isaiah 54:5). Jonah learned the same truth when he was sent to preach repentance to the people of Nineveh. The angel told the shepherds that the good tidings were for all people.

The good tidings were that the Savior had come. They needed somebody who could bring them back into fellowship with God, because the blood of bulls and goats could not do this in any permanent way. But the blood of the Savior could. The angel message was that God had come, redemption was possible, the Lord had visited His people with salvation. What a testimony to the evangel this was. And it was further validated when the angel who was accompanied by "a multitude of the heavenly host" began to chant or sing, "Glory to God in the highest, and on earth peace, good will toward men." Where could there be sweeter music? What hymn writer could match those words?

ANGELS AND THE EVANGEL IN THE BOOK OF ACTS

We might call two wonderful instances "case studies" of how angels see to it that unbelievers hear the gospel, respond to it, and become saved. It shows again the concern of angels for the evangel and the steps they take to implement it.

The first case is that of the Ethiopian nobleman, a man of great authority. While reading the Old Testament Scriptures, he came to Isaiah and, unable to understand what the prophet meant, needed someone to interpret the Scripture to him. An angel knew of this situation. But the angel did not and could not do what the Ethiopian needed. He could not preach the gospel. But he could assist the Ethiopian eunuch by sending someone to him who could.

So the Scripture tells us that the angel spoke to Philip and specifically instructed him to go "toward the south unto the way that goeth down from Jerusalem unto Gaza, which is desert" (Acts 8:26). Philip obeyed the angel and approached the chariot. Then he interpreted the Scripture for the Ethiopian. Later the angel led him up and took him away. And the Ethiopian went on his way rejoicing. If the angel had been unconcerned about the evangel, he would not have sent Philip to preach the gospel to this interested inquirer.

The second instance has to do with Peter and the conversion of Cornelius. In this case, the situation is reversed. The angel had told Philip what to do so the Ethiopian could be saved. Here, he did not tell Peter what to do, but rather ordered Cornelius to send for Peter, who would then tell him the story of the gospel so he could be saved. Would it not have been much easier for the angel to have preached the gospel to Cornelius than to have had him send for Peter? After all, Peter was not a willing witness. He had the notion that it was wrong to preach the gospel for the salvation of Gentiles. Cornelius, however, followed the word of the angel and sent for Peter. Then God had to appear in a dream and convince Peter that it was all right for him to witness to a Gentile. Peter finally went, and Cornelius was wonderfully saved. But it was done through the auspices of the angel who was deeply concerned with the evangel, and for the salvation of this Roman soldier.

One other story in the Acts of the Apostles is somewhat different, though no less worthy of consideration. It has to do with Paul on his way to Rome. He was shipwrecked en route. But while it appeared that the ship would sink with all hands lost, an angel of the Lord appeared to Paul at night. The angel told those aboard the ship that they would all be saved. Then he said something that illuminates the concern of angels for the salvation of men and the witness of Christians to the unsaved. "Fear not, Paul; thou must be brought before Caesar" (Acts 27:24). Here we see that same principle. The angel could not witness to Caesar, but

Paul could. And God in His providence was sending him to Rome for precisely this purpose. If Paul had not fully known the will of God before, it was clear at this moment. God intended that Caesar should hear the gospel. And the angel, by bringing the message, revealed his own interest in the evangel.

THE SOUND OF ANGEL VOICES

The keynote of evangelism is couched in the heavenly proclamation I have mentioned, "Unto you is born this day . . . a Saviour which is Christ the Lord." And the task of world evangelization will be completed by men and women whom the Holy Spirit uses. But wherever and whenever we see the gospel working in its power to transform, there is a possibility that in some ways angels may be involved. This is a mystery that we will never quite understand until we get to heaven.

It is not unreasonable to ask, "What did the angel voices sound like?" And "What did they say when they spoke?" Angels seemed to communicate terse commands. Often the angel messengers urged haste, and this is understandable since they were communicating a directive from God. Dr. Miller points out that the contemporary expression "Hurry up" would fit most angel commands. The words "Get up" were sometimes literally used. The angel said to Peter, "Rise quickly." The angel said to Gideon, "Arise and go in this thy might." The angel said to Joseph, "Go quickly," and to Philip, "Arise and go."

In the same way, any evangelistic ministry sounds the note of urgency concerning the gospel. We have no time to waste because we can never reclaim this moment. We may never have a second chance to witness if we neglect the first.

We can illustrate this from the sinking of the *Titanic*. The greatest ship of its day, weighing 46,000 tons, it was considered unsinkable. But on the night of April 14, 1912, while moving through the ocean at 22 knots, it struck an iceberg. Because it carried only half as many life jackets as passengers, when it sank, 1,513 people drowned. Even though this event occurred more than seventy years ago, there is still a great fascination about it. The discovery of the hulk of the *Titanic* has revived our interest in the whole tragic story.

Out of tragedy, however, God can still bring triumph.

One passenger, John Harper, was on his way to preach at Moody Church in Chicago. Trying to stay afloat in the ocean he drifted toward a young man holding on to a plank. Harper asked, "Young man, are you saved?" The man said, "No." A wave separated them. After a few minutes they drifted within speaking distance of each other, and again Harper called to him, "Have you made your peace with God?" The young man said, "Not yet." A wave overwhelmed John Harper and he was seen no more, but the words, "Are you saved?" kept ringing in the young man's ears.

Two weeks later a youth stood up in a Christian Endeavor meeting in New York, told his story, and said, "I am John Harper's last convert."

11

Angel Ministries
in the Life of Jesus

It would take an entire book to spell out in detail how the life of Jesus was intertwined with the attending ministry of angels. Before He was here, they followed His orders. And since He ascended into heaven, they have worshiped Him before the throne of God as the Lamb slain for our salvation.

To prepare for the coming of Jesus, an angel appeared to Zacharias to inform him that his wife would be the mother of John the Baptist (Luke 1:13). Gabriel, one of the mighty angels of God, announced to Mary that she would give birth to the Messiah. An angel and a multitude of the heavenly host spread the good news of Jesus' coming to the shepherds in the field (Luke 2:9). These angelic incidents preceded and accompanied His birth, but when Jesus began His public ministry, angels were intimately involved in His life as well.

Perhaps the most difficult period in the life of Jesus before His crucifixion was His temptation by the devil in the wilderness. After He had fasted forty days and nights, Satan tried to break Him down. In Christ's weakened human condition, Satan began his attack, seeing this as his greatest opportunity to defeat the program of God in the world since his victory in the Garden of Eden. He was out to shipwreck the hope of the human race. Wishing to prevent the salvation of sinners, he struck at the moment when Christ's physical weakness made Him most susceptible to temptation. Satan always directs his sharpest attack at his victim's weakest point. He knows where the Achilles heel may be, and he does not fail to strike at the opportune time.

Three times Satan attempted to defeat Jesus. Three times Jesus quoted Scripture, and three times Satan went down to defeat. Then the Bible declares that "he [Satan] departed from him [Jesus] for a season" (Luke 4:13). It was at this point that angels came to His assistance—not to help Him resist Satan as they help us, for He did that by Himself, but to help Him after the battle was won. The angels "ministered" to Jesus. The Greek word *diakoneo* says it well, for they served Him as a deacon would serve. "Behold, angels came and ministered unto him" (Matthew 4:11). Angelic ambassadors supported, strengthened, and sustained Him in that trying hour. From that moment on, our Lord Jesus Christ, "who has been tempted in every way, just as we are—yet was without sin" (Hebrews 4:15 NIV), could sympathize and help Christian believers for the ages to come and lead them to victory in their hour of temptation.

THE ANGEL WITH JESUS IN THE
GARDEN OF GETHSEMANE

The night before His crucifixion, Jesus was in the Garden of Gethsemane. Only a short time later He was to be seized by the soldiers, betrayed by Judas Iscariot, set before the rulers, beaten, and at last crucified. Before He was hung on the cross, He went through the terrible agony in the garden made Him sweat, as it were, drops of blood. It was in this situation that the Son of Man needed inner strength to face what no other being in heaven, hell, or earth had ever known. In fact, He was to face what no created being could have faced and gone through in victory. He was about to take upon Himself the sins of men. He was to become sin for us.

Jesus had taken Peter, James, and John with Him to the Garden. They could have provided Him with reinforcement and encouragement, but instead they fell asleep. The Son of Man was all alone. He prayed, "Father, if thou be willing, remove this cup from me: nevertheless not my will, but thine, be done" (Luke 22:42). Then it was at that crucial moment that the angel came to assist Him, "strengthening Him." The Greek word for strengthening is *eniskuo*, which means to make strong inwardly. Whereas the disciples of the Lord Jesus had failed to share His agony, as they slept, the angel came to help.

ANGELS WAITING AT THE CROSS

The tragedy of sin reached its crescendo when God in Christ became sin. At this point, He was offering Himself as the sacrifice required by the justice of God if man was to be redeemed. At this moment Satan was ready to try his master stroke. If he could get Christ to come down from the cross, and if Christ allowed the mockery of the crowd to shame or anger Him, then the plan of salvation would be jeopardized. Again and again they shouted, "If thou be the Son of God, come down from the cross" (Matthew 27:40). He knew He could come down if He chose; He knew He could get help from more than twelve legions of angels who hovered about with drawn swords.

Yet for our salvation, He stayed there. The angels would have come to the cross to rescue the King of kings, but because of His love for the human race and because He knew it was only through His death that they could be saved, He refused to call for help. The angels were under orders not to intervene at this terrible, holy moment. Even the angels could not minister to the Son of God at Calvary. He died alone to take the full death penalty you and I deserved.

We can never plumb the depths of sin, or sense how terrible human sin is, until we go to the cross and see that it was "sin" that caused the Son of God to be crucified. The ravages of war, the tragedy of suicide, the agony of the poverty-stricken, the suffering and irony of the rejected of our society, the blood of the accident victim, the terror of rape and mugging victims of our generation—these all speak as with a single voice of the degradation that besets the human race at this hour. But no sin has been committed in the world today that can compare with the full cup of the universe's sin that brought Jesus to the cross. The question hurled toward heaven throughout the ages has been, "Who is He and why does He die?"

The answer comes back, "This is My only begotten Son, dying not only for your sins but for the sins of the whole world." To you sin may be a small thing; to God it is a great and awful thing. It is the second largest thing in the world; only the love of God is greater.

When we comprehend the great price God was willing to pay for the redemption of man, we only then begin to see that something is horribly wrong with the human race. It must have a Savior, or it is doomed! Sin cost God His very best. Is it any wonder that the angels veiled their faces, that they were silent in their consternation as they witnessed the outworking of God's plan? How inconceivable it must have seemed to them, when they considered the fearful depravity of sin, that Jesus should shoulder it all. But they were soon to unveil their faces and offer their praises again. A light was kindled that day at Calvary. The cross blazed with the glory of God as the most terrible darkness was shattered by the light of salvation. Satan's depraved legions were defeated and they could no longer keep all men in darkness and defeat.

THE ANGELS AT THE RESURRECTION

The Bible says that on the third day after Jesus' death, "there was a great earthquake; for the angel of the Lord descended from heaven, and came and rolled back the stone from the door, and sat upon it. His countenance was like lightning, and his raiment white as snow: And for fear of him the keepers did shake, and became as dead men" (Matthew 28:2–4).

Though some Bible students have tried to estimate how much this stone weighed, we need not speculate, because Jesus could have come out of that tomb whether the stone was there or not. The Bible mentions it so that generations to come can know something of the tremendous miracle of resurrection that took place. I have often wondered what those guards must have thought when, against the brightness of the rising sun, they saw the angel rolling away the gigantic boulder with possibly the lightest touch of his finger! The guards, though heavily armed, were paralyzed with fear.

As Mary looked into the tomb, she saw "two angels in white sitting, the one at the head, and the other at the feet, where the body of Jesus had lain" (John 20:11–12). Then one of the angels who was sitting outside the tomb proclaimed the greatest message the world has ever heard: "He is not here, but is risen" (Luke 24:6). Those few words changed the history of the universe. Darkness and despair died; hope and anticipation were born in the hearts of men.

ANGELS AND THE ASCENSION OF JESUS

We find the story of the ascension of Jesus in Acts 1. Verse 9 says, "And when he had spoken these things, while they beheld, he was taken up; and a cloud received him out of their sight." Jesus had been accompanied to earth by an angelic host. I believe that the word "cloud" suggests that angels had come to escort Him back to the right hand of God the Father.

The watching disciples were sad and despondent. Tears filled their eyes. But again two angels, looking like men and dressed in white raiment, appeared and said, "Ye men of Galilee, why stand ye gazing up into heaven? This same Jesus, which is taken up from you into heaven, shall so come in like manner as ye have seen him go into heaven" (Acts 1:11).

Thus, the angels escorted the resurrected Lord of glory back to be seated at the Father's right hand; then even the morning stars ascribed honor, glory, and praise to Him as the Son of the living God. On the other hand, some angels remained behind to assure those early disciples that they would always be near, ready to help God's people throughout the ages to come—until Christ returns in person with the angelic host.

12

ANGELS IN PROPHECY

Angels have an important role in future events! Human history began at Eden where God planted a garden and made man for His eternal fellowship. Angels were there. They have never failed to attend the human scene. And they will continue on the scene throughout the succeeding ages till time runs into eternity.

Just as millions of angels participated in the dazzling show when the morning stars sang together at creation, so will the innumerable hosts of heaven help bring to pass God's prophetic declarations throughout time and into eternity.

When God decrees it, Satan (Lucifer) will be removed from the world of disorder so God can establish righteousness everywhere and a true theocracy. Not until that event takes place will the human race know perfect peace on earth. Paul tells us in

Romans 8 that the whole creation groans and travails as it awaits the day of Christ's victory.

The prophets spoke of a wonderful day when God would lift the curse, when lion and lamb would lie down together, and when nations would learn war no more (Isaiah 2:4; 11:6). Angel hosts will fulfill His royal decrees and oversee God's purpose in the universe. Christ is coming in great power, and all His holy angels will be with Him. In Acts 1:10–11 angels gave counsel to the disciples after Jesus had ascended to heaven. As we have already seen, when He had left the Mount of Olives, angels appeared, saying, "Ye men of Galilee, why stand ye gazing up into heaven? This same Jesus . . . shall so come in like manner as ye have seen him go into heaven" (Acts 1:11). Angels encouraged those downcast believers who had seen Jesus Christ disappear from their view into a cloud. After this, angels figure prominently in the prophetic plan of God that continued on into the future events of Bible prophecy.

In every age, the true believers have asked, "Will this conflict of the ages ever end?" Each period of history seemingly has its own trials and convulsions. Each generation seems to have to "fight it out." Behind it all is the unseen struggle of the ages. We thought that modern technology would solve many of the great problems of the human race. In some ways it has, by eliminating the fear of diseases like polio and smallpox. But it has also given us Frankenstein weapons of destruction. Poverty, hunger, greed, injustice, prejudice, terrorism, lust, war, and death are still with us. This is the same war that began mysteriously in the heart of Lucifer. It seems that our world is on a suicidal course; but God has other plans. Light shines at the end of the tunnel. Someday

Satan and his demons will go down in defeat. The Bible declares that righteousness will eventually triumph, Utopia will come to earth, the kingdom of God will ultimately prevail. In bringing all this about, angels will have a prominent part.

A little girl heard a clock strike thirteen times. Breathlessly she ran to her mother and said, "Mother, it's later than it's ever been before." Almost everyone throughout the world will agree: It's later than it's ever been before. The human race is rushing madly toward some sort of climax, and the Bible accurately predicts what the climax is! A new world is coming. Through modern technology and scientific achievement we are catching glimpses of what that new world is. If it were not for depraved human nature, man could achieve it himself. But man's rebellion against God has always been his stumbling block. The penalty for man's rebellion is death. The best leaders and the best brains have many times been stopped by death. The Bible teaches that "it is appointed unto men once to die" (Hebrews 9:27). Today the world longs for a leader such as Abraham Lincoln, but death took him from us.

God will use the angels to merge time into eternity, creating a new kind of life for every creature. Even today's intellectual world speaks of a point when time will be no more. Most scientists agree that the clock of time is running out. Ecologically, medically, scientifically, morally, time seems to be running out. In almost every direction we look, man's time on earth seems to be running out. Self-destruction is overtaking us as a human race.

Will man destroy himself? No! God has another plan! Since the beginning of time, man has been interested in what lies beyond the short span of life. Modern man is turning to the occult, Eastern mysticism, palm readers, and every other kind of help available to tell him about the future. Strangely, only a minority turn to the Bible, the only book that accurately foretells the future. The Bible teaches that Jesus Christ is coming back again with His holy angels. It refers to His coming as like "a thief in the night" (2 Peter 3:10), a day of wrath (Romans 2:5), and the judgment of the great day (Jude 6), with many other references both direct and indirect. The age of utopia will be preceded by unparalleled events of suffering for the human race—totalitarianism, poverty, disease, earthquakes, moral collapse, war—until men's hearts will fail them for fear (Luke 21:26).

Luke 21 says there will be "wars and commotions. . . . Nation shall rise against nation, and kingdom against kingdom: And great earthquakes shall be in divers places, and famines, and pestilences; and fearful sights and great signs shall there be from heaven" (verses 9–11).

Believing Christians and believing Jews alike will be persecuted. Men will deliver "you up to the synagogues, and into prisons, being brought before kings and rulers for my name's sake. . . . And ye shall be betrayed both by parents, and brethren, and kinsfolk, and friends; and some of you shall they cause to be put to death. And ye shall be hated of all men for my name's sake. . . . And when ye shall see Jerusalem compassed with armies, then know that the desolation thereof is nigh. . . . And there shall be signs in the sun, and in the moon, and in the stars; and upon the earth distress of nations, with perplexity; the sea and the waves roaring; men's hearts failing them for fear, and for looking after those things which are coming on the earth: for the powers of heaven shall be shaken" (Luke 21:12–26).

Jesus continued in verse 27, "And then shall they see the Son of man coming in a cloud with power and great glory."

Even as in the beginning of time angelic forces waged war in heaven (Revelation 12:7–9), so in the very last days angels will wage still another war; Satan will make his last stand. As the time draws near, he intensifies his activities.

But it will be a victorious day for the universe, and especially planet Earth, when the devil and his angels are thrown into the lake of fire, never again to tempt and destroy man. God has assigned this task to the angels , and Scripture assures us that they will be victorious (Matthew 13:41–42).

ANGELS WILL GATHER GOD'S ELECT

Linked to this idea Jesus says that "when the Son of man shall come in his glory, and all the holy angels with him, then shall he sit upon the throne of his glory" (Matthew 25:31). In other words, when Jesus returns, He will be accompanied by the hosts of heaven. The holy angels will be with Him! As He says in Matthew 13:41–42, "The Son of man shall send forth his angels, and they shall gather out of his kingdom all things that offend, and them which do iniquity; and shall cast them into a furnace of fire: there shall be wailing and gnashing of teeth."

Earlier in this same chapter, Jesus has related a significant little story commonly called the parable of the tares and wheat (Matthew 13:24–30, 36–43). Both had been allowed to grow together until the harvest, but then the reapers were to gather them up in bundles. The tares were to be burned; the wheat gathered. We often wonder why God permits so much sin in the world, why He withholds His right arm of judgment. Why doesn't God put an end to sin now? We can give an answer from this text where Jesus said, "Let both grow together," the evil with the good (verse 30). If we were to try to wipe all evil from the face of the earth, who could count on justice? Pure justice does not exist here, because everyone is guilty, including the judges who sit in judgment. We are all guilty of sin.

Man must do his best in meting out justice, but his best is not complete justice. To angels will be delegated the ministry of separating the good from the bad, discerning even attitudes. God's judgment will be so pure that even those who are condemned will bow their knee and confess, "Thou art just." As someone has said, "When I die I do not want justice—I want mercy!" That mercy has been provided by the Lord Jesus Christ.

So angels will not only accompany Christ when He returns, but will be assigned the responsibility of gathering out of His kingdom all things that offend and work iniquity, that they might be judged (Matthew 13:47–50).

It boggles the mind to try to imagine the kind of earth this is going to be when God eliminates the devil and sin. Our minds are staggered at the thought of "Christ on the throne." The great southward moving Sahara Desert of Africa will bloom and blossom. Mankind will be able to grow new foods; land that today is useless will grow twelve crops a year. The urge in man's heart toward immorality will have vanished. In that day the great drive in man will be a thirst for righteousness.

It takes a great deal of faith in these days of despondency to believe this, but it is the clear teaching of the Bible. Without this hope of the future I do not know what modern man does, except turn to drugs and alcohol.

Today we have the choice of whether or not to receive the ministry of angels. In choosing to follow Jesus Christ, we also choose the protective watch and care of the angels of heaven. In the time of the Second Coming, we will no longer be afforded the privilege of choice. If we delay now, it will be too late, and we forfeit forever the gracious ministry of angels and the promise of salvation to eternal life.

ANGELS IN OUR FUTURE

Dr. Miller asks the question, "What does the future hold for this weary old world? . . . for the physical earth? The answers to such questions are not to be found in astrology or necromancy but in the divinely inspired Word of God. And we may be certain that, as the passing of time fulfills the prophetic Scriptures, the holy angels will be deeply involved in the fulfillment." God will renovate the earth, order the New Jerusalem to descend from heaven, and give redeemed man a position above the angels—what a future!

Elijah was one of the greatest prophets, suddenly appearing on the scene in one of Israel's darkest hours (1 Kings 17). He was a strong, suntanned son of the desert. At times he could be bold as a lion, and at times crushed with frustration. On one occasion he challenged the prophets of the heathen god Baal to a duel to see who was the true God (1 Kings 18:19). When the prophets of

Baal could get no answer from their false god, and Elijah's God answered by fire, Queen Jezebel, unable to accept the prophet's verdict, determined to take his life and pursued him with her chariot for many miles. Elijah, weary from his flight and desperately hungry, lay down under a juniper tree to rest. Feeling extremely sorry for himself, he went to sleep, to be wakened by an angel's touch. Then food was set before him to eat, and the angel said, "Arise, eat."

"And he looked, and, behold, there was a cake baken on the coals, and a [jar] of water at his head. And he did eat and drink, and laid him down again. And the angel of the Lord came again the second time, and touched him, and said, Arise and eat; because the journey is too great for thee. And he arose, and did eat and drink, and went in the strength of that meat forty days and forty nights unto Horeb the mount of God" (1 Kings 19:6–8).

God did not let his faithful prophet down. He provided just what he needed physically, psychologically, and spiritually. Many of us despair of coping with the pressures of our lives, but if we are living Spirit-filled and Spirit-directed lives, we can claim God's promises. The prophetic Scriptures give us "hope." Without Scripture's plan of God for the future and the hope it brings, I do not know what the average thinking person does. Certainly a person will not find the answer by wringing his hands, or by committing suicide, or by turning to the occult. We find the answer to the future in Holy Scripture. It is summed up in the person of Jesus Christ. God has centered all our hopes and dreams on Him. He is the Commander-in-Chief of these angelic armies that will accompany Him on His return.

ANGEL AUTHORITY

New Testament writers have reaffirmed the badge of authority given to angels to fulfill the prophetic dictates of God. The apostle Peter emphasized this truth when speaking of Christ, who was at the right hand of God, having gone into heaven after "angels and authorities and powers [had been] made subject unto him" (1 Peter 3:22). The time is coming when the twenty-four elders of His angelic creation will fall down before the Lamb and sing their new song (Revelation 5:9–10). Thereafter, the holy angels will gather round the throne and join in a great testimony to the Lamb, expressing praise with such words as, "Worthy is the Lamb that was slain to receive power and riches and wisdom and might and honor and glory and blessing" (Revelation 5:12 NASB). While angels have tremendous authority, it is limited to doing only the will of God. They never deviate from God's message, never dilute His message, never change God's plan. Throughout the ages they have glorified only Him, never themselves.

The Bible teaches that the demons are dedicated to control-ling this planet for their master, Satan. Even Jesus called him "the prince of this world" (John 12:31). He is the master-organ-izer and strategist. Many times throughout biblical history, and possibly even today, angels and demons engage in warfare. Many of the events of our times may very well be involved in this unseen struggle.

We are not left in doubt about who will ultimately triumph. Time after time Jesus has assured us that He and the angels would be victorious. "When the Son of man shall come in his glory, and all the holy angels with him, then shall he sit upon the throne of his glory" (Matthew 25:31). The apostle Paul wrote, "The Lord Jesus shall be revealed from heaven with his mighty angels in flaming fire" (2 Thessalonians 1:7,–8).

Jesus also taught that "Whosoever shall confess me before men, him shall the Son of man also confess before the angels of God" (Luke 12:8). It is impossible to comprehend one's suffering of eternal loss when he learns that angels do not acknowledge him because he has been false in his claims to know Christ. But what a moment it is going to be for believers throughout all the ages, from every tribe, nation, and tongue, when they are presented in the court of heaven. Scripture calls it "the marriage supper of the Lamb" (Revelation 19:9). This is the great event when Jesus Christ is crowned King of kings and Lord of lords. Both believers of all ages and all the angelic hosts will join in bowing their knees and confessing that He is Lord.

The book of Revelation, from chapter 4 to 19, gives us a picture of judgments to befall the earth such as the world has never known. Angels will be involved in all of these judgments. But after these terrifying events, Christ will come with His holy angels to set up His kingdom.

Whether the battle between the forces of Satan and the forces of God involve other planets and galaxies we do not know. But we do know that the earth is the scene of the conflict; however, it is a struggle that affects the entire universe. It is mind-boggling that you and I, with such a short period of time on this planet, play a part in this battle of the ages. It is incredible to us that supernatural beings from outer space are engaged in a struggle for this planet.

It all started in the Garden of Eden, a place located somewhere between the Tigris and the Euphrates rivers in the Middle East. It is significant that the nations prominent in early history are once again becoming prominent: Israel, Egypt, Syria, Iran, and so on. In that garden God gave a great promise, "And I will put enmity between thee and the woman, and between thy seed and her seed; it shall bruise thy head, and thou shalt bruise his heel" (Genesis 3:15). As we approach the end of the age, the head of Satan is being battered and bruised as the forces of God gain momentum. Under the command of God, Michael the archangel is now organizing his forces for the last battle—Armageddon. The last picture in the Bible is one of heaven.

Many years ago I was visiting the dining room of the United States Senate. As I was speaking to various people, one of the senators called me to his table. He said, "Billy, we're having a discussion about pessimism and optimism. Are you a pessimist or an optimist?" I smiled and said, "I'm an optimist." He asked, "Why?"

I said, "I've read the last page of the Bible."

The Bible speaks about a city whose builder and maker is God, where those who have been redeemed will be superior to angels. It speaks of "a pure river of water of life, clear as crystal proceeding out of the throne of God and of the Lamb" (Revelation 22:1). It says, "And they shall see his face; and his name shall be in their foreheads. And there shall be no night there; and they need no candle, neither light of the sun; for the Lord God giveth them light: and they shall reign for ever and ever" (verses 4–5).

The next verse has a thrilling last word to say about angels: "These sayings are faithful and true: and the Lord God of the holy prophets sent his angel to shew unto his servants the things which must shortly be done."

Christian and non-Christian alike should meditate on the seventh verse, where God says, "Behold I come quickly: blessed is he that keepeth the sayings of the prophecy of this book."

13

THE ANGELS AND DEATH

The angel who came to the garden where Jesus' body lay rolled away the stone and permitted fresh air and morning light to fill His tomb. The sepulcher was no longer an empty vault or dreary dormitory; rather, it was a life-affirming place that radiated the glory of the living God. No longer was it a dark prison but a transformed reminder of the celestial light that sweeps aside the shadows of death. Jesus' resurrection changed it.

An unknown poet has said of the tomb, "'Tis now a cell where angels used to come and go with heavenly news." No words of men or angels can adequately describe the height and depth, the length and breadth of the glory to which the world awakened when Jesus came forth to life from the pall of death. As Charles Wesley says in his hymn:

'Tis mystery all! Th' Immortal dies!
Who can explore His strange design?
In vain the first-born seraph tries
To sound the depths of love Divine!
'Tis mercy all! Let earth adore!
Let angel minds inquire no more.

In contrast to Jesus, we all still have to die. Yet just as an angel was involved in Christ's resurrection, so will angels help us in death. Only one thin veil separates our natural world from the spiritual world. That thin veil we call death. However, Christ both vanquished death and overcame the dark threats of the evil fallen angels. So now God surrounds death with the assurance of angelic help to bring pulsing life out of the darkness of that experience for believers. We inherit the kingdom of God.

CHRISTIANS AT DEATH

Death for the Christian cuts the cord that holds us captive in this present evil world so that angels may transport believers to their heavenly inheritance. Death is the fiery chariot, the gentle voice of the King, the invitation to nonstop passage into the banquet house of the world of glory.

In another connection I have already mentioned Lazarus, whom angels escorted to Abraham in heaven. This story has always been a tremendous comfort to me as I think about death. I will actually be taken by angels into the presence of God. These ministering spirits who have helped me here so often will be with me in my last great battle on earth. Death is a battle, a profound crisis event. Paul calls it "the last enemy" (1 Corinthians 15:26). While the sting of death has been removed by the work of Christ on the cross, and by His resurrection, yet the crossing of this valley still stimulates fear and mystery. However, angels will be there to help us. Could not the "rod and staff," which help us in the valley of the shadow of death (Psalm 23:4), be these holy angels?

We who have made our peace with God should be like the evangelist D. L. Moody. When he was aware that death was at hand, he said, "Earth recedes, heaven opens before me." It appeared as though he was dreaming. Then he said, "No, this is no dream . . . it is beautiful, it is like a trance. If this is death, it is sweet. There is no valley here. God is calling me, and I must go."

After having been given up for dead, Moody revived to indicate that God had permitted him to see beyond that thin veil separating the seen from the unseen world. He had been "within the gates, and beyond the portals," and had caught a glimpse of familiar faces whom he had "loved long since and lost awhile." Then he could remember when he had proclaimed so vociferously earlier in his ministry, "Some day you will read in the papers that D. L. Moody of East Northfield is dead. Don't you believe a word of it. At that moment I shall be more alive than I am now. I shall have gone up higher, that is all—out of this old clay tenement into a house that is immortal; a body that death cannot touch, that sin cannot taint, a body fashioned like unto His glorious body. . . . That which is born of the flesh may die. That which is born of the Spirit will live forever" (*The Life of Dwight L. Moody* by W. R. Moody). If Moody were to witness to us now, he would surely tell us of the glowing experience that became his as the angelic hosts ushered him into the presence of the Lord.

Phillips Brooks, the writer of "O Little Town of Bethlehem," was one of the greatest pulpit orators and best-loved preachers of the nineteenth century. No greater tribute could be paid him than the words of a five-year-old Boston girl, who exclaimed after her mother had told her that the beloved Mr. Brooks had died, "Mother, how happy the angels will be!"

Death is not natural, for man was created to live and not to die. It is the result of God's judgment because of man's sin and rebellion. Without God's grace through Christ, it is a gruesome spectacle. I have stood at the bedside of people dying without Christ; it was a terrible experience. I have stood at the bedside of those who were dying in Christ; it was a glorious experience. Charles Spurgeon said of the glory that attends the death of the redeemed, "If I may die as I have seen some die, I court the grand occasion. I would not wish to escape death by some by-road if I may sing as they sang. If I may have such hosannas and alleluias beaming in my eyes as I have seen as well as heard from them, it were a blessed thing to die."

Death is robbed of much of its terror for the true believer, but we still need God's protection as we take that last journey. At the moment of death the spirit departs from the body and moves through the atmosphere. But the Scripture teaches us that the devil lurks then. He is "the prince of the power of the air" (Ephesians 2:2). If the eyes of our understanding were opened, we would probably see the air filled with demons, the enemies of Christ. If Satan could hinder the angel of Daniel 10 for three weeks on his mission to earth, we can imagine the opposition a Christian may encounter at death.

But Christ on Calvary cleared a road through Satan's kingdom. When Christ came to earth, He had to pass through the devil's territory and open up a beachhead here. That is one reason He was accompanied by a host of angels when He came (Luke 2:8–14). And this is why holy angels will accompany Him when He comes again (Matthew 16:27). Till then, the moment of death is Satan's final opportunity to attack the true believer; but God has sent His angels to guard us at that time.

In telling the story in Luke 16, Jesus says that the beggar was "carried by the angels." He was not only escorted; he was carried. What an experience that must have been for Lazarus! He had lain begging at the gate of the rich man until his death, but then suddenly he found himself carried by the mighty angels of God!

Once I stood in London to watch Queen Elizabeth return from an overseas trip. I saw the parade of dignitaries, the marching bands, the crack troops, the waving flags. I saw all the splendor that accompanies the homecoming of a queen. However, that was nothing compared to the homecoming of a true believer who has said good-bye here to all of the suffering of this life and been immediately surrounded by angels who carry him upward to the glorious welcome awaiting the redeemed in heaven.

The Christian should never consider death a tragedy. Rather he should see it as angels do: They realize that joy should mark the journey from time to eternity. The way to life is by the valley of death, but the road is marked with victory all the way. Angels revel in the power of the resurrection of Jesus, which assures us of our resurrection and guarantees us a safe passage to heaven.

Hundreds of accounts record the heavenly escort of angels at death. When my maternal grandmother died, for instance, the room seemed to fill with a heavenly light. She sat up in bed and almost laughingly said, "I see Jesus. He has His arms outstretched toward me. I see Ben [her husband who had died some years earlier] and I see the angels." She slumped over, absent from the body but present with the Lord.

When I was a student in a Bible school a godly young missionary volunteer was suddenly taken ill. The physician said she had only a few hours to live. Her young husband and one or two faculty members were in the room when she suddenly exclaimed, "I see Jesus. I can hear the singing of the angels."

The Reverend A. A. Talbot, missionary to China, was at the bedside of a dying Chinese Christian. Suddenly the room was filled with heavenly music. The Chinese Christian looked up with a radiant smile exclaiming, "I see Jesus standing at the right hand of God, and Margaret Gay is with Him." (Margaret Gay was the Talbots' little daughter who had died months before.)

Susanna Wesley said, "When I am gone, sing a song of praise to God."

Dying patients are given so many drugs today that we do not hear as many of these stories now. But to those who face death in Christ, it is a glorious experience. The Bible guarantees every believer an escorted journey into the presence of Christ by the holy angels.

The angelic emissaries of the Lord are often sent not only to catch away the redeemed of the Lord at death, but also to give hope and joy to those who remain, and to sustain them in their loss. He has promised to give "the oil of joy for mourning, the garment expressive of praise instead of a heavy, burdened and failing spirit."

Today man has been overtaken by an increasing sense of gloom about life. In his Responding to Suicidal Crisis, Doman Lum quotes Minna Field on the inadequacy of the counsel and treatment given by those who merely "attempt to escape what is to them an unbearable prospect by a pat on the back and by telling the patient that he is talking nonsense." Death seminars are now being held in major medical centers, and teams of psychiatrists, psychologists, and therapists are constantly encouraged to become involved. Robert J. Lifton, in studying the cessation of life, points out in the same book some interesting views held by survivors of the atomic destruction of Hiroshima. He says that "there was a lasting sense of an overwhelming and permanent encounter with death. As a result, there was a breakdown of faith or trust in any human structure, a psychological closure in which people literally numbed themselves to any emotional feelings regarding death, and an overwhelming sense of guilt and self-condemnation as if they were responsible for the tragedy. . . . We are obsessed with the fear of sudden death . . . and recognize the unpredictable nature of life."

In popular thinking you and I have heard people speaking of death as "crossing the Jordan." It is found in spirituals and in some hymns of the Christian faith. It comes, of course, from the victorious march of the Israelites who crossed the Jordan to enter the Promised Land. They passed over Jordan on dry ground. By analogy we can consider that the ministering angels will see us safely across the Jordan River of death as we enter the promised land of heaven. So the Christian does not sorrow as those who have no hope (1 Thessalonians 4:13).

When the apostle Paul spoke of his own approaching death, he said, "We are confident, I say, and willing rather to be absent from the body, and to be present with the Lord" (2 Corinthians 5:8). When that glorious physical and spiritual separation takes place, the angels will be there to escort us into the presence of our Savior with abounding joy, and it will mean "life everlasting."

THE WONDERFUL WELCOME TO COME

I believe that death can be beautiful. I have come to look forward to it, to anticipate it with joy and expectation. I have stood at the side of many people who died with expressions of triumph on their faces. No wonder the Bible says, "Precious in the sight of the Lord is the death of his saints" (Psalm 116:15). No wonder David said, "Even though I walk through the valley of the shadow of death, I will fear no evil, for you are with me" (Psalm 23:4 NIV).

You may be filled with dread at the thought of death. Just remember that at one moment you may be suffering, but in another moment, you will be instantly transformed into the glorious likeness of our Savior. The wonders, beauties, splendor, and grandeur of heaven will be yours. You will be surrounded by these heavenly messengers sent by God to bring you home where you may rest from your labors, though the honor of your works will follow you (Revelation 14:13).

No wonder the apostle Paul said, "Therefore, my dear brothers, stand firm. Let nothing move you. Always give yourselves fully to the work of the Lord, because you know that your labor in the Lord is not in vain" (1 Corinthians 15:58 NIV).

Are you ready to face life? Are you ready to face death? No one is truly ready to die who has not learned to live for the glory of God. You can put your confidence in Jesus because He died for you, and in that last moment—the greatest crisis of all—He will have His angels gather you in their arms to carry you gloriously, wonderfully into heaven.

14

ANGEL SPECTATORS

How would you live if you knew that you were being watched all the time, not only by your parents, wife, husband, or children, but by the heavenly host? The Bible teaches in 1 Corinthians 4:9 that angels are watching us.

Paul says we are a "spectacle" to them. A. S. Joppie points out that the word referred to the arenas where first-century crowds went to see animals killed for sport, men battle to the death and, later, Christians torn apart by lions. In using the word spectacle, Paul is picturing this world as one vast arena. All true Christians participate in this great drama as they seek to obey Christ since this throws them into severe conflict with the forces of evil, who are bent on humiliating them. Yet Scripture says, "They did not love their lives so much as to shrink from death" (Revelation 12:11 NIV).

During this conflict, which was not limited to the arena, the angels were watching them, longing to hasten to their rescue to set free those men and women who often went joyfully to their death. Yet God forbade the angels to rush in as armies of deliverance. Nor had He allowed them to rescue Jesus at the cross when He tasted the death of separation from God the Father. The angel spectators were poised and ready to intervene; the attack order never came. Why? Because God's moment of final victory over the vicious forces of evil had not yet come.

As I mentioned earlier we face many perplexing questions today, such as, Why does God permit evil? Why doesn't God intervene and punish sin? Why does God allow disease? Why does God permit catastrophe? Yet God's timing is precise! Angel hosts who witness everything that transpires in our world are not free to bear up the righteous and deliver the oppressed until God gives the signal. One day He will. Christ has reminded us that the wheat and the tares, the righteous and the unrighteous, are to grow in the field together until the harvest time when the holy angels gather God's elect and bring them into His kingdom.

ANGELS AT ATTENTION

As God's angels have watched the drama of this age unfolding, they have seen the Christian church established and expand around the world. They miss nothing as they watch the movements of time, "to the intent that now unto the principalities and powers in heavenly places might be known by the church the manifold wisdom of God" (Ephesians 3:10). Dr. Joppie reminds us that the word "now" actually covers the vast expanse of this church age. Angel hosts have witnessed the formation of the church of Christ Jesus and have watched the walk of each believer as the Lord worked His grace, love, and power into each life. The angels are observing first-hand the building of the body of the true church in all places of His dominion this very hour.

But what are they thinking as we live in the world's arena? Do they observe us as we stand fast in the faith and walk in righteousness? Or may they be wondering at our lack of commitment? These two possibilities seem evident from Ephesians 3:10: "(The purpose is) that through the church the complicated, many-sided wisdom of God in all its infinite variety and innumerable aspects might now be made known to the angelic rulers and authorities (principalities and powers) in the heavenly sphere" (AMP).

Our certainty that angels right now witness how we are walking through life should mightily influence the decisions we make. God is watching, and His angels are interested spectators too. The Amplified Bible expresses 1 Corinthians 4:9 this way: "God has made an exhibit of us . . . a show in the world's amphitheater—with both men and angels (as spectators)." We know they are watching, but in the heat of the battle, I have thought how wonderful it would be if we could hear them cheering.

INCENTIVES FOR RIGHTEOUSNESS

The charge to live righteously in this present world sobers us when we realize that the walk and warfare of Christians is the primary concern of heaven and its angelic hosts. Paul said, "I solemnly charge you in the presence of God and of Christ Jesus and of the chosen angels, that you guard and keep (these rules)" (1 Timothy 5:21 AMP). Paul was stirring up Timothy to remember that the elect angels were constantly watching how he served the Savior and lived the Christian life. What fact could provide a greater motivation to righteous living than that? I must say to myself, "Careful, angels are watching!"

It must give the angels great satisfaction to watch the church of Jesus Christ minister the unsearchable riches of Christ to lost men everywhere. If the angels rejoice over one sinner who repents (Luke 15:10), then the angel hosts are numbered among the spectators in the heavenly grandstands. They are included among those who are referred to as "so great a cloud of witness" (Hebrews 12:1); and they never miss any of the details of our earthly pilgrimage. Yet they do not jeer as did the Greek crowds of Paul's day. Rather, as we declare the gospel and see our friends saved, they rejoice with us.

In his book *Though I Walk Through the Valley*, Dr. Vance Havner tells of an old preacher who worked into the night on a sermon for his small congregation. His wife inquired why he spent so much time on a message that he would give to so few. To this the minister replied, "You forget, my dear, how large my audience will be!" Dr. Havner adds, "Nothing is trivial here if heaven looks on. We shall play a better game if, 'seeing we are encompassed,' we remember who is in the grandstand!"

Our valleys may be filled with foes and tears; but we can lift our eyes to the hills to see God and the angels, heaven's spectators, who support us according to God's infinite wisdom as they prepare our welcome home.

15

ANGELS IN OUR LIVES TODAY

In the early days of World War II, Britain's air force saved it from invasion and defeat. In her book *Tell No Man*, Adela Rogers St. John describes a strange aspect of that weeks-long air war. Her information comes from a celebration held some months after the war, honoring air chief marshal Lord Hugh Dowding. The king, the prime minister, and scores of dignitaries were there. In his remarks, the air chief marshal recounted the story of his legendary conflict where his pitifully small complement of men rarely slept, and their planes never stopped flying. He told about airmen on a mission who, having been hit, were either incapacitated or dead. Yet their planes kept flying and fighting; in fact, on occasion pilots in other planes would see a figure still operating the controls. What was the explanation? The air chief marshal said he believed angels had actually flown some of the planes whose pilots sat dead in their cockpits.

That angels piloted planes for dead men in the battle for Britain we cannot finally prove. But we have already seen from Scripture some of the things angels have certainly done, can do, and are yet going to do as history approaches its climax. The important question for each of us is how angels can assist us in our lives here and now: How do they help us attain victory over the forces of evil? What is our continuing relationship to them?

We know that God has given His angels charge over us so that without their help we could never get the victory over Satan. The apostle Paul said, "For we wrestle not against flesh and blood, but against principalities, against powers, against the rulers of the darkness of this world, against spiritual wickedness in high places" (Ephesians 6:12). Let's consider how we can gain help from God through angels.

THE GOD OF THIS AGE

Lucifer, our archenemy, controls one of the most powerful and well-oiled war machines in the universe. He controls principalities, powers, and dominions. Every nation, city, village, and individual has felt the hot breath of his evil power. He is already gathering the nations of the world for the last great battle in the war against Christ—Armageddon. Yet Jesus assures us that Satan is already a defeated foe (John 12:31; 16:11). In 2 Timothy 1:10, Paul says that Jesus Christ has abolished death and brought life and immortality to light through the gospel. Peter declares that Jesus "has gone into heaven and is at God's right hand—with angels, authorities and powers in submission to him" (1 Peter 3:22 NIV).

THE DEFEAT OF SATAN

While Satan is a defeated foe in principle, obviously God has not yet eliminated him from the world scene. The Bible teaches, however, that God will use angels to judge and totally eliminate him from the universe. In Revelation 12, we read of Satan's earlier defeat: "Michael and his angels fought against the dragon; and the dragon fought and his angels, and prevailed not; neither was their place found any more in heaven. and the great dragon was cast out, that old serpent, called the Devil, and Satan, which deceiveth the whole world: he was cast out into the earth" (verses 7–9).

In chapter 20 John describes how Satan's present earthly rule will be temporarily restricted: "And I saw an angel come down from heaven, having the key of the bottomless pit and a great chain in his hand. And he laid hold on the dragon, that old serpent, which is the Devil, and Satan, and bound him a thousand years, and cast him into the bottomless pit, and shut him up, and set a seal upon him, that he should deceive the nations no more. . . ." John then tells us that after a temporary release followed by the last great battle, God will cast Satan into the lake of fire and brimstone, there to be tormented forever (Revelation 20:10).

Some will say, "It is well and good to talk about the final defeat of the devil, but until that happens it doesn't help me because I have to contend with him every day." But this is not the whole story. We have been given specific instructions in Scripture about how to get victory over the devil.

We are told, for example, "Do not give the devil a foothold". (Ephesians 4:27 NIV). In other words, don't leave any vacant places in your heart for him. The apostle Peter taught, "Be sober, be vigilant; because your adversary the devil, as a roaring lion, walketh about, seeking whom he may devour" (1 Peter 5:8). Thus, we cannot be too careful. This includes the injunction to join God's resistance movement: "Whom resist stedfast in the faith" (1 Peter 5:9). And James says, "Resist the devil, and he will flee from you" (James 4:7).

But these admonitions to be vigilant and to resist tell only part of the story. We are not in the battle alone, nor must we rely on our strength alone. Instead, we are to rely on the Holy Spirit, who dwells within us and is willing and able to help us in every situation if we will turn to Him. In addition we can count on the powerful presence of angels many times more numerous and powerful than Satan and his demons. As Increase Mather wrote centuries ago in *Angelographia*, "Angels both good and bad have a greater influence on this world than men are generally aware of. We ought to admire the grace of God toward us sinful creatures in that He hath appointed His holy angels to guard us against the mischiefs of wicked spirits who are always intending our hurt both to our bodies and to our souls."

We have already considered Elisha at Dothan, ringed by apparently overwhelming enemy forces.

Yet if we, like his servant, had open spiritual eyes, we would see not only a world filled with evil spirits and powers—but also powerful angels with drawn swords, set for our defense.

At Dothan thousands of soldiers surrounded the city and intended to do Elisha harm. Yet he had peace. His servant, however, did not, and needed his eyes opened. We, who are troubled, confused, fearful, frustrated Christians need God to open our eyes this very moment. As Vance Havner says, "Our primary problem is not light, but sight. Light is of no value to a blind man. Reading books galore on the subject will not reveal the angels unless our eyes are touched by faith."

We must not get so busy counting demons that we forget the holy angels. Certainly we are up against a gigantic war machine. But we are encompassed by a heavenly host so powerful that we need not fear the warfare—the battle is the Lord's. We can boldly face Satan and his legions with all the confidence of the old captain who, when told that his outfit was completely surrounded, shouted, "Good, don't let any of them escape." If your valley is full of foes, raise your sights to the hills and see the holy angels of God arrayed for battle on your behalf.

When Abraham sent his eldest servant back to his blood relations to look for a bride for Isaac, he urged him to go confidently because of God's angel: "he shall send his angel before thee, . . . and prosper thy way" (Genesis 24:7, 40). Isaiah the prophet said, "In all their affliction he [the Lord] was afflicted, and the angel of his presence saved them" (63:9). God promised Moses in the midst of all his exasperations, "Mine angel shall go before thee" (Exodus 23:23). The Bible also says we may see the angels God has sent but fail to recognize them: "Be not forgetful to entertain strangers: for thereby some have entertained angels unawares" (Hebrews 13:2). Angels, whether noticed by men or not, are active in our twentieth-century world too. Are we aware of them?

It was a tragic night in a Chinese city. Bandits had surrounded the mission compound sheltering hundreds of women and children. On the previous night the missionary, Miss Monsen, had been put to bed with a bad attack of malaria, and now the tempter harassed her with questions: "What will you do when the looters come here? When firing begins on this compound, what about those promises you have been trusting?" In his book *1,000 New Illustrations*, Al Bryant records the result. Miss Monsen prayed, "Lord, I have been teaching these young people all these years that Thy promises are true, and if they fail now, my mouth shall be forever closed; I must go home."

Throughout the next night she was up, ministering to frightened refugees, encouraging them to pray and to trust God to deliver them. Though fearful things happened all around, the bandits left the mission compound untouched.

In the morning, people from three different neighborhood families asked Miss Monsen, "Who were those four people, three sitting and one standing, quietly watching from the top of your house all night long?" When she told them that no one had been on the housetop, they refused to believe her, saying, "We saw them with our own eyes!" She then told them that God still sent angels to guard His children in their hour of danger.

We have also noted the provision of angels. On occasion they have even given food, as we know from the life of Elijah, following his triumph over the priests of Baal. Fearful, tired and discouraged, "as he lay and slept under a juniper tree, behold, then an angel touched him, and said . . . Arise and eat" (1 Kings 19:5–7). God has promised, "Are they not all ministering spirits, sent forth to minister for them who shall be heirs of salvation?" (Hebrews 1:14). Need we think this provisioning by angels ceased thousands of years ago?

When I was visiting the American troops during the Korean War, I was told of a small group of American marines in the First Division who had been trapped up north. With the thermometer at twenty degrees below zero, they were close to freezing to death. And they had had nothing to eat for six days. Surrender to the enemy seemed their only hope of survival. But one of the men, a Christian, pointed out certain verses of Scripture and taught his comrades to sing a song of praise to God. Following this they heard a crashing noise and turned to see a wild boar rushing toward them. As they tried to jump out of his way, he suddenly stopped in his tracks. One of the soldiers raised his rifle to shoot, but before he could fire, the boar inexplicably toppled over. They rushed up to kill him only to find that he was already dead. That night they feasted on meat and began to regain their strength.

The next morning just as the sun was rising, they heard another noise. Their fear that an enemy patrol had discovered them suddenly vanished as they found themselves face to face with a South Korean who could speak English. He said, "I will show you out." He led them through the forest and mountains to safety behind their own lines. When they looked up to thank him, they found he had disappeared.

ANGELS IN JUDGMENT

As we continue to study how to gain the help of angels in our lives today, we need to look soberly once again at the relation of angels to judgment.

Just before fire and brimstone fell on Sodom because of its sins, the angel said, "For we will destroy this place . . . the LORD hath sent us to destroy it" (Genesis 19:13).

In Daniel 7:10 the Word of God says, "A fiery stream issued and came forth from before him . . . the judgment was set, and the books were opened." In scores of places in the Bible God tells us that He will use angels to execute His judgments on all those who have refused to obey His will by failing to receive Christ as Savior and Lord. As Jesus said, "The Son of man shall send forth his angels, and they shall gather out of his kingdom all things that offend, and them which do iniquity; and shall cast them into a furnace of fire: there shall be wailing and gnashing of teeth" (Matthew 13:41–42). Jesus also said, "It shall be more tolerable for Tyre and Sidon at the day of judgment, than for you" (Matthew 11:22). And again, "every idle word that men shall speak, they shall give account thereof in the day of judgment" (Matthew 12:36). "For there is nothing covered, that shall not be revealed; neither hid, that shall not be known" (Luke 12:2).

God is recording not only the words and actions but all the thoughts and intents of our hearts. Someday you and I will have to give an account, and our final destiny will be determined by whether we have received or rejected Jesus. Paul said that God would give "to you who are troubled rest with us, when the Lord Jesus shall be revealed from heaven with his mighty angels, in flaming fire taking vengeance on them that know not God and that obey not the gospel of our Lord Jesus Christ" (2 Thessalonians 1:7–8).

Justice demands that the books of life be balanced, but without a final judgment this would be impossible. Laws too are meaningless unless accompanied by a penalty for those who break them. Reason alone should tell us that there must come a time when God will call upon the Hitlers and the Idi Amins of the world for an accounting. Otherwise there is no justice in the universe.

Thousands of wicked men have lived evil lives and perpetrated their evil designs upon others without seeming to pay any penalty for their misdeeds in this life. However, the Bible says that a time will come when the crooked places will be made straight (Isaiah 45:2). In the great day of God's judgment men will call on Him for mercy, but it will be too late. In that day if men were to seek God, they would not be able to find Him. It would be too late. They could cry out for angels to deliver them, but it would be of no avail.

ANGELS REJOICE IN THE SALVATION OF SINNERS

While angels will play an important role in executing the judgment of God on those who refuse Jesus Christ as Savior and Lord, yet at the same time the Bible informs us that they also rejoice in the salvation of sinners. Jesus tells several striking stories in Luke 15. In the first, a man had a hundred sheep. When one was lost, he left the ninety-nine in the wilderness to seek it. When he found the sheep he slung it over his own shoulders and brought it back to the fold. At home he summoned all his friends, saying, "Rejoice with me: for I have found my sheep which was lost" (verse 6). Jesus said, "I say unto you, that likewise joy shall be in heaven over one sinner that repenteth, more than over ninety and nine just persons, which need no repentance" (verse 7).

His second story is that of a woman who lost a valuable silver coin. She looked everywhere. She swept her house carefully. At last when she recovered the coin she called all her friends and neighbors, saying, "Rejoice with me; for I have found the piece which I had lost" (verse 9). "Likewise, I say unto you, there is joy in the presence of the angels of God over one sinner that repenteth" (Luke 15:10).

In these two parables is not Jesus telling us that the angels of heaven have their eyes on every person? They know the spiritual condition of everybody on the face of the earth. Not only does God love you, but the angels love you too. They are eager for you to repent and turn to Christ for salvation before it is too late. They know the terrible dangers of hell that lie ahead. They want you to turn toward heaven, but they know that this is a decision that you and you alone will have to make.

A rich young ruler came running to kneel before Christ one day and asked, "Good Master, what shall I do that I may inherit eternal life?" (Mark 10:17). When Peter had preached his great sermon at Pentecost, Luke says the people were "pricked in their heart, and said unto Peter, . . . what shall we do?" (Acts 2:37). The African nobleman riding in the chariot across the desert talked with Philip the evangelist. Suddenly the nobleman stopped his chariot and said, "What doth hinder me to be baptized?" (Acts 8:36). At midnight the Philippian jailer asked Paul and Silas, "Sirs, what must I do to be saved?" (Acts 16:30). Modern man forever asks this same question. It is old but always new. It is just as relevant today as it was in the past.

Just what must you do to cause the angels to rejoice? How do you become reconciled to God? How do you repent of your sin? A simple question demands a simple answer. Jesus made everything so simple, and we have made it so complicated. He spoke to people in short sentences, using everyday words, illustrating His message with never-to-be-forgotten stories. He presented the message of God in such simplicity that many were amazed at what they heard. They could hardly believe their ears because the message was so simple.

In the Acts of the Apostles, the Philippian jailer asked the apostle Paul, "What must I do to be saved?" Paul gave him a very simple answer, "Believe on the Lord Jesus Christ, and thou shalt be saved" (Acts 16:30–31). This is so simple that millions stumble over it. The one and only way you can be converted is to believe on the Lord Jesus Christ as your own personal Lord and Savior. You don't have to straighten out your life first. You don't have to try to give up some habit that is keeping you from God. You have tried all that and failed many times. You can come "just as you are." The blind man came just as he was. The leper came just as he was. The thief on the cross came just as he was. You can come to Christ right now wherever you are and just as you are—and the angels of heaven will rejoice!

Some of the greatest and most precious words recorded in all of Scripture were spoken by Satan himself (not that he intended it to be so). In his discussion with God about Job, he said, "Hast not thou made an hedge about him, and about his house, and about all that he hath on every side? thou hast blessed the work of his hands, and his substance is increased in the land" (Job 1:10).

As I look back over my life, I remember the moment I came to

Jesus Christ as Savior and Lord. The angels rejoiced! Since then I have been in thousands of battles with Satan and his demons. As I yielded my will and committed myself totally to Christ—as I prayed and believed—I am convinced that God "put a hedge about me," a hedge of angels to protect me.

The Scripture says there is a time to be born and a time to die. And when my time to die comes an angel will be there to comfort me. He will give me peace and joy even at that most critical hour, and usher me into the presence of God, and I will dwell with the Lord forever. Thank God for the ministry of His blessed angels!

HOW TO BE
BORN AGAIN

BILLY GRAHAM

THOMAS NELSON
Since 1798

NASHVILLE DALLAS MEXICO CITY RIO DE JANEIRO

HOW TO BE BORN AGAIN

Published in Nashville, Tennessee, by Thomas Nelson. Thomas Nelson is a registered trademark of Thomas Nelson, Inc.

Thomas Nelson, Inc. titles may be purchased in bulk for educational, business, fund-raising, or sales promotional use. For more information, please e-mail SpecialMarkets@ThomasNelson.com.

Unless otherwise noted, Scripture quotations are from *The New American Standard Bible* (© 1960, 1962, 1963, 1968, 1971 by the Lockman Foundation and used by permission). Scripture quotations marked *The Living Bible* are from *The Living Bible, Paraphrased* (Wheaton: Tyndale House Publishers, © 1971) and are used by permission. Scripture quotations marked NIV are from the *New International Version* of the Bible (© 1973, 1978, 1984 by International Bible Society). The quotation marked Goodspeed is from *The New Testament: An American Translation* by Edgar J. Goodspeed (© 1923, 1948 by the University of Chicago). The quotation marked TEV is from the *Today's English Version* of the Bible (© 1976 American Bible Society). The quotations marked Phillips are from *The New Testament in Modern English* (rev. ed.), (© 1958, 1960, 1972 by J. B. Phillips).

ISBN 978-0-8499-3160-4 (TP)
ISBN 978-0-8499-1127-9 (TP)

Library of Congress catalog card number: 77-76057

Printed in the United States of America

10 11 12 13 14 EPAC 24 23 22 21 20

CONTENTS

PREFACE

Today being "born again" is big news. *Time* magazine carries a feature story on "Born Again Faith." Political candidates give the subject as much attention as the latest economic statistics or the energy crisis. A former Black Panther leader and radical of the 1960s returns from exile and announces, "My life has turned 180 degrees. I have been born again." A man who was deeply involved in one of the most publicized political scandals of our time writes a bestseller explaining the change in his life as a result of being born again. A Gallup poll comes up with the astonishing conclusion that "more than one-third of those who are old enough to vote have experienced born again religious conversions."

Born again!

Is it possible? Can life be transformed?

What's it all about? What does it mean?

Is it real? Will it last?

How is a person "born again"?

The expression "born again" is not a new term, invented by modern journalists to describe recent religious trends. The term "born again" is almost two thousand years old. One dark night, in the ancient city of Jerusalem, Jesus turned to one of the best-known intellectuals of his time and said, "I say to you, unless one is born again he cannot see the kingdom of God" (John 3:3). In those words Jesus told us of both the necessity and the possibility of new birth—of spiritual transformation. Since that time untold millions throughout the ages have attested to the reality and the power of God in their lives through being born again.

A young Marine Corps officer, a veteran of the Vietnam War, described publicly the night battle in Vietnam when he and his troops came under enemy attack. Only a few were lifted out alive by helicopter. The sixteen surgical operations he endured had helped to restore his physical powers, but now he was speaking of the spiritual rebirth he had received since returning home. He said, "We bear an allegiance to the flag of our country, but unless we have been born again through faith in Christ, all our religion is worth nothing."

This lieutenant had been born again.

I think of the great Dutch Christian, Corrie ten Boom, who is now in her eighties. Her story of courage in the midst of Nazi persecution has inspired millions. She tells of an experience when she was only five years old when she said, "I want Jesus in my heart." She described how her mother took her little hand in hers and prayed with her. "It was so simple, and yet Jesus Christ says that we all must come as children, no matter what our age, social standing, or intellectual background."[1]

Corrie ten Boom, at the age of five, had been born again.

I have had countless people tell me, in person and by letter, how they were born again and their lives were changed. A man from Milwaukee wrote, "Tonight my wife and I had come to the brink of ending our marriage. We felt we could no longer stay together under the conditions in which we were living. Both of us admitted that we thought we no longer loved each other. I no longer enjoyed her company nor appreciated my home life. We made bitter statements about each other. We could make no compromise, nor could we agree on how to improve our marriage even if we were to try.

"I believe it was God's will that I turned on the television and listened to your message about spiritual rebirth. As my wife watched with me, we began to search our hearts and felt a new life within us. I prayed that God would come into my heart and truly make me a new man and help me begin a new life. Our troubles seem rather slight now."

Both this man and his wife were born again.

What does it mean to be born again? It is not just a remodeling job, performed somehow by us on ourselves. Today we hear a lot about recycling, reconstruction, and reshaping. We renovate houses and add on more rooms. We tear down old buildings and build new ones in our cities, calling it urban renewal. Millions and millions of dollars are spent every year on health spas, beauty resorts, and exotic cosmetics—all by people hoping to reshape their faces or renew their bodies.

In like manner, people frantically pursue all sorts of promised cures for the renewal of their inner lives. Some people hunt for renewal at the psychiatrist's office. Others search for spiritual renewal in exotic oriental religions or processes of inward meditation. Still others seek inner peace and renewal in drugs or alcohol. Whatever the path, however, they eventually come to a dead end. Why? Simply because man cannot renew himself. God created us. Only God can re-create us. Only God can give us the new birth we so desperately want and need.

I believe this is one of the most important subjects in the entire world. Governments may be elected or may topple. Military machines may advance and retreat. Men may explore outer space or probe the ocean depths. All of these events are part of the grand plan for humans on this planet.

But the central theme of the universe is the purpose and destiny of every individual. Every person is important in God's eyes. That is why God is not content to stand with His arms folded (as it were) and simply watch the human race wallow in misery and destruction. The greatest news in the universe is that we can be born again! "For God so loved the world, that He gave His only begotten Son, that whoever believes in Him shall not perish, but have eternal life" (John 3:16).

This new birth happens in all kinds of ways. It may seem to happen over a period of time or in a moment. The paths that people take to reach that point of decision may be very direct or very circuitous. Whatever the path, we always find Christ at the end to welcome us. And that encounter with Christ, that new birth, is the beginning of a whole new path in life under His control. Lives can be remarkably changed, marriages excitingly improved, societies influenced for good—all by the simple, sweeping surge of individuals knowing what it is to be born again.

It may be that down inside you sense an unnamed need you cannot describe. Perhaps you have been consciously searching all your life to fill a void in your heart and to find a purpose for living. Perhaps outwardly you have been very successful in life, but you know it has not brought you peace and true happiness. Perhaps your life is an unbroken chain of heartaches and shattered dreams. Maybe you are just curious.

Whatever your background may be, I pray that God will use this little book to give you hope—to show you that you, too, can be born again.

How to Be Born Again is not for the theologians or the philosophers. There are many learned works of theology that probe the meaning of the new birth (or "regeneration," as theologians often call it). I know there have been different emphases among theologians concerning the new birth. Some have stressed the importance of what God does to bring us to faith. Some have stressed the importance of man's search for faith. Some have thought of the new birth as a single event in time, while others use the term to speak of all God wills to do in our lives. Ultimately there is a mystery about the new birth; we cannot understand everything about it, for our minds are finite.

However much the theologians may disagree about fine points of doctrine, the central truth of the new birth is clear: Man apart from God is spiritually dead. He needs to be born again. Only by God's grace through faith in Christ can this new birth take place.

My concern has been to make this book practical. Although we may not be able to say everything possible about the new birth, I have wanted to say everything that was necessary to help people who really want to know God. I want to help them come to have this life-changing experience. I want them—I want you—to be born again. I believe God wants you to be born again.

I was already working on this book when the term "born again" became big news. I have sensed the blessing of God as I have continued writing, and have sensed also that God may have led me to write this book at just the right time as millions wonder about being born again.

I gave my original manuscript to my friends Paul Fromer and Carole Carlson—and asked for help. Then with the added help of my wife and of Cliff and Billie Barrows, we finished it in a little apartment provided by dear Mexican friends while I recuperated from an illness.

Thus, my deepest appreciation to Bill and Vivian Mead of Dallas, Texas, and our wonderful friends, the Servitje family in Mexico, for making our working, recuperating period possible; to Paul Fromer, professor at Wheaton College, and to my secretary, Stephanie Wills, who typed and retyped the manuscript; for the wonderful encouragement and help from my wife, Ruth; for the comments of Dr. John Akers and Mrs. Millie Dienert; but especially to Carole Carlson for the magnificent work she did in helping to simplify what may have been too deep and theological for people all over the world who I pray will read this book and experience "the new birth."

Billy Graham
Montreat, North Carolina
May 1, 1977

Author's Note: I am using the words *born again* and *regeneration* in their widest possible terms in this book. I recognize that in one sense they can be narrowly defined theologically, and in another sense cover the whole range of what we mean by "salvation." (The term *new birth* has been used in a wide and in a restricted sense; it may signify the whole process of salvation including the preparatory work of conviction and the concluding work of discipleship and, ultimately, glorification; or it can be used only for that act of imparting spiritual life, excluding the preparation phase and the lifetime phase.)

I recognize that different denominations have slightly different interpretations. For example, the Roman Catholic Church regards *regeneration* as meaning everything in the transition from a position of condemnation on earth to a state of salvation in heaven. The Augsburg Confession and the Formula Concordie use the *new birth* or *regeneration* in the wide meaning but distinguish between justification and sanctification. In the Reformed Churches, such as the Presbyterians, the term is used in the wide significance, but also distinguishes between justification and sanctification. Thus reformed theologians include not only the new birth but all that comes from it. Calvin taught that the new birth was the restoration of the Divine image within us. He believed that the new birth came not only by an instantaneous act of Divine life being infused to the spiritually dead, but also the various processes of spiritual growth that followed. The Westminster Confession of Faith never used the term *regeneration*, but used the term *effectual calling*. This meant the entire work of the Holy Spirit in the application of total redemption.

Sometimes these uses of the terms *new birth* and *regeneration* have led to semantic differences. In this book I am not making these distinctions but simply stating what most denominations basically believe historically—that man needs regeneration and to be born again—and how he may go about it if he lacks the assurance or if he has never made this commitment, whether he is a church member or not.

PART ONE

MAN'S PROBLEM

1

WHY AM I SO EMPTY?

When the Viking landed on Mars, the world exclaimed, "Unbelievable! Magnificent!" The mysterious Red Planet had been penetrated. An ingeniously designed robot which was the result of one billion dollars and the probing minds of hundreds of scientists had accomplished a task that man had dreamed about for generations.

Exploring the great mysteries of the universe, trying to predict the quirks of nature, attempting to predict a trend in society or politics are all modern concerns.

In the business world, for instance, men search for ways to improve their efficiency. On office walls and on bulletin boards of sales organizations we see slogans like "Plan Ahead" or "Plan Your Work and Work Your Plan." Corporations hire firms at large fees to determine how they can improve their planning. Business, world politics, and economics change so fast that in a few days the direction of an entire country can change. Companies called "Think Factories" project thinking a decade or more in advance to keep abreast of the changing times.

In our daily lives we keep a calendar, trying to mark down appointments and schedule our days. If there were no planning, children would never get to the dentist, mothers would never make the community meeting, businesses and labor unions would collapse. We are always searching for ways to streamline our lives, to simplify daily living.

But what about the greater issues of life and death? Do we plan? Do we need to search for answers to the deep moral and spiritual questions so that our lives are more orderly? Man has always thought so, which is why we have philosophers, psychologists, and theologians. Today, however, much of the world in search of knowledge and fulfillment ignores God!

I knew a brilliant young lawyer who did not seem to find a need for God during his intense years of concentration as a student. Later, he began to write a book about a famous person. While he was working on this book we had a conversation during the course of which I detected that he was on a personal spiritual quest. He hoped to find somewhere in the life of the man who was the subject of his book a spiritual fulfillment which he himself wanted. He knew this person believed in God and had accepted Christ into his heart. He also seemed reassured that the one about whom he was writing had doubts from time to time.

This young man who has been searching for so long has now

become interested in spiritual things. In my earlier contacts with him I thought he was an agnostic, interested only in gaining knowledge at the university and later at law school. Now I suspect that all through adolescence and his twenties he was searching for God without knowing it.

THE SELF-MADE MAN

We are taught to be independent, to make it on our own. As we look at an individual we may say, "Now there's someone who's made it!" We admire him and respect his ability to "pull himself up by his bootstraps."

We have even had a well-known TV commercial that says, "Please, Mother, I'd rather do it myself."

And yet within each of us is a deep-seated frustration: "I ought to be better. I believe I was made for something more; there must be more to life than this. Why am I so empty?"

Such feelings, often subconscious, cause us to struggle toward some unknown, unnamed goal. We may try to evade this quest, we may detour into a fantasy world, we may even regress to lower levels of life and seek to escape. We may throw up our hands in disgust and say, "What's the use? I'm okay just working and keeping out of trouble." But somehow, deep inside is a compulsion which invariably leads us to take up the search again.

This is one of the reasons the nation became fascinated by *Roots*, the product of Alex Haley's ten-year search for identity. My friend Rod McKuen felt rootless and a strange "vacuum" in his heart as he began his search for his true father. The oldest book in the possession of the human race is *Job*, and Job once exclaimed, "Oh that I knew where I might find Him" (Job 23:3).

This search transcends race, age, economic status, sex, and educational background. Either man began nowhere and is looking for someplace to go, or he began somewhere and lost his way. In either case, he's searching. None of us will ever find "total satisfaction" until we find that our roots are in eternity.

A famous scientist at an Eastern university asked to see me. Somewhat surprised, I met him in a quiet room at the Student Union. Suddenly this brilliant man, admired by many and respected as a leader in his field, broke down. When he regained his composure he told me: "I'm at the point of ending my life . . . My home is a wreck, I'm a secret alcoholic, my children don't respect me. I've never really had a guiding principle in my life except to be recognized in my field of physics. I've come to realize that I don't really know the true values of living. I've watched you on TV and although I don't understand all your're trying to communicate, I have a conviction that you know what the real meaning of life is."

He hesitated, and I'm sure the next thing this famous, self-made man said was very difficult for him: "I've come to you for help." It was a desperate cry.

From every culture, every country—from those who cannot read to Nobel Prize winners—there is the age-old phenomenon, the mystery of *anthropos*, the "upward-looking one," the one who is searching, inquiring for life's deeper and often hidden meaning.

In airports, on planes, in hotel lobbies across the world, people have come to me with serious questions about broken family relationships, ill health, or financial catastrophes. But more often they reveal empty souls. On an airplane flight a man poured out his life story to me. It was a saga of shattered dreams, broken hopes, and emptiness. Before we parted he had said "yes" to Christ. Tremendous relief came over his face as he whispered, "Thank you."

When we landed, I watched him embrace his wife and talk excitedly to her at the same time. I don't know what their conversation was, but from his expression he was evidently telling her of his new relationship with the Lord. I can only imagine how amazed she must have been at the change, because he had told me how his temper and unfaithfulness had just about broken their marriage.

I don't know if his marriage was put back together, because I never saw him again, but his direction was certainly changed on that plane trip.

FAME AND FORTUNE

One of our best-known show biz personalities asked me to come to his dressing room after a show on which I had appeared. He motioned me in and said, "I make people laugh . . . but inside I feel like hell. I've been married twice, both marriages have broken up. It's been mostly my fault, I guess, but I don't think I could make a go of a third marriage unless I could find some sort of fulfillment, which I don't know how to get."

He stopped and looked at me. "Do you think what I'm really looking for is summed up in the word *God?*"

All of his fame and money had not satisfied his searching heart.

A man who was destined to be very influential in the life of Charles Colson, of Watergate fame, was Tom Phillips. Colson writes in his book, *Born Again*, that Phillips said: "It may be hard to understand . . . but I didn't seem to have anything that mattered. It was all on the surface. All the material things in life are meaningless if a man hasn't discovered what's underneath them . . .

"'One night I was in New York on business and noticed that Billy Graham was having a Crusade in Madison Square Garden,' Tom continued. 'I went—curious, I guess—hoping maybe I'd find some answers. What Graham said that night put it all into place for me. I saw what was missing—the personal relationship with Jesus Christ, the fact that I hadn't ever asked Him into my life, hadn't turned my life over to Him. So I did it—that very night at the Crusade.'"[1]

Once again a man was forced to examine his soul.

I was in another country at one time and was invited to have lunch with a man who, materially speaking, had everything this world could offer. In fact, he expressed to me how he could buy anything he wanted. He had traveled extensively in business; everything he touched seemed to turn to gold. He was leader of his social set, and yet in his own words he said, "I'm a miserable old man, doomed to die. If there is a hell, that's where I'm headed."

I looked through the beautiful old windows at the snow falling gently on the manicured lawn and thought about others, like him, who had expressed to me similar thoughts about the emptiness of life without God—the meaninglessness of life for a man who has everything to live with, but nothing to live for. My attention came back with a start as I heard him say, "I've asked you here today to read the Bible to me and to talk to me about God. Do you think it's too late? My father and mother were strong believers in God and often prayed for me."

The verse from Matthew 4:4 flashed across my mind: "Man shall not live on bread alone." And Luke 12:15 tells us, "Not even when one has an abundance does his life consist of his possessions."

We read every day about the rich, the famous, the talented, who are disillusioned. Many of them are turning to the occult, or Transcendental Meditation, or Eastern religions. Some are turning to crime. The questions they thought were answered are left dangling: What is man? Where did he come from? What is his purpose on this planet? Where is he going? Is there a God who cares? If there is a God, has He revealed Himself to man?

IS THE INTELLECTUAL SEARCHING?

The men and women who are considered part of the intellectual community are searching for the same meaning, the same sense of fulfillment, but many are hampered by their own sense of pride. They would like to save themselves, because pride nourishes self-esteem, making us believe we can manage ourselves without God.

Famous English writer and philosopher Bertrand Russell wrote prolifically concerning ethics, morals, and human society, trying to prove what he believed were the fallacies in the Bible. When it came to the pride of the intellectual, Russell wrote, "Every man would like to be God, if it were possible; some few find it difficult to admit the impossibility."[2]

From the very beginning of time, man has said, like Lucifer, "I will be like the most High" (Isa. 14:14, KJV).

The search continues. The heart needs filling, and most intellectuals come to a point in their lives when the academe, the scientific community, the business or political activities are no longer enough.

A brilliant analyst of the cultural scene wrote: "Man, being human, however, tries again and again to evade the logic of his own position, and searches for his true self, his humanity, his freedom, even if he can only do so by means of sheer irrationality or completely unfounded mysticism."[3]

We see the results of man searching for his true self in mystic experiences, new cults, and what is called the New Consciousness. "Man today wants to experience God. It is not faith or knowledge which is the key word, but experience."[4]

As the desire for this experience increases, the false philosophers and false gods become acceptable. A European intellectual says: "For centuries there has been the search for the attainment of that ideal which the Greeks called ataraxia, the idea of quiet calm, of deep inner contentment, beyond the restlessness, frustrations, and tensions of normal living. Many searched for this via philosophy and religion, but always there has been the parallel search for short cuts."[5]

An American scholar writes, "As man's search for experiences, new leaders, new hopes, increases in intensity, there will be that continued desire to find an alternative route into what appears to be a dark future."[6]

Men desperately want peace, but the peace of God is not

absence from tension or turmoil, but peace in the midst of tension and turmoil.

In Calcutta, India, I wanted to see a great woman of God who is known to the world as Mother Teresa. I arrived early in the evening and the sisters hated to disturb Mother Teresa, because three men had died in her arms that day and she had just gone to her room to get a bit of rest. However, the official who brought me there sent a note to Mother Teresa, and in a few minutes she was there. I immediately had the impression of this saintly woman as a person who has peace in the midst of turmoil. It's the peace that passes all understanding, and all misunderstanding, too.

How desperately we need that kind of peace during a generation which is being torn apart by internal unrest and despair. The daily newspapers are classics in negative outlook. Terrorism, bombings, suicide, divorce, and general pessimism are the diseases of the day, because in his pride man refuses to turn to God!

The honest intellectual, however, the one who keeps an open mind along with his searching heart, is the one who makes a thrilling discovery. Dr. Rookmaaker says: "We cannot understand God fully, nor know His work completely. But we are not asked to accept in blind faith. On the contrary: We are asked to look around us, and know that the things He tells us through His Son and His prophets and apostles are true, real, and of this world, the cosmos He has made.

"Therefore our faith can never be just 'out of the box,' irrational. Faith is not a sacrifice of the intellect if we believe in the biblical account of history."[7]

WHO NEEDS HELP?

In the rash of disaster movies in the middle seventies there was one called *Earthquake*. When the devastating quake hit, two of the main characters in the movie found shelter under a sturdy car from the flying debris and the terror of unleashed nature. At that moment they didn't reason about what had happened; they didn't analyze what they were going to do; they knew they needed help and dove for shelter.

The person who is on the bottom of life's circumstances wants help immediately. He doesn't need to analyze and examine how help comes; he only knows he needs to be saved.

When it comes to the disasters of our inner earthquakes some intellectuals want to know the source of help and all the details concerning that source. The intellectual has a certain set of beliefs which are self-sufficient and he believes his system is complete. Other intellectuals accept blindly the counterfeits which may be veiled in such complex language and thought patterns that the denial of their premises would sound ignorant. It's very difficult for some to say, "That doesn't really make good sense, and I don't understand what is being said."

Nevertheless, many intellectual searchers have opened their minds and hearts to the truth of the good news and found new life.

A young Hindu who was doing graduate study in nuclear medicine at UCLA was just beginning her second year of study when she came to a crusade. At the end of the service she accepted Christ as her Savior and was born again.

A brilliant surgeon who came to a crusade heard me say that if gaining heaven depended upon good deeds I wouldn't expect to get there. He had devoted his life to helping humanity, but at that moment he realized his training, his years of hard work and devotion, his sleepless nights with patients, and his love for his profession wouldn't earn him a place with God. This man, who had seen many births himself, knew what it was to be born twice.

Many people think Christ talked only to down-and-outers or children. One of His greatest encounters during His teaching ministry was with an intellectual. This man, whose name was Nicodemus, had a very rigid philosophical and theological system, and it was a good plan, with God at the center. However, this "intellectual" structured his philosophical religious system without the new birth—found only in Jesus Christ!

What did Jesus, the carpenter from Nazareth, tell this well-educated man? He said, in words like these, "Nicodemus, I'm sorry I can't explain it to you. You have seen something that troubles you, that doesn't fit your system. You admit I am more than an ordinary man, that I act with the power of God. This may not make sense to you, but I can't explain it to you because your assumptions do not allow for a starting point. Nicodemus, to you it's not 'logical.' Nothing in your thought patterns permits it. You cannot see with spiritual insight until you are born spiritually. You will just have to be born again."

Nicodemus was baffled. "'And how can a man who's getting old possibly be born?' replied Nicodemus. 'How can he go back into his mother's womb and be born a second time?'" (John 3:4, Phillips).

The intellectual asks, "How can a man be born twice?"

If anyone is to find the answer to his search he must reject much of his old system and plunge into a new one. He will see the possibility of what he thought was impossible.

"That is also why only this uniquely 'impossible' faith—with a God who is, with an Incarnation that is earthly and historical, with a salvation that is at cross-purposes with human nature, with a Resurrection that blasts apart the finality of death—is able to provide an alternative to the sifting, settling dust of death and through a new birth open the way to new life."[8]

In the mountains near our home there was a small plane lost with four people on board. At the same time a fifteen-year-old girl was lost in approximately the same area in the Great Smoky Mountains. It was a sad time for our little community because the four were killed and the girl was never found.

As my wife talked to a man who tells us about the tragic events of these people, he told her a story from his own experience. He was born and raised in these mountains, he said, and thought he could never get lost. The mountains were his playground as a child and his hunting area as an adult. One day, however, he found himself groping through the brush and clambering over the rocks, hopelessly confused. He wandered and retraced his steps and suddenly, to his relief, came upon an old man in a mountain cabin. He told Ruth that he would never forget the advice the old man gave him: "When you find yourself lost in the mountains, never go down—always go up. At the top of the ridge you can get your bearings and find your way again."

We can become lost in the mountain of life. We have two choices; we can either go down and get caught in drugs, depression, emptiness, and confusion, or we can keep heading up. The direction we go will determine whether we find ourselves or not.

In this Age of Quest the most important is our personal search for answers concerning life and about God. That search will propel us in the only true direction, in only one way, and we will be embarked on that journey when we are born again.

2

CAN ANYONE TELL ME
WHERE TO FIND GOD?

A drunk was looking for something on the sidewalk one night under a streetlight. He groped along the ground, feeling the cement, occasionally grabbing the pole for support. A passerby asked what he was looking for. "Lost my wallet," the drunk replied. The passerby offered to help him look, but with no success.

"Are you sure you lost it here?" he asked the drunk.

"Course I didn't!" the drunk replied. "It was half a block back there."

"Then why aren't you looking back there?"

"Because," answered the drunk with baffling logic, "there ain't no streetlights back there."

Searching is important, but it doesn't do any good unless we search in the right places.

The governor of one of our states entertained us in his home and after dinner asked to talk to me privately. We went into his study and I could see that he was struggling with his emotions, but finally he said, "I'm at the end of my rope. I need God. Can you tell me how to find Him?"

A young man, toughened in the Green Berets, so strong that his hands had been insured as lethal weapons, fell upon the floor of his room one night, weeping like a helpless child. "God, God, where are You?"

From the ghetto to the mansion, from community leader to prisoner on death row, a man wonders if there is a God. And if there is, what is He like?

A remarkable fact for all seekers of God is that belief in some kind of God is practically universal. Whatever period of history we study, whatever culture we examine, if we look back in time we see all peoples, primitive or modern, acknowledging some kind of deity. During the past two centuries archaeology has unearthed the ruins of many ancient civilizations, but none has ever been found that did not yield some evidence of a god who was worshiped. Man has worshiped the sun and carved idols. Man has worshiped a set of rules, animals, and other men. Some seem to worship themselves. Man has made gods out of his imagination, although basically through a fog of confusion he believes that God does exist.

Some people give up the pursuit of God in frustration, calling themselves "atheists" or "agnostics," professing to be irreligious. Instead they find it necessary to fill the vacuum left within them with some other kind of deity. Therefore man makes his own "god"—money, work, success, fame, sex, or alcohol, even food.

Today many use their nation as an object of worship, espousing the gospel of nationalism. They mistakenly attempt to displace the true and living God with the religion of nationalism. Others make a god of their cause. Although many radical groups deny faith in God, thousands willingly lay down their lives and suffer privation and poverty because of their belief in "the cause" or "the revolution."

Failing to find the true God, millions declare their allegiance to lesser gods and causes. They find no ultimate answers or satisfaction, however. Just as Adam was made for fellowship with God, so are all men. Jesus commented on the First Commandment by saying, "And you shall love the Lord your God with all your heart, and with all your soul, and with all your mind, and with all your strength" (Mark 12:30).

He meant that man, unlike a stone or an animal, has the capacity to love God.

Two-Way Search

Although the wise person seeks God, we have seen that he doesn't have the intellectual capacity to reason his way through to God. He must raise a serious personal question: "Is there any hope of being successful in this search? Can I really know God?"

Once when being interviewed by Ludovic Kennedy on BBC in London, I was asked, "Who made God?" The answer was simple. "No one made God." God is self-existent.

"In the beginning God" are the words which build the cornerstone of all existence. Without God there would have been no beginning and no continuing. God was the creating power and the cohesive force that brought cosmos out of chaos. By divine fiat He brought form out of shapelessness, order out of disorder, and light out of darkness.

Scientists cannot see God in a test tube or a telescope. God is God and the mind of man is too small!

Blaise Pascal, the celebrated seventeenth-century French physicist, said, "A unit joined to infinity adds nothing to it any more than one foot added to an infinite length. The finite is swallowed up by the infinite and becomes pure zero. So are our minds before God."

As we seek this great God, what route are we to take? How can a created, finite human being, limited by time and space, understand an infinite God?

Our failure to comprehend God fully should not strike us as strange. After all, we live surrounded by mysteries we cannot explain—mysteries far simpler. Who can explain why objects are always attracted to the center of the earth? Newton formulated the law of gravity, but he couldn't explain it. Who can explain reproduction? For years scientists have tried to reproduce a living cell and solve the mystery of procreation. They believe they are coming close, but as yet they are without success.

We have become accustomed to accepting as fact many mysteries we cannot explain. I am amazed when my wife mixes cornmeal, shortening, eggs, baking powder, and buttermilk, and I see the soupy mixture slowly rise in the oven and come out light and fluffy with a crispy brown crust. I don't understand it, but I accept the results.

God is far more complex than some of the earthly phenomenon we cannot understand. However, we could present many arguments before a very skeptical jury which would suggest the existence of God. In the scientific realm we know that whatever is in motion must be moved by something else, since motion is the response of matter to power. Yet in the world of matter there can be no power without life, and life presupposes a being who produces the power to move such things as tides and planets.

Another argument says that nothing can be the cause of itself. It would be prior to itself if it caused itself to be, and that is an absurdity!

Consider the law of life. We see objects that have no intellect, such as stars and planets, moving in a consistent pattern, cooperating ingeniously with one another. It is evident that they achieve their movements not by accident but by design.

Whatever lacks intelligence cannot move intelligently. What gives direction and design to these inanimate objects? It is God. He is the underlying, motivating force of life.

Many evidences and arguments suggest God's existence, yet the plain truth is that God cannot be proved by intellectual arguments alone. If the human mind could fully prove God, He would be no greater than the mind that proves Him!

Ultimately you must come to God by faith. Faith is the link between God and man. The Scriptures say you must believe that *He is*. "Faith" is used many times in the Bible, and God has taken it upon Himself to encourage that faith. God continues to pursue man—just as man is searching for Him.

In spite of man's repeated rebellion, God loves man with an

everlasting love. Some earthly fathers give up on their children when they fall into habits and company that are despicable. A father might order his son or daughter out of the house and tell them never to return. On the other hand, some fathers and even mothers deny their children before they are even born. We know young people—even grown ones—whose lives are scarred by parental rejection. The only way such a person can be healed is to accept the fact and ask the Lord to supply the lack. The Bible says, "When my father and my mother forsake me, then the LORD will take me up" (Ps. 27:10, KJV).

God has never forsaken man. The most dramatic quest of the centuries is God's loving and patient pursuit of man.

When man chose in the Garden of Eden to defy God's law, to break the line of communication between himself and God, he could no longer have fellowship. Light and darkness could not live side by side. Why did this barrier come between God and His creation? The cause is a characteristic of God that the average person does not comprehend. God is absolute "holiness."

Long ago God said to Israel, "I the LORD your God am holy" (Lev. 19:2).

In the book of Revelation the cry in heaven night and day is, "Holy, holy, holy, is the Lord God, the Almighty, who was and who is and who is to come" (Rev. 4:8).

A holy God recoils from our evil; He cannot look upon sin because it is ugly and revolting to Him. Because man was stained with sin, God could no longer have fellowship with him. However, *God loves us—in spite of ourselves.*

God had a plan to restore fellowship with man, in spite of his sin. If God didn't have a plan, certainly no one else can! He had said to Adam and Eve at the very beginning when they broke His law, "You will surely die" (Gen 2:17). In a later chapter we will discuss the three dimensions of death. Man had to die or God would have had to go back on His word, and God cannot be a liar or He would no longer be God.

We can see that because man still sins, still defies authority, and still acts independently of God, a great gulf exists between him and God. Twentieth-century men and women are no different from Adam and Eve. We may have added some sophisticated technology, built a few skyscrapers, and written several million books, but there is still a chasm between sinful man and holy God. Yet across this dark, barren abyss, God calls, even pleads, with man to be reconciled to Him.

God loves us.

The apostle John said that "God is love" (1 John 4:8).

The prophet Jeremiah quotes God as saying, "'I have loved you with an everlasting love; therefore I have drawn you with lovingkindness'" (Jer. 31:3).

Another prophet, Malachi, said, "'I have loved you,' says the LORD" (Mal. 1:2).

In every good novel or play there must be conflict. But even Shakespeare could not have created a more powerful plot than the divine dilemma. We know that man is sinful and separated from God. Because God is holy, He couldn't automatically forgive or ignore man's rebellion. Because God is love, He couldn't completely cast man aside. Conflict. How could God be just and the justifier? This is the question Job posed: "But how can a man be in the right before God?" (Job 9:2).

GOD SPEAKS

Radio was just coming of age when I was a boy. We would gather around a crude homemade set and twist the three tuning dials in an effort to establish contact with the transmitter. Often all the sound that came out of the amplifier was the squeak and squawk of static. It wasn't very exciting to listen to all those senseless sounds, but we kept at the controls with anticipation. We knew that somewhere out there was the unseen transmitter, so if contact was established and the dials were in adjustment we could hear a voice loud and clear. After a long time of laborious tuning the far distant sound of music or a voice would suddenly break through and a smile of triumph would brighten the faces of everyone in the room. As last we were tuned in!

Perhaps you have been puzzled that the prophets said God spoke to them. Does He speak to us? Does He tell us where He is—how we can find Him—how we can be right with Him? How God has answered these questions in His Word is the subject of part 2 of this book, which deals with the kind of person Jesus Christ was and the work He did. God has solved the problem, He does tell us about Himself and His loving concern. The key is a line of communication which is "revelation."

Revelation means "to make known" or "to unveil." Revelation requires a "revealer," who in this case is God. It also requires "hearers"—the chosen prophets and apostles who recorded in the

Bible what He told them. Revelation is communication in which God is at one end and man is at the other.

In the revelation that God established between Himself and us we can find a new dimension of living, but we must "tune in." Levels of living we have never attained await us. Peace, satisfaction, and joy we have never experienced are available to us. God is trying to break through. The heavens are calling and God is speaking!

Have you heard God's voice? At the same time you are searching for God, He is speaking to you.

3

DOES GOD REALLY SPEAK TO US?

God has spoken to us from the beginning. Adam heard the voice of the Lord in the Garden of Eden. God also spoke to Eve, and she knew who was speaking and must have trembled because she knew she had disobeyed Him.

Two people, a man and a woman, chose to disobey God and plunged into a world that was spiritually dark and dead—and physically unproductive except by hard work and suffering. The world was under the judgment of God. The Bible teaches that man is in a period of spiritual blackout. "The god of this world has blinded the minds of the unbelieving" (2 Cor. 4:4).

Isaiah, the great Hebrew prophet, said, "We grope along the wall like blind men, we grope like those who have no eyes; we stumble at midday as in the twilight, among those who are vigorous we are like dead men" (Isa. 59:10).

Isaiah was giving a vivid description of what sounds like physical blindness, but which is the darkness of the spirit.

To be trapped in physical darkness can be an uncanny experience. When Cliff Barrows and I were in England just after World War II, we drove down the streets in fog so thick that one of us had to walk in front of the car to prevent it from running into the curb. This was a new experience, a type of "blackout" which was frightening.

How much worse it is to be forever spiritually blacked-out and trapped! There are those who have physical blindness and yet are able to "see" better than a sighted person.

There is a beautiful Korean girl with a voice that has been described as "electric." She also plays the piano beautifully, and yet she is physically blind. Kim sees more than many with 20-20 vision and does not consider her blindness a handicap, but a gift from God. I have found her to have mental, psychological, and spiritual insights which are amazing.

Man is also spiritually deaf. Another great prophet said people have "ears to hear but do not hear" (Ezek. 12:2). Jesus said it with more force: "If they do not listen to Moses and the Prophets, they will not be persuaded even if someone rises from the dead" (Luke 16:31).

The difference between physical deafness and spiritual deafness is illustrated to me vividly at the crusades. We have a section for the deaf and I have often stopped to shake hands with these men and women. At one crusade about a dozen deaf persons were brought to see me in my office and I sat and talked to them through an interpreter. The light of Christ was quite obvious on the faces of many of them.

The world of the physically deaf is one which those of us with normal hearing find difficult to comprehend. But we walk in the world of the spiritually deaf every day.

Spiritually, many men and women are more than deaf and blind, they are dead. "You were dead in your trespasses and sins" (Eph. 2:1).

For the spiritually dead there is no communication with God. Millions of persons long for a world of joy, light, harmony, and peace; instead they are engulfed in a world of pessimism, darkness, discord, and turmoil. They search for happiness, but it eludes them, just as a sunbeam or a shaft of light eludes a child who tries to catch it.

Many give up and give in to pessimism. Often their despondent attitude leads to a circle of cocktail parties or bars where they obliterate the reality of their world with the unreality of alcohol. Sometimes they are led to drugs or an all-consuming pursuit of a hobby or a sport. All these are symptoms of the great escapist disease caused by an insidious infection called sin.

Many persons want to dissect God under their own microscopes. After establishing their own methods of analysis they come to no conclusions. God remains the great cosmic silence, unknown and unseeing. However, God does communicate with those who are willing to obey Him. He penetrates the dark silence with free, life-giving discoveries in nature, the human conscience, Scripture, and the Person of Jesus Christ.

GOD SPEAKS IN NATURE

I was present when our youngest son was born, and our three sons-in-law and our oldest son were present at the births of their children. We all felt that we had experienced a miracle. As one of the doctors said, "How can anyone deny the existence of God after witnessing birth?"

In its own language, nature speaks of God's existence, whether it is the cry of a baby or the song of a meadowlark. It is the language of order, beauty, perfection, and intelligence. The intricacies of a flower are God's work; the instincts of the birds are within His plans. God speaks in the regularity of the seasons; in the movements of the sun, moon, and stars; in the balance of the elements which allow us to breathe. "The heavens are telling of the glory of God; and their expanse is declaring the work of His hands. Day to day pours forth speech, and night to night reveals knowledge" (Ps. 19:1–2).

The very size of the universe has always been incomprehensible to man, but as twentieth-century exploration has taken man into space our minds have become boggled. Every scientist who lacks belief in God must be completely baffled when he surveys how small man is on this earth—part of an estimated 100 billion galaxies, with 100 billion stars and planets in each galaxy.

With the exploration of the universe this generation has also looked at the other end of the scale. The electron microscope and biochemical research have enabled investigators to examine cells which have been magnified up to 200,000 times. There are so many molecules in one drop of water that if they could be transformed into grains of sand there would be enough sand to pave a road from Los Angeles to New York!

The apostle Paul said, "For since the creation of the world His invisible attributes, His eternal power and divine nature, have been clearly seen, being understood through what has been made" (Rom. 1:20).

God says that we can learn a great deal about Him just by observing nature. Since He has spoken through His universe men and women are without excuse for not believing Him. This is the reason the psalmist writes, "The fool has said in his heart, 'There is no God'" (Ps. 14:1).

God speaks in nature but we cannot know Him simply by sitting under a tree and gazing at the sky. He has another avenue of revelation for us which is often called that "still small voice."

GOD SPEAKS IN OUR CONSCIENCE

What is a conscience? A dictionary definition is "the sense of right and wrong; ideas and feelings within a person that tell him when he is doing right and warn him of what is wrong."

"Let your conscience be your guide" is sometimes wise advice, but not always. God shows Himself in our conscience. Sometimes it is a gentle teacher, prodding us in the right direction like the usher in a darkened theater leading us to our seats. Other times our conscience is our worst enemy, torturing us day and night with agonizing unrest.

Paul describes the working of conscience in this way: "For when Gentiles who do not have the Law do instinctively the things of the Law, these, not having the Law, are a law to themselves, in that they show the work of the Law written in their hearts, their conscience bearing witness, and their thoughts alternately accusing or else defending them" (Rom. 2: 14–15).

"A man's conscience is the LORD's searchlight exposing his hidden motives" (Prov. 20:27, *The Living Bible*).

When we realize that God takes a powerful light and shines it into the darkest recesses of our minds, examining not just our actions but the motives behind those actions, it becomes clear that God does indeed speak through our conscience.

Even people who are not Christians realize the existence of something within themselves which is a guiding force. Thomas Jefferson wrote almost two hundred years ago that "the moral sense, or conscience, is as much a part of man as his leg or arm. It is given to all human beings in a stronger or weaker degree, as force of members is given them in a greater or less degree."

Some persons, even without God, have a stronger sense of conscience than others. But the one with a seared or dead conscience is like an airplane without a pilot or a boat without a rudder—confused and directionless, on a collision course with circumstances. Through sin the conscience can become hardened, and even dead.

GOD SPEAKS IN SCRIPTURE

The Bible is the textbook of revelation. In God's great classroom there are three textbooks—one called nature, one called conscience, and one named Scripture. The laws God revealed in nature have never changed. In the written textbook of revelation—the Bible—God speaks through words. The Bible is the one book which reveals the Creator to the creature He created! No other book that man has conceived can make that statement and support it with fact.

The Bible is unique in its claims, its teachings, and its survival. Today there are many persons who are looking at books which are supposed to give answers to the great questions of life and death; many of these books are products of Eastern religions or humanistic philosophy. In his book *Evidence That Demands a Verdict*, Josh McDowell quotes a former professor of Sanskrit who spent forty-two years studying Eastern books and said this in comparing them with the Bible: "'Pile them, if you will, on the left side of your study table; but place your own Holy Bible on the right side—all by itself, all alone—and with a wide gap between them. For, . . . there is a gulf between it and the so-called sacred books of the East which severs the one from the other utterly, hopelessly, and forever . . . a veritable gulf which cannot be bridged over by any science of religious thought.'"[1]

Skeptics have attacked the Bible and retreated in confusion. Agnostics have scoffed at its teaching, but are unable to produce an intellectually honest refutation. Atheists have denied its validity, but must surrender to its historical accuracy and archaeological verification.

I picked up a reputable news magazine and read that a certain head of state made a remark about the economic trends. Nothing very startling about that. You and I read statements made by men and women every day. If we hear them from several different sources, we are inclined to believe that they're true and to tell someone else.

If we were confronted with a book which said in hundreds of different situations that, for instance, the Queen of England spoke, we would believe that she actually had been making statements. No doubt about it!

The writers of the Bible spoke in many ways to indicate that God gave them their information. In the Old Testament alone they said three thousand times that God spoke! Just in the first five books of the Bible we find such phrases as these:

"The LORD God called to the man."

"The LORD God said to the woman."

"The LORD said to Noah."

"God spoke until Israel."

"God said."

"The LORD spoke saying."

"The LORD commanded."

"Hear the words of the LORD."

"Says the LORD."

Did God speak to these men as they were inspired to write? If He didn't, then they were the most blatant and consistent liars the world has ever known, or they were mentally deranged. Would a variety of men from different areas, many of them not knowing each other, tell more than three thousand lies on one subject? If they were mistaken in this area, why should we believe anything they said? If we cannot believe that God spoke to men in the Bible, then we cannot believe that the prophecies of these great men came true—and yet they did!

If someone lies to you two or three times, you begin to distrust him. You find it difficult, if not impossible, to believe anything he says. However, we would have to negate everything in the Bible if we thought that the Bible writers lied when they said God spoke.

Jesus quoted frequently from the Old Testament. He knew it well and never doubted the Scriptures. He said, "Scripture cannot be broken" (John 10:35).

The apostles often quoted the Old Testament Scriptures. Paul said, "All Scripture is inspired by God" (2 Tim. 3:16). Peter said, "For no prophecy was ever made by an act of human will, but men moved by the Holy Spirit spoke from God" (2 Pet. 1:21).

Many people get their belief about the Bible from secondhand sources. A smattering of biblical movie epics, some television reruns, hearsay, and courses on comparative religion give them man's view of Scripture. In high school or college classes students take courses in "the Bible as literature." Many times these classes are used to undermine the faith of young people unless there is a teacher who understands the Bible and has a strong faith in God. I know students who have studied such topics as the "Myths and Discrepancies of the Bible."

Secondhand sources will not do.

A verse or a story in the Bible may speak to someone in a way someone else could not imagine. It was a firsthand source in a secondhand bookstore that changed the lives of an entire family.

My wife has a weakness for books—especially old, choice religious books which are now out of print. At one time Foyles in London had a large secondhand religious book department. One day during the 1954 London Crusade she was browsing though the books in Foyles when a very agitated clerk popped out from behind the stacks and asked if she was Mrs. Graham. When she told him that she was, he began to tell her a story of confusion, despair, and frustrations. His marriage was on the rocks, his home was breaking up, and business problems were mounting. He explained that he had explored every avenue for help and as a last resort planned to attend the services at Harringay arena that night. Ruth assured him that she would pray for him, and she did. That was in 1954.

In 1955 we returned to London. Again my wife went into Foyles' secondhand book department. This time the same clerk appeared from behind the stacks, his face wreathed in smiles. After expressing how happy he was to see her again, he explained that he had gone to Harringay that night in 1954 as he had said he would, that he had found the Savior, and that the problems in his life had sorted themselves out.

Then he asked Ruth if she would be interested in knowing what verse it was that "spoke to him." She was. Again he disappeared behind all the books and reappeared with a worn Bible in his hand. He turned to Psalm 102, which I had read the night that he had attended the crusade. He pointed out verse 6, "I am like a pelican of the wilderness: I am like an owl of the desert" (KJV). This had so perfectly described to him his condition that he realized for the first time how completely God understood and cared. As a result he was soundly converted to the Lord Jesus Christ. And subsequently so was his entire family.

My wife was in London during 1972 at the time of a Harringay reunion. As the ceremonies closed, a gentleman came up to speak to her, but he didn't have to introduce himself. She recognized the clerk from Foyles. He was radiantly happy, introduced his Christian family, and explained how they were all now in the Lord's work—all because God spoke to him when he was "an owl of the desert!"

Make use of this tool of communication by which God speaks to us—namely, the Bible! Read it, study it, memorize it. It will change your entire life. It is not like any other book. It is a "living" book that works its way into your heart, mind, and soul.

SPEAKING IN DARK PLACES

In places where there is easy accessibility to the Bible, it may gather dust on the shelf. In countries where the Bible is subversive literature, God speaks in unusual ways.

A famous violinist was invited years ago by Chow En Lai to teach at one of the famous universities in the People's Republic of China. He was told that if he wanted to leave he would be able to do so. After seven years this violinist was completely disillusioned.

When he went to the exit permit office to apply for the right to leave, he was refused. However, he returned every day, and one day a piece of paper was slipped into his pocket. On returning home he found it there and pulled it out, only to discover that it was a page from the Bible. He read it with interest and found that it strangely spoke to his heart. On one of his subsequent visits a man came up to him and asked if he would like another page from the Bible. He said he would.

Each day when he returned to the exit permit office he was

supplied with another page from the Bible. There in the People's Republic of China he was soundly converted to Jesus Christ. Ultimately he received his exit permit and went to Hong Kong. He is now a professor in another country.

When Corrie ten Boom was in Ravensbruck prison camp, it was the studying and teaching of the Word of God that kept her mind clear so that when she was released she was mentally alert. Many inmates upon their release were little more than vegetables and had to be cared for until they regained some form of normalcy.

A similar story is told of a missionary who was imprisoned by the Japanese in China. At this concentration camp the penalty for owning even a portion of the Scriptures was death. However, a small Gospel of John was smuggled to her in a winter coat. At night when she went to bed she pulled the covers over her head and with her flashlight read a verse and then put herself to sleep memorizing that verse. In this way, over a period of time, she memorized the entire Gospel of John.

When she went to wash her hands she would take one page at a time, dissolve it in the soap and water, and flush it down the drain. "And that is the way," she said, "that John and I parted company."

This little missionary was interviewed by a *Time* reporter just before the prisoners were released. The reporter happened to be standing at the gates when the prisoners came out. Most of them shuffled along, eyes on the ground, little more than automatons. Then out came the little missionary, bright as a button. One of the reporters was heard to ask, "I wonder if they managed to brainwash her?"

The *Time* reporter overheard the remark and said, "God washed her brain!"

The Word of God hidden in the heart is a stubborn voice to suppress. Ruth had another experience in London which emphasizes this fact. During the meetings in Earls Court in 1966 she made friends with a little Cockney beatnik. Each night as we arrived, this thoroughly likable, irrepressible little rebel would be waiting for Ruth. During the Earls Court crusade she would frequently sit with Ruth, or sometimes just walk with her to her seat. They began an unusual, but lasting, friendship.

Ruth learned that the girl had, previous to her conversion, been on drugs. Ruth told her to memorize several verses which she felt would be important to her, like John 3:16, 1 John 1:8, and the last two verses of Jude. One night she even warned her that, because of her past background, when she hit a snag in life she would have two choices: one was to go back on drugs, the other was to go forward with the Lord Jesus Christ.

One night during the service the usher gave my wife a note saying, "I am on drugs and I need you. Please come help me." It was signed by this young friend.

Ruth slipped out of the meeting and found her waiting—white-faced, hollow-eyed, and obviously drugged. Ruth, having had little previous experience with drug users, thought that they were handled as drunks and took her to a coffee stand to get her a cup of coffee. She didn't realize that was the last thing she should have done. On the way she asked the girl why she had done this, only to receive the reply, "Me best friend died on an overdose today."

Ruth wanted her to hear the sermon, and they sat down on a

step within earshot of the service. The girl was in no condition to hear. Realizing that her little friend was fast passing out, Ruth wrote on the little card found at the bottom of a pocket package of Kleenex something to this effect: "God loves me. Jesus died for me. No matter what I have done, He will forgive me if I repent and ask Him to forgive me."

The following year, 1967, we were back in London at Earls Court for another series of meetings. One evening Ruth was having tea with her young beatnik friend. The girl fished into her sack and brought out the crumpled Kleenex card on which Ruth had written the words the previous year. She asked Ruth when she had written these words. Ruth told her, but the girl had no recollection of what had happened that night. Then she repeated the verses of Scripture that Ruth told her to learn and asked when it was that she had learned them. Ruth explained to her, but she didn't remember the occasion. It is interesting that the drugs could cause amnesia up to a certain point, but they had not been able to take away the Word of God which she had hidden away in her heart.

A similar situation happened when Ruth fell out of a tree while trying to build a pipeslide for our grandchildren. She suffered a severe concussion and was unconscious for the better part of a week. As she regained consciousness, the thing that concerned her the most was that she could remember so little. Her greatest loss was that of the Bible verses which she had memorized down through the years.

In her notebook she has written how one night as she was fuzzily praying about this fact, out of nowhere came the words, "I have loved thee with an everlasting love, therefore with loving kindness have I drawn thee." There was no recollection of when or where she had memorized the verse, for her mind was still foggy. And yet—there it was!

GOD SPEAKS IN JESUS CHRIST

God speaks most clearly in the person of His Son, Jesus Christ. "God . . . in these last days has spoken to us in His Son" (Heb. 1:1–2).

Throughout the ages many people have believed that God is a spirit within everyone. Tolstoy, the great Russian writer, said, "Every man recognizes within himself a free and rational spirit, independent of his body. This spirit is what we call God."

Philosophers have found God in everything. In the first century the Roman philosopher Seneca set the stage for belief throughout the ages when he wrote, "Call it nature, fate, fortune: all are but names of the one and same God."

Seneca was, of course, wrong. But so have millions of men throughout the ages been equally mistaken.

In most religions of the world we find some references to a belief that God would visit the earth. There have been many men who have come claiming they are God. One man from Korea during our time has drawn many followers by claiming to be the "Lord of the Second Advent."

However, it was not until the "fullness of time" when all the conditions were right, when all the prophecies were fulfilled, that God "sent forth His Son, born of a woman" (Gal. 4:4).

In a little town in the Middle East almost two thousand years ago, the prophecy in Micah 5:2 was fulfilled when God "was revealed in the flesh" (1 Tim. 3:16). This revelation came in the person of Jesus Christ.

The Scripture says about Christ, "In Him all the fullness of Deity dwells in bodily form" (Col. 2:9).

This revelation is the most complete God ever gave to the world. Do you want to know what God is like? All you have to do is look at Jesus Christ.

Nature has perfection and beauty; we see order, power, and majesty in the physical world around us. All of these descriptions apply to Jesus Christ. In the working of our conscience and the magnificence of the written Scriptures we find justice, mercy, grace, and love. These are attributes of Jesus Christ. "The Word [logos] became flesh, and dwelt among us" (John 1:14).

To His disciples and to all of us living in this twentieth-century world, Jesus said, "Believe in God, believe also in me" (John 14:1). This sequence of faith is inevitable. If we believe in what God made and what God said, we must believe in the One whom God sent.

How can we believe? The means of understanding these facts of salvation is "faith." We are not always challenged to understand everything, but we are told to believe. "But these have been written so that you may believe that Jesus is the Christ, the Son of God; and that believing you may have life in His name" (John 20:31).

Every need to know God, every expectation of eternal life, every desire for a new social order—all must be tied to the only

One who can accomplish these goals—Jesus Christ. When we come to Jesus Christ, the unknown becomes known; we experience God Himself.

When our groping, darkened lives experience the light of the eternal presence of God, we are able to see that another world stretches beyond the confusion and frustration of the world we live in.

A small child, not even old enough for school, went into one of those mirrored mazes at an amusement park. When her father discovered that she had slipped away, he saw her trying to find her way out and beginning to cry in fear. She became increasingly confused by all the paths, until she heard her daddy call out, "Don't cry, darling. Put your hands out and reach all around. You'll find the door. Just follow my voice."

As he spoke the little girl became calm and soon found her way out and ran to the security of her father's outstretched arms.

God has revealed Himself to the human race on this little planet through nature, conscience, the Bible—and fully in the person of Jesus Christ.

4

BUT I'M NOT RELIGIOUS!

The question is often heard, "What about all the other religions of the world? Isn't one religion as good as another?"

Few terms in the language of man have been so distorted and misunderstood as that of *religion*. Eighteenth-century German philosopher Immanuel Kant described religion as "Morality or moral action." Hegel, the philosopher who influenced Hitler's thinking, said religion was "a kind of knowing."

"Religion" has many meanings for many people. It can mean the sadistic symbolism of the Manson girls, who cut an "x" on their foreheads; it can be the rituals of Transcendental Meditation or the chants of various cults; or it can suggest quiet meditation within the comforting walls of a church.

Many people say rather proudly, "I'm not very religious," but in spite of some of his own objections, man is a religious being. The Bible, anthropology, sociology, and other sciences teach us that people long for some sort of religious experience.

My major in college was anthropology, which the dictionary explains as a science dealing with the races, customs, and beliefs of mankind. I have also had the privilege of traveling extensively on every continent. I have found from personal experience that what I learned from anthropology is true: Man has naturally and universally a capacity for religion—and not only a capacity, for the vast majority of the human race practices or professes some form of religion.

Religion can be defined as having two magnetic poles, the biblical and the naturalistic. The biblical pole is described in the teachings of the Bible. The naturalistic pole is explained in all the man-made religions. In humanistic systems there are always certain elements of truth. Many of these faiths have borrowed from Judeo-Christianity; many use portions and incorporate their own fables. Other religions or faiths have in fragments what Christianity has as a whole.

The apostle Paul described the naturalistic pole when he said that men "exchanged the glory of the incorruptible God for an image in the form of corruptible man and of birds and four-footed animals and crawling creatures" (Rom. 1:23).

All false religions cut away parts of God's revelation, add ideas of their own, and come out with various viewpoints that differ from God's revelation in the Bible. Natural religion does not come from God, but from the natural world He created and that turned away from Him in its pride.

A false religion is like the imitation of high fashion. I've read that after an exclusive showing of original designs in one of the fashion centers of the world like Paris, copies will soon appear in the mass merchandising stores under different labels. The very presence of counterfeits prove the existence of the real. There would be no imitations without a genuine product.

God's original design has always had imitators and counterfeits!

THE BIRTH OF RELIGION

How did all the religions of the world get started? A famous military conqueror from the past was able to state a truth, without realizing that he had charged right past the real Truth. Napoleon Bonaparte stated, "I would believe in a religion if it existed ever since the beginning of time, but when I consider Socrates, Plato, Muhammad, I no longer believe. All religions have been made by man."

Paul Bunyan once said, "Religion is the best armor that a man can have, but it's the worst cloak."

When did man invent this maze of religion? It began with a couple of fellows who are rather well known. When Adam and Eve had their sons, we might have thought they would have been able to instill in both of them the importance of a right relationship with God. However, Cain wanted to do it his own way. He approached the first altar with his offering of "the fruit of the ground," trying to regain "paradise" without accepting God's plan of redemption. Cain brought what he had grown, the distinctive elements of his own culture. Today we would call Cain's gift his attempt at salvation by works. But God never said we could work our way to heaven.

His brother, Abel, obeyed God and humbly offered the first of his flock in a sacrifice of blood. Abel agreed with God that sin deserved death and could be covered before God only through the substitutionary death of a guiltless sacrifice. Cain deliberately rejected this plan. God demanded a blood sacrifice.

The Bible writers knew that blood was absolutely essential for life. A person or an animal might get along without a leg or an eye. But no animal or man could live without blood. That is why the Old Testament said, "For the life of the flesh is in the blood" (Lev. 17:11).

Thus, the Bible teaches that atonement for sin comes only through the shedding of blood. "In fact, the law requires that nearly everything be cleansed with blood, and without the shedding of blood there is no forgiveness" (Heb 9:22, NIV).

When we speak of the blood of Christ, therefore, we are saying that He died for us. Blood sacrifice underlined the seriousness of sin. Sin was a life-and-death matter. Only the shedding of blood could atone for sin. The death of Christ also underlined the principle of substitution. In the Old Testament a sacrificed animal was seen as a substitute; the innocent animal took the place of the guilty person. In the same way, Christ died in our place. He was innocent, but He freely shed His blood for us and took our place. We deserved to die for our sins, but He died in our place.

Because of Christ's death for us, we can know His life—now and eternally. "Knowing that you were not redeemed with perishable things . . . but with precious blood . . . of Christ" (1 Pet. 1:18–19).

When Cain chose to go his way, not God's way of blood, something bitter happened to his heart. He began to hate his brother, Abel. Just as the true Christian believer will often not be accepted by those who have their man-made religion, Abel was not accepted by Cain, and this hatred festered until Cain killed his brother.

Pride, jealousy, and hatred have been in the human heart in all cultures and all ages. Many years ago when I was a student in Florida, a young man killed his older brother in a fit of jealousy. His father and mother had both been killed in an automobile crash, and when the will was read it indicated that the older brother had received two-thirds of an orange grove, leaving only a third to the younger brother. He became moody and depressed, angry at his deceased parents, and intensely jealous of his brother. Then the older brother disappeared, and about six weeks later his body was found tied with wire to the trunk of a cypress tree in a river.

Times haven't changed. Millions want salvation, but on their own terms; they want to chart their own courses and devise all kinds of routes to lead to God.

If Christianity is true, it is not a religion. Religion is man's effort to reach God. The dictionary describes *religion* as a "belief in God or gods . . . or worship of God or gods." Religion can be anything! But true Christianity is God coming to man in a personal relationship.

The modern interest in the occult and in Eastern religions is indicative of man's eternal search for God. We cannot escape the fact that man is instinctively religious, but God has chosen to reveal Himself to us through nature, conscience, the Scriptures, and through Jesus Christ. The Scripture says there is no excuse for a person not to know God!

IN THE NAME OF "RELIGION"

It's no wonder that people say with satisfaction, "I'm not religious." Extreme cruelties and great injustices have been perpetrated in the name of religion.

In China when my wife was growing up, frequently babies who died before cutting their teeth were thrown out to be eaten by pariah dogs. The people feared that if evil spirits thought they cared too much for the children they would come and take another one. They tried to prove their indifference in this crude way. "Religion" impressed Ruth as being grim and joyless, and often cruel.

I once saw a man in India lying on a bed of spikes. He had been there for many days, eating no food and drinking little water. He was attempting to atone for his sins. Another time in Africa I saw a man walk on coals of fire. Supposedly, if he came through unscathed, he was accepted by God; if he was burned, he was considered to be a sinner in need of more repentance.

In India a missionary who passed the banks of the Ganges noticed a mother sitting by the riverbank with two of her children. On her lap was a beautiful new baby and whimpering beside her was a painfully retarded child of about three. On her return home that night, the missionary saw the young mother still sitting at the riverbank, but the baby was gone and the mother was trying to comfort her little retarded child. Horrified at what she thought might be true, the missionary hesitated a moment and then walked over to the mother and asked her what had happened. With tears streaming down her cheeks, the mother looked up and said, "I don't know about the god in your country, but the god in mine demands the best." She had given her perfect baby to the god of the Ganges.

People have made human sacrifices in the name of religion. They have worshiped all types of idols, from brass monkeys to trees. In some of the Pacific islands, for instance, some of the islanders believe that the souls of their ancestors are in certain trees. Offerings are made to the tree, and they believe that if any injury occurs to the tree, some misfortune will come upon the village. They fear that if the tree were cut down, the village and all its inhabitants would inevitably perish.

In the name of religion, kings, emperors, and leaders of nations and tribes have been worshiped as gods. One English scholar wrote, "At a certain stage of early society the king or priest is often thought to be endowed with supernatural powers or to be an incarnation of a deity; . . . he is held responsible for bad weather, failure of the crops, and similar calamities."[1]

An example of the class of monarchs worshiped as deity was the Mikado, the spiritual emperor of Japan. In an official decree he received the title of "manifest or incarnate deity." An early account says of the Mikado: "It was considered as a shameful degradation for him even to touch the ground with his foot. . . . None of the superfluities of the body were ever taken from him, neither his hair, his beard, nor his nails were cut."[2]

Many people will shrug at "religion" and agree with the philosophy professor from a prestigious American university who wrote:

"The term 'religion' has come into use as a label for referring all at once to Judaism, Christianity, Islam, Buddhism, Hinduism, Taoism, and Confucianism, as well as a great many other siblings, some of whom have proper names and some of whom do not, but all of whom are taken to be sufficiently similar to the seven mentioned here to make it useful to lump them together."[3]

Can we really lump Christianity with every "religion" of the world?

WITHOUT EXCUSE

From the very beginning of time, "natural" religion was introduced onto the human stage as a substitute for God's plan. The apostle Paul describes his phenomenon in his letter to the Romans, using references to images resembling birds, animals, and serpents to illustrate man-made religion. But this doesn't describe all its forms. Today there are many new and more sophisticated religious expressions—especially at some universities—but they are really from the same root: man seeking God consciously or unconsciously.

Paul describes man's corruption of God's revelation: "For since the creation of the world His invisible attributes, His eternal power and divine nature, have been clearly seen, being understood through what has been made, so that they are without excuse. For even though they knew God, they did not honor Him as God or give thanks; but they became futile in their speculations, and their foolish heart was darkened. Professing to be wise, they became fools. . . . For they exchanged the truth of God for a lie, and worshiped and served the creature rather than the Creator, who is blessed forever" (Rom. 1:20–25).

Paul was simply saying that all men everywhere possess at least a primitive knowledge of God. Some people greet this idea with cynicism, which initiates the inevitable question: What about the pagans who have never heard of Jesus?

What about the pagans on Main Street, U.S.A., or the pagans at Oxford or the Sorbonne? God created all of us in His image; everyone is answerable to the light that He revealed to them. How can a just God condemn people who have never had the opportunity to hear the gospel? The answer is in Genesis 18:25: "Shall not the Judge of all the earth do right?" (KJV).

God's nature will bear witness of a divine power and person to whom everyone will answer. On the other side, God's justice will be exhibited against those who fail to live up to the light that He has given them.

In my lifetime, I have heard of many instances in which people have been given insight into the "eternal power and divine nature" of God, without benefit of a Bible or an evangelistic crusade.

In the mid 1950s, we held a major crusade in Madras, India. One man walked over 120 miles to attend these meetings. I was told that this man came from a village that had never had a missionary and, so far as anyone knew, the gospel of Christ was completely unknown. Yet he longed with all his heart to know the true and living God. He heard that a "guru" from America was going to be speaking, and his desire for God was so intense that he came and found Christ. Eight months later when Bishop Newbigin of the Church of South India (who told me the story) visited the village, he found the entire community had been turned into a church. Everyone had been led to Christ by this one man.

When we were preaching in northeast India in 1972, people walked for as much as ten days, carrying all their belongings on their shoulders, bringing their entire families from such places as Nepal, Sikkim, and Burma. We were told that a number of those people had never heard the name of Jesus Christ. They just heard that a religious meeting was going to be held and they wanted to come and see what it was about. Many stayed to find Christ.

I am convinced that when a man sincerely searches for God with all his heart, God will reveal Himself in some way. A person, a Bible, or some experience with believers will be used by God to reach the one who seeks.

A famous Bible teacher, Dr. Donald Barnhouse, told about a boat trip he had to take through the middle of Africa on a river. When he got into the boat, he noticed a chicken and thought it was probably for their next meal. After two or three hours he heard a roar in the distance and realized that they were approaching very turbulent water. The nationals who were rowing the boat steered it over to the bank, got out, and took the chicken into the woods. There they made a very crude altar. Preparatory to sacrificing the chicken, they chopped off its head and sprinkled the blood over the front of the boat. Dr. Barnhouse said he realized once more that even without a missionary and without God's Word having been taught to those people, they knew a sacrifice was necessary.

So Paul says that God has seen to it that all people everywhere possess basic knowledge of Him, His attributes, power, and divine nature. Through what they can observe, and through their consciences, they can respond to Him if they wish.

But humankind has turned away from Him. Their minds did not love the truth enough, their wills didn't desire to obey Him, their emotions were not excited by the prospect of pleasing Him.

What happened? What is still happening? Man suppresses the truth, mixes it with error, and develops the religions of the world.

Humanistic religions are often offended by biblical faith, which is the belief that accepts the Bible as the authoritative source of what sin is, and how through the life and atoning death of Christ, God can declare sinners "just." Natural religion contains just enough truth to make it deceptive. It may contain elements of the truth, or high ethical standards. Some of its followers at times use terms which sound like the language of the Bible. The English scholar C.S. Lewis said that all religions are really a preview or perversion of Christianity.

Religion of man may have a very pleasant sound. Thomas Paine wrote, "The world is my country, all mankind are my brethren, and to do good is my religion." While morality or "do-goodness" may win the approval of men, it is not acceptable to God, nor does it reflect His full moral demands. In fact, some of the crudest immorality in human history has had the approval of natural religion.

There is a great counterfeiter who adapts himself to every culture, even deceiving true believers at times. He doesn't charge on the scene clothed in red and wearing a hideous mask but charms his way as an "angel of light." This is how Satan operates. Thousands of people have entered churches without discovering a vital experience with Jesus Christ. The substitutes have been handed them in the guise of religious rituals, good works, community effort, or social reform, all of which are commendable actions in themselves, but none of which can gain a person a right relationship with God.

There are many people who say, "I guess I'm a Christian," or "I try to be a Christian." There's no guess or "try to" in the Christian life. Even some of the great intellects of our time have not come to grips with this truth: The simplicity of the gospel can reach the mentally retarded as well as the geniuses.

THE COMPROMISERS

Where there is truth and error there is always compromise. Within some churches there is a movement to reshape the Christian message to make it more acceptable to modern man. A view held by many is that "the Christian churches have been, and still are, fountainheads of anti-intellectualism and opposition to critical thinking."[4]

Books are written and sermons preached scoffing at the Bible and the basic beliefs of the Christian faith. One thick volume is called *Bible Myths* and the chapter titled "The Miracles of Christ" starts this way: "The legendary history of Jesus of Nazareth, contained in the books of the New Testament, is full of prodigies and wonders. These alleged prodigies, and the faith which the people seem to have put in such a tissue of falsehoods, indicate the prevalent disposition of the people to believe in everything, and it was among such as class that Christianity was propagated."[5]

Time magazine, in a lengthy article on the Bible, said, "Questions about the Bible's truth are nothing new; they have arisen from its earliest days."[6]

I knew an archaeology professor at Wheaton College who was also studying at the University of Chicago. Frequently the Chicago professor would bring up some point to undermine the trustworthiness of the Scriptures. On each occasion the archaeology teacher would bring out some archaeological find which proved the authenticity of the Scriptures. At one point the professor at the University of Chicago exclaimed in exasperation, "That's the trouble with you evangelical archaeologists! You're always digging up something to prove us wrong and the Bible right!"

Archaeology has never uncovered anything that disproved the Scriptures.

Among some of those who are theologians but who fail to agree among themselves on which part of the New Testament to retain and which part to reject. Some of them seem to agree that the miracles were myths. They regard the resurrection as a subjective experience of the disciples rather than an objective historical event. They question that Jesus Christ was supernatural and reject any explanation that says part of His excellence came from the fact that He was God as well as man.

C.S. Lewis was baffled by biblical critics who would pick and choose among the supernatural events they accepted. "He wondered at the selective theology of the Christian exegete who, 'after swallowing the camel of Resurrection, strains at such gnats as the feeding of the multitudes.'"[7]

THE DECEIVERS

From compromise to deceit is a small step. All through the Bible we are warned about false prophets and false teachers. Jesus said, "Beware of the false prophets, who come to you in sheep's clothing, but inwardly are ravenous wolves. . . . So then, you will know them by their fruits" (Matt. 7:15, 20).

Sometimes the "sheep's clothing" is a clergyman's robe. He may be a liberal or a fundamentalist. The liberal is like the Sadducees of old, denying biblical truth. The extreme fundamentalists, like the Pharisees of old, may accept sound theology but add so much nonbiblical material to it. Other times the clothing may be worn by someone with a string of degrees, who speaks with logical-sounding phrases. It's difficult sometimes for a Christian to discern a false teacher, since in some ways he resembles the true teacher. Jesus spoke of false prophets who "show great signs and wonders, so as to mislead, if possible, even the elect" (Matt. 24:24).

The person behind the Great Deception is Satan himself. He is crafty and clever, working in such subtle and secretive ways that no Christian should brag that he is beyond the assaults of Satan.

The apostle Paul warned Timothy, "But evil men and imposters will proceed from bad to worse, deceiving and being deceived" (2 Tim. 3:13). He also warned the church at Ephesus, "Let no one deceive you with empty words" (Eph. 5:6); and again, "As a result, we are no longer to be children, tossed here and there by waves and carried about by every wind of doctrine, by the trickery of men, by craftiness in deceitful scheming" (Eph. 4:14).

A woman who now leads hundreds of women each week in a Bible class in California said that for years her pseudointellectualism had her grabbing onto every "religious thought" that was presented. After accepting Jesus Christ as her Savior and being born again spiritually, she said, "I'm no longer a child . . . carried about by every wind of doctrine."

This is a time when more false teachers will appear. We may be living in a time in history when this age may be drawing to an end. The apostle Peter said: "But false prophets also arose among the people, just as there will also be false teachers among you, who will secretly introduce destructive heresies, even denying the Master who bought them, bringing swift destruction upon themselves. And many will follow their sensuality, and because of them the way of the truth will be maligned; and in their greed they will exploit you with false words; their judgment from long ago is not idle, and their destruction is not asleep" (2 Pet. 2:1–3).

When we realize that the heresies and the deceptions are secretly introduced, it should make us even more alert. The Sunday school, the Bible class, the pulpit, the classroom, and the mass media are being invaded en masse. Some of the terms of Christianity are even being used, for example, *peace, love,* and *born again.* Watch for the words which pepper secular literature and have entirely different meanings: *messiah, a Christ, redemption, regenerate, genesis, conversion, mercy, salvation, apostle, prophet, deliverer, savior, a spiritual leader.* Even great theological terms like *evangelical, infallible Bible,* etcetera, are rapidly losing their former meaning.

Thousands of untaught Christians are being deceived today, as are millions of people who are rejecting or ignoring the true Christ.

Deceivers with intellectual arguments which sound like the epitome of scholarship are beguiling many.

Paul is not gentle with the false teachers. He says, "But the Spirit explicitly says that in later times some will fall away from the faith, paying attention to deceitful spirits and doctrines of demons, by means of the hypocrisy of liars" (1 Tim. 4:1–2).

The Bible is very clear that many have turned away because they listened to Satan's lies and deliberately chose to accept the doctrines of devils rather than the truth of God.

BACK TO BASICS

Church members and spiritually thirsty non-church members have been hungry for a personal, vital experience with Jesus Christ. Many have been turning to other forms of worship in addition to the church service.

I wrote in my book *World Aflame* that "unless the church quickly recovers the authoritative biblical message, we may witness the spectacle of millions of Christians going outside the . . . church to find spiritual food." This is exactly what has happened.

We now estimate that there are over two million prayer groups and Bible study groups meeting in homes and churches in the United States that were not meeting ten years ago. One of the great hopes we see is that denominational leadership is beginning to recognize this and promote Bible studies conducted on a lay level with adequate leadership.

Our own crusade preparation has revealed in recent years a far greater increase in actual home prayer meeting groups. In our most recent crusades we established a prayer group on every block in the city. The result is that thousands of additional prayer meeting groups are being held in connection with the crusades—in some cities as many as five thousand.

With nearly fifty million adult Americans having experienced "born again" religious conversions, I believe it is important to have a clear understanding of what this is all about.

AN OLD CLICHÉ

Nothing could be more grossly wrong than the old cliché that "any religion will do, as long as you're sincere." What if the same line of reasoning were used with a baby? The mother would say, "I don't have any milk, but I truly want my baby to be fed, so I'll just put some coke or a little wine in the bottle. After all, they're all liquids." Ridiculous as that may sound, it is no more so than the old "sincerity" answer.

Who invented religion? Let's go back to the brothers again. The two altar fires outside Eden illustrate the difference between true and false religion. One belonged to Abel, who made an offering to the Lord God from the firstborn of his flock. Abel acted in love, adoration, humility, reverence, and obedience. And the Bible says that the Lord held Abel and his offering in high regard.

His older brother, Cain, brought a bloodless, cheap offering to the altar, and the Bible says of God that "for Cain and for his offering He had no regard" (Gen. 4:5).

Was God being unfair? After all, didn't Cain attempt to please God? Wasn't he sincere?

This story was put in the Bible to teach us that there is a right way and a wrong way to make contact with God. Abel brought a sacrifice of blood as God had instructed: Cain made his vegetable sacrifice selfishly and superficially, disobeying God by coming without faith. When God didn't bless his sacrifice, Cain killed his brother. Cain's worship was empty religiosity, hollow as his whole life became. He left his family and walked the earth as a bitter man, crying out to the Lord, "My punishment is too great to bear!" (Gen. 4:13).

Cain was sincere—but wrong.

Humanistic religion emerges under the very noses of great men of God. While Moses was on Mount Sinai receiving the tablets of stone "written with the finger of God," false religion was erupting in the camp of Israel. The people said to Aaron, "Come, make us a god who will go before us." Aaron was carried along with the idea of a new religion and said, "Tear off the gold rings which are in the ears of your wives, your sons, and your daughters, and bring them to me." Out of this gold he made a molten calf and the people said, "This is your god, O Israel, who brought you up from the land of Egypt" (Exod. 32:1–4).

Throughout time other idolatrous beliefs have eroded the foundations of truth. Whether ancient or modern, all have posed alternatives to the biblical way of approaching God.

Men and women may devise plans to satisfy their inner longings, but in the midst of all the "religions" of the world, God's way is available in the Bible for all who will come to Him on His terms.

For the person who searches, the answers are available.

5

WHAT IS THIS THING CALLED SIN?

There's a story about a jet which was traveling from Chicago to Los Angeles. As the gigantic plane leveled out at forty thousand feet, the passengers heard a voice over the loudspeaker.

"This is a recording. You have the privilege of being the first to fly in a wholly electronic jet. This plane took off electronically. It is now flying at forty thousand feet electronically. It will land in Los Angeles electronically.

"This plane has no pilot, no copilot, no flight engineer. But don't worry. Nothing can go wrong . . . go wrong . . . go wrong . . . go wrong . . . go wrong . . ."

Something has gone wrong with our jet age. It's supposed to be scientifically sophisticated and morally liberated. But it isn't. What's gone wrong?

In every major city in America and Europe crime is up. The crime wave has hit the world with hurricane force. A news magazine reported that in the United States "in the past 14 years, the rate of robberies has increased 255%, forcible rape 143%, aggravated assault 153% and murder 106%."[1]

Statistics are cold until they happen to you. I was told that at a fine private university in a small town in the West the girls don't go out of their rooms at night for fear of mugging or rape. The father who told me this said he had sent his daughter there to get her away from the dangerous areas of the large cities. This was worse.

There is no longer a safety zone in any city. A woman may be pistol-whipped while parking her car in an underground structure, or a man beaten on his way out of his office. Criminals have no respect for age, with older citizens living in many areas in a nightmare of fear. In New York City, police charged a gang of six teenagers—one of whom was thirteen—with murdering three elderly and penniless men by asphyxiation. One man died with his prayer shawl stuffed into his mouth.

Man is a contradiction. On one side is hatred, depravity, and sin; on the other side is kindness, compassion, and love. Man is a helpless sinner on one hand and has capacities which would relate him to God on the other. No wonder Paul spoke of man's disease as "the mystery of iniquity."

Some people don't like the word *sin*. They believe this is for the other person, not them. But everyone recognizes that the human race is sick and that whatever the disease is, it has affected all of life.

What is this thing called sin? The Westminster Confession defines it as "any want of conformity to or transgression of the law of God." Sin is anything contrary to the will of God.

THE BEGINNING OF SINNING

Where did sin begin and why did God allow it? The Bible hints at the answer to this riddle when it teaches that sin did not originate with man, but with the angel whom we know as Satan. This was no ordinary angel, but the most magnificent of creatures!

The prophet Ezekiel describes this noble being this way: "'You were the anointed cherub who covers, and I placed you there. You were on the holy mountain of God. . . . You were blameless in your ways from the day you were created *until unrighteousness was found in you*'" (Ezek. 28:14, 15, emphasis mine). Here is a glimpse of where it started. In some unknown past, sin was found in the heart of this magnificent creature of heaven.

The prophet Isaiah gives us another hint of the origin of evil: "'How you have fallen from heaven, O star of the morning [Lucifer], son of the dawn! You have been cut down to the earth, you who have weakened the nations! But you said in your heart, '*I will* ascend to heaven; *I will* raise my throne above the stars of God, and *I will* sit on the mount of assembly in the recesses of the north. *I will* ascend above the heights of the clouds; *I will* make myself like the Most High.' Nevertheless you will be thrust down to Sheol, to the recesses of the pit" (Isa. 14:12–15, emphasis mine).

There's the picture. Lucifer's sin was that of the five "I wills." He fell and became Satan because of his undue ambition. He wanted to be like God! He wanted to be equal to God. This was conceit in its strongest form. The New Testament gives us a glimpse of the sin of pride or conceit when it speaks of a person who might "become conceited and fall into the condemnation incurred by the devil" (1 Tim. 3:6).

FROM SATAN TO SINNERS

Sin began with the revolt of Lucifer and continued with man's revolt against God. In place of "living for God," sin substitutes "living for self."

The Bible makes it quite clear how sin entered the human race. In that luscious garden of Eden there were many trees. One tree symbolized the knowledge of good and evil, and God in His wisdom said, "You shall not eat." Adam and Eve with one or two bites violated what they knew to be God's will (see Rom. 5:12–19; Gen. 3:1–8; 1 Tim. 2:13–14).

God could have created us as human robots who would respond mechanically to His direction. Obviously this would be a response over which man had no control. But instead, God created us in His image, and He desires that the creature worship the Creator as a response of love. This can be accomplished when "free will" is exercised. Love and obedience which are compelled do not satisfy. God wanted sons, not machines.

A pastor friend who was having dinner with us one evening told us about his son who was attending a state university and becoming "very wise." "Dad," he said to his father one day, "I'm not sure that when I get out of school I will be able to follow you in your

simple Christian faith." Our friend looked his son in the eyes and
replied, "Son, that is your freedom—your terrible freedom."

And that is what God gave Adam and Eve—and what He
gives us—our freedom to choose. Our "terrible freedom." God
gave humankind the gift of freedom. Our first parents had the
choice: whether to love God or rebel and build their world without Him. The tree of knowledge of good and evil was their test—
and they flunked.

SIN IS REBELLION

Why did Adam and Eve, with all of Paradise to enjoy, choose to
rebel? The cause of rebellion was "the lust of the flesh and the lust
of the eyes and the boastful pride of life" (1 John 2:16). And this
is the type of lust to which Eve submitted. "When the woman saw
that the tree was good for food, and that it was a delight to the
eyes, and that the tree was desirable to make one wise, she took
from its fruit and ate; and she gave also to her husband with her,
and he ate" (Gen. 3:6).

Centuries later, Christ faced the same three temptations in the
wilderness. He overcame all of them and thereby showed us that
it is possible to resist temptations of Satan (Matt. 4:1–11).

The Ten Commandments tell us not to covet or lust. However, all moral law is more than a test; it's for our own good.
Every law which God has given has been for our benefit. If a person breaks it, he is not only rebelling against God, he is hurting
himself. God gave "the law" because He loves man. It is for man's
benefit. God's commandments were given to protect and promote

man's happiness, not to restrict it. God wants the best for man. To ask God to revise His commandments would be to ask Him to stop loving man.

Children usually accuse their parents of "not understanding" and being too strict. When a father says to his teenager, "Be in at eleven o'clock, and let me know exactly where you are going to be," he is protecting his child, not punishing him. God is a loving father.

When Adam and Eve broke God's commandment, they died spiritually and faced eternal death. The consequences of that act were immediate and fearful. Sin became and is the stubborn fact of life.

In our universe we live under God's law. In the physical realm, the planets move in split-second precision. There is no guesswork in the galaxies. We see in nature that everything is part of a plan which is harmonious, orderly, and obedient. Could a God who made the physical universe be any less exacting in the higher spiritual and moral order? God loves us with an infinite love, but He cannot and will not approve of disorder. Consequently, He has laid down spiritual laws which, if obeyed, bring harmony and fulfillment, but, if disobeyed, bring discord and disorder.

What were the results of Adam and Eve's sin? When both Satan and Adam challenged God's law, they did not break it; they broke themselves upon it. The life of beauty, freedom, and fellowship that Adam had known was gone; his sin resulted in a living death. Nature became cursed and the poison of sin infected the entire human family. The whole of creation was thrown into disharmony and the earth was now a planet in rebellion!

MISSING THE TARGET

One of the translations of the term *sin* in the New Testament means "a missing of the target." Sin is failure to live up to God's standards. All of us miss the target; there is not one person who is capable of fulfilling all of God's laws at all times.

For some people, even the standards of the world seem unattainable. One of the most intense and exciting spectacles we ever view is the World Olympics. Athletes who have trained for years, disciplining their minds and bodies to attain greater and greater goals, often fall short of their target. One of the finest figure skaters said she was particularly afraid that a fall would ruin her performance. She said, "Think how much time I've put into this, and how much other people have to help me. With one mistake, it could all go down the drain."[2]

In our spiritual lives we are constantly falling. There is no way we can turn in a perfect performance. King David said, "They have all turned aside, together they have become corrupt; there is no one who does good, not even one" (Ps. 14:3).

The prophet Isaiah confessed, "All of us like sheep have gone astray, each of us has turned to his own way" (Isa. 53:6).

We have all been touched by the sin of Adam. David said, "Behold, I was brought forth in iniquity, and in sin my mother conceived me" (Ps. 51:5). This doesn't mean that he was born out of wedlock, but that he inherited the tendency to sin from his parents.

Why do we have to be punished for what Adam did? Think about it. Would you have done any better than Adam? I know I wouldn't have.

We are all sinners by choice. When we reach the age of accountability and face the choice between good and evil, we will slip. We may choose to get angry, to lie, or to act selfishly. We will gossip or slander someone's character. None of us can really trust his heart, any more than we can trust a lion. In an animal preserve in East Africa the lions are allowed to roam around as if they were in their native habitat. People drive their cars or jeeps through the area, watching the lions, but are warned not to get near them. One woman rolled down her car window to get a better look, and without warning a lion charged, critically mauling her. That lion looked so tame, acted so docile, and yet became ferocious in one frightening instant.

The Bible applies this principle like this: "Sin is crouching at the door" (Gen. 4:7). Most of us are capable of almost anything, given the right circumstances. David was a classic example. Under circumstances of fleshy desire he took a woman who belonged to another man, then saw to it that her husband was murdered by putting him in the front line of battle.

You may be saying, "You make everyone out to be so rotten, and that isn't really true." Of course it isn't. A person may be a very moral individual and yet lack the love for God which is the fundamental requirement of the law.

Because we fail to meet God's requirements, we are guilty and under condemnation. Being guilty means that we deserve punishment. The very holiness of God reacts against sin: "For the wrath of God is revealed from heaven against all ungodliness and unrighteousness of men . . ." (Rom. 1:18).

GUILTY OF WHAT?

The Bible says that sin is falling short of the glory of God. Many people are unaware of the nature of the target, so they can't understand why they are told that they are missing it. Let's imagine that someone puts a blindfold around your eyes and ties it so tight that you are completely in the dark. Then you are told there is a dartboard across the room and you are to hit it with a dart. You throw in exactly the direction you are told, but when the blindfold is removed you find that your dart is stuck in a lampshade, three feet from the target. You aimed in the right direction, but you missed.

This is where the world is today, missing the target. It's what Solomon meant when he said, "There is a way which seems right to a man, but its end is the way of death" (Prov. 14:12).

When God begins to open our blindfolds so that a small amount of light begins to seep through, we may begin to see an outline, at least, of the target. We can see, for instance, how God was beginning to reveal a general sense of direction to a girl who wrote me: "I'm not in any serious trouble or anything, but I do need the help of Jesus Christ. This is my first attempt to reach out to Him. I'm seventeen, and seriously want to consider myself a Christian. I'm reaching out . . . please don't disappoint me."

Her letter shows that she senses "something" is wrong with her present life. Just what is wrong in her life and right in Christ's life she isn't yet able to say, but her life without Christ carries a kind of odor of death to it, and she wants to replace it by the fragrance of Christ. When she says she isn't in any "serious trouble," she means that she hasn't been arrested, or shamed before the community. But she has an uneasiness in her heart.

To help us see that something is terribly wrong in our lives and that death—spiritual death—will result, God gives us "the law," that is, a set of standards to sharpen our moral judgment so that we can recognize sin. The Ten Commandments form the backbone of the law. They are a giant x-ray machine to reveal the bone structure of our sinfulness. The first four x-ray plates concern our direct relationship to God. The last six concern our relationships with others.

READING THE X-RAYS

"You shall have no other gods before Me" (Exod. 20:3). Another god is not necessarily a brass Buddha or a carved totem pole. Whatever captures our highest interest is our god. Sports can be a god—or work, or money. Sex may be a god to some, while travel may be a god to another. But our highest interest should be God. He alone is worthy of our worship. Jesus said that the greatest commandment was to love God with all our heart, soul, mind, and strength. If we were able to do this, we would be demonstrating that we have no other god except the Lord.

"You shall not make for yourself an idol" (Exod. 20:4). The first commandment dealt with whom we worship. This one concerns how. We are told to worship sincerely, with a heart for God. "Man looks at the outward appearance, but the LORD looks at the heart" (1 Sam. 16:7). When we sit in a church, full of piety, but ignoring God, we make an idol of the church building.

You shall not take the name of the LORD *your God in vain"* (Exod. 20:7). This does not just apply to swearing, but even using the name for deity, such as God or Lord, without thinking of God Himself. If we vaguely mouth the words of a hymn, or call ourselves Christians without knowing Christ personally, we take the name of God in vain.

There is a story of Alexander the Great who met a disreputable character whose name was also Alexander. Alexander the Great said, "Either change your way of life or change your name."

"Remember the sabbath day, to keep it holy" (Exod. 20:8). A day in seven set apart for special worship and rest is called for in Scripture. Jesus said, "The Sabbath was made for man, and not man for the Sabbath" (Mark 2:27). This means that we need that special day. God in His wisdom tells us that our bodies need it for rest, just as our spirits need it for worship. The practice of turning weekends into long periods of leisure and entertainment to the exclusion of worship means that we lose the advantage of both leisure and worship.

We know that a nation or an individual that works seven days a week suffers physically, psychologically, and spiritually. All machinery needs occasional rest.

"Honor your father and your mother" (Exod. 20:12). This passage sets no age limit on such honor. In addition, it does not say they must be honorable to be honored. This doesn't necessarily mean that we must "obey" parents who may be dishonorable. Not only while we are children, but as long as our parents live, we must honor them if we are to obey God. Honor has many shapes: affection, humor, financial aid, respect. And yet harsh words are often

heard in the home more than anywhere else. We say things to our parents that we would never say to our friends at work or in church.

"You shall not murder" (Exod 20:13). In the older translation of this command the word *kill* was used, but the original Hebrew properly refers to murder. The outward act of murder is the final act of many emotions. Behind it are the attitudes of irritation, envy, and hatred. Jesus said, "You have heard that the ancients were told, 'You shall not commit murder, and whoever commits murder shall be liable to the court.' But I say to you that everyone who is angry with his brother shall be guilty before the court; and whoever says to his brother, 'You good-for-nothing,' shall be guilty before the supreme court; and whoever says, 'You fool,' shall be guilty enough to go into the fiery hell" (Matt. 5:21–22).

Is anyone able to say that he has never been angry with someone else? We all stand condemned before such a law, even if we have never forcefully taken someone's life.

"You shall not commit adultery" (Exod. 20:14). One scholar said: "One of the extraordinary things is that in the non-Christian religions time and time again immorality and obscenity flourish under the very protection of religion. It has often been said and said truly that chastity was the one completely new virtue which Christianity brought into this world."[3] Although that may be true, this commandment goes beyond chastity. It involves more than dishonoring a wife or husband by having sexual relations with others; it deals with the mentality which is occupied with sex. It means even looking at a man or woman with an attitude of desire or lust. To God, purity is first a matter of the heart, then of action.

Put in those terms you might say, "That's ridiculous. No one can live up to that commandment." And you would be right.

"You shall not bear false witness against your neighbor" (Exod. 20:16). We think of a witness as one being in court. If we were to lie on a stand and say, "But, your honor, my dog was provoked into biting my neighbor. He started to hit my animal with a large stick and so he attacked in self-defense," when, in fact, your dog had taken a chunk out of your neighbor's leg without provocation, then you would be bearing false witness.

But what if you gossip in a "harmless" way? The commandment is just as shattered!

"You shall not covet" (Exod. 20:17). When we take something that belongs to another, that's stealing. It is an act. Coveting is an attitude. When we desire something that belongs to someone else, that's coveting. How many marriages have ended in divorce because a man replaced thoughts about his own wife with thoughts about the desirability of his neighbor's wife? We are told not to covet anything, and that means our neighbor's new house, his car, his TV set, or the camper in his driveway.

RESULTS OF THE X-RAYS

Can anyone read the Ten Commandments with insight and not feel condemned by them? They reveal our hearts. The apostle James made the comment that even one commandment broken would be enough to destroy us. If we are suspended over a pit by a chain of ten links, how many links have to break for us to fall into the pit? "For whoever keeps the whole law and yet stumbles in one point, he has become guilty of all" (James 2:10).

The Bible and our consciences tell us that we have seriously missed the target and are sinners. What does a holy God do? How does God deal with our sin?

We see a glimpse of this in the words of a young man who became painfully aware of the commandment, "You shall not steal." He said, "My life was not a rosy one. Before I was thirteen years old I was a thief in heart, word, and action. I had been arrested many times. I spent time in a boy's reformatory and less than a week after I left I was stealing again." He said that his family gave up on him and thought that his future was destroyed. One night he heard the gospel on television, found a Bible, and started to read it. As a result he asked Christ to forgive him for his past. He is now looking to Christ to build a new foundation and give him a new future.

How can God forgive us? What happens if sin becomes a pattern in our lives? What if we are really caught up in the sin syndrome? Is there any hope?

If there weren't any hope I wouldn't be writing this book! If there weren't any answers, you probably wouldn't be reading!

6

Does God Have a Cure for Spiritual Disease?

A doctor in Australia told me of a conversation between a man and his barber. As the scissors worked, the barber said, "Hmm—I see you have a sore on your lip."

"Yep," said the man. "My cigarettes have done that."

"Well," said the barber, "it doesn't seem to be healing."

"Oh, it will—it will," replied the man confidently.

A month later he came into the shop again. His lip was split and ugly.

"Don't worry about it," he told the barber, "I've switched to a cigarette holder. It'll heal soon."

The barber had been concerned about his customer so he obtained some medical photographs that showed what lip cancer looked like. He urged his friend to compare them in the mirror with his own lip.

"Well, they look a lot alike," admitted the man, "but I'm not worried."

On the third month the man failed to come for his regular haircut. When the barber called his friend's home to inquire about him he was told, "Oh, didn't you know? He died of cancer two days ago."

Sin is like cancer. It destroys step by step. Slowly, without realizing its insidious onslaught, it progresses until finally the diagnosis is pronounced: sick to death.

A man was describing to us how he had been brought up in a godly European home, had come to this country as a young man to seek his fortune, had been converted to Christ, and then had gotten sidetracked. Temptation yielded to another temptation until finally he found himself in what he thought was a hopeless condition. I'll never forget how he described the process. "It was like being in the ocean when there is a strong undertow," he said. "You don't realize how far you're drifting from shore until all of a sudden you find yourself beyond your depth, trying desperately to swim, but unable to hold your own against the outgoing tide."

But, unless we know some of the signs of danger, how can we seek help? We can find the help the Bible provides when we know the parts of a person that sin strikes and corrupts.

MIND ATTACK

A person may be brilliant in some areas, but inadequate about spiritual realities. The Bible teaches us that a veil lies over our minds and that before we can know Christ this veil must be lifted. Without this spiritual sight we cannot come to God.

You may have heard someone ask, "How can any intelligent person believe in the Bible and all those myths and contradictions?" (implying that the gospel of Jesus Christ is anti-intellectual). The implication is contrary to truth. Understanding demands the use of the mind, but when the mind is diseased by sin it is clouded and confused.

Joel Quinones was a living example of a person whose mind was under attack. I met him in San Diego and heard his amazing story.

Joel was first thrown into prison at the age of eight for trying to kill a sadistic man who had beaten him and burned him with cigarettes. When Joel was released, he came out a bundle of hatred and from then on did everything he could to show his scorn to society. As a result Joel found himself in San Quentin at the age of nineteen and spent the next eleven years there. He was turned over to the prison psychiatrists who examined him, gave him shock treatments, and finally diagnosed him as "criminally insane."

Joel was placed with the incorrigibles. When they were fed, the food was placed on what appeared to be a large shovel with the handle long enough to push it under two separate security doors. "You don't even feed a tiger that way," Joel told us, "but that's the way they fed us."

After all those years in San Quentin, it was decided to get rid of the undesirable aliens, and Joel, along with a number of other Mexicans, was taken across the border and turned loose. He had a godly mother, a cook at a Bible school, who had been in the courtroom when Joel had been convicted for the first time. She had said to him then, "Joel, this isn't the end. Jesus has work for you to do."

When he was released in Mexico, his mother was there to greet . him. Putting her arms around him, she said, "Joel, you need the Lord Jesus; you need to ask Him to forgive your sins, to give you a new heart and a new life."

Joel struggled with this, but before the Lord was finished with him he was a transformed person. He went to Bible school, married one of the graduates, and is today a prison chaplain in Mexico. He has won so many prisoners to Christ that he is busy trying to build a halfway house, a "City of Refuge" to which these prisoners can come for rehabilitation before returning to normal life.

Sin had affected Joel's mind, but the transforming power of Christ had given him new gifts.

As I write this, I'm looking at a bone-handled knife with a five-inch blade that once belonged to Joe Medina. Joe's story is one of the most unbelievable, comic, awe-inspiring demonstrations of the power of God in what the ordinary person would have termed a hopeless life that I have ever heard. Mind attack? Joe simply couldn't think straight.

Joe was brought up in a Bronx ghetto. His mother and both of his grandmothers were spirit mediums. The streets of New York had been his home since babyhood, and gang warfare, knife fighting, stealing, and lying were simply a way of life. He was one of those disenchanted, rebellious youths of the sixties—a drug user and accomplished thief.

Joe, however, went to a meeting at which Akbar Haqq, one of our associate evangelists, was speaking. Before the evening was over, Joe had given his heart to Jesus Christ. The day after his conversion, one of his best buddies was trying to induce Joe to go with him to get drugs and Joe didn't want to be bothered. The friend pulled a knife and threatened to cut Joe up. That was a big mistake. Joe was small, but like lightning, with a knife, and before he knew what had happened, he had plunged the knife (yes, the one on my desk) into his buddy. The boy he attacked was in the hospital for two weeks.

Joe had no Christian background to fall back on and he had many ups and downs in his spiritual life. He enrolled in a small college near us but quit school before the year was up. I'm still not sure what his reason was, but I think he had some vague notion that he had to get back to share his faith with his buddies in the Bronx.

My wife talked to Joe before he left and urged him to come to Madison Square Garden, where we were having a meeting. I found out later that Joe had rounded up some of his tough buddies and gotten to the Garden at 7:30, only to find it closed because it was full, and the policeman wouldn't let him in. There had been a threat on my life that night and the policemen were taking a dim view of any suspicious-looking characters. Joe and his friends qualified for that description.

They went into a huddle and decided to rush the police. They succeeded in getting to the top floor of the Garden but suddenly found themselves face-to-face with a wall of plainclothesmen advancing on them. Turning to run the other way, they confronted another formidable wall of police. They were thrown out of the Garden without further ceremony. When I heard about this later I thought, *Oh, no! Just the ones we were trying to reach!*

However, Joe was undaunted and brought his sister and brother the next night. They both came forward to receive Christ.

Joe had a lot of trouble for a while getting values straightened out. He called Ruth one time and said he had to see her. When he arrived, she could tell something was wrong. "What have you done now, Joe?" she asked.

"Ruth, I robbed a filling station."

"Oh, Joe, why did you do that?"

"Well, it's this way—I have this buddy, you know. Well, he needed some money and he'd never robbed a filling station before. Golly, Ruth, I just felt it was my Christian duty to help him."

Ruth asked him how much he had taken and then asked him if his buddy was a Christian. He was not, Joe said. Ruth explained to Joe that he would have to be responsible for returning the entire amount. Joe looked as if she had hit him in the stomach with her fist. She then asked him point-blank if he had anything else in his possession that he had stolen. He looked at her in amazement and exclaimed, as if that were the dumbest question ever asked, "Everything I own!"

Joe returned all the stolen goods. After more advances and retreats in his Christian growth than I care to relate, he was finally admitted to Columbia Bible College. In his senior year he became vice president of the student body and is today a graduate student there with an amazing knowledge and love of the Bible.

On a recent weekend he came to visit us, and the Presbyterian pastor of our community, Calvin Thielman, asked him to give his testimony and talk about his ministry. Joe told how he related to the drug users, the dropouts, the rebels. His story was full of such wit, humor, and compassion that the audience was left with the reassurance that "nobody's hopeless."

Only those who knew Joe from the beginning can fully appreciate the marvels of the new birth in this young man's life. His mind had been so attacked by sin that it took a long time for the healing process. We are born again as babies, not mature Christians, and babies need a lot of love and patience!

The Bible teaches that sin affects the mind, whether that mind is of superior intelligence or average. A person may be intellectually brilliant, but spiritually ignorant. "A natural man does not accept the things of the Spirit of God; . . . and he cannot understand them, because they are spiritually appraised" (1 Cor. 2:14).

An intellectual mind can be turned into a first-class mind when Christ penetrates the heart. Gerhard Dirks, one of the most brilliant men in the world, is reported to have an IQ of 208. He has over 140 patents with IBM and has even attempted theoretically to reconstruct the human brain. He became completely bewildered and shaken, however, when confronted with the complexity and utter impossibility of such a reconstruction. He didn't know what to do or where to run. His choice was twofold: either the human brain came about by a fantastic chance or by intelligent planning. When faced with the alternative he knew he had only one choice, and he became a believer in God as it was revealed to him through Jesus Christ, whose intellect he could not surpass.

Dr. Boris Botsenko, a brilliant Russian physicist-mathematician, was attending a conference of scientists in Edmonton, and in his hotel he picked up a Gideon Bible. He read it and through it accepted Jesus Christ and was born again. He is now in the research department of the University of Toronto.

ATTACK ON THE WILL

Sin attacks another facet of our being—will. Jesus said, "Everyone who commits sin is the slave of sin" (John 8:34). Even in countries where there is political freedom, there are millions who live under the tyranny of pride, jealousy, or prejudice. Countless others are slaves to alcohol, barbiturates, or narcotics. They possess traits or are consumed by desires they hate but are powerless in their grip. They want to be free, and some search for freedom through avenues offered by other men. But Christ said, "You will know the truth, and the truth will make you free" (John 8:32). Christ is the truth.

I have known many persons who found freedom from the bondage of will and desire. On May 9, 1972, in a little church outside of Nashville, Tennessee, a pastor gave a gospel invitation and a man named Johnny Cash got up and went down the aisle and knelt at the altar of the church. Johnny Cash says that he gave his life to Jesus Christ that day. Here is a man whose life had been hurt by drugs and imprisonment, and who has become a hero in the world of country music. He is now a force for good in the world and is being used in the cause of Christ.

I have in my possession a hashish pipe as a reminder of a young man who was a slave to drugs. He had made a terrible mess of his life and also the life of the girl he loved. As a result, he drove to a lonely, deserted parkway where he slit his wrists. Evidently he didn't do a very good job, because the blood wasn't coming out fast enough and he thought at that rate it was going to take him too long to die. So he crawled under the tailpipe of his car with the motor still going, covered himself with a blanket, and proceeded to inhale the fumes.

He said that while he became drowsy from the fumes he uttered a prayer asking God to forgive him for what he was doing. Suddenly a horrible black feeling came over him and he knew that what he was about to do did not please God. In his weakness, with bleeding wrists and a drugged mind, he drove to a pastor's home. The pastor took him to the hospital. After the young man was treated, the pastor explained to him that Christ alone can make atonement for our sins and give us release from guilt and the joy of being forgiven.

This young man is now happily married and is a positive influence on the lives of others.

Unresolved hatred is a tyranny which can make anyone a slave to sin as it attacks the will. Just a few years ago Dr. William P. Wilson, then Professor of Psychiatry at Duke University Medical Center, systematically took Bibles away from his patients at the center. But his life and medical practice have been transformed by the power of Jesus Christ, and he now uses the insights he has gained from the gospel in treating his patients. He keeps copies of the Bible in his office and gives them out. Dr. Wilson says, "One of the greatest causes of mental illness is unresolved guilt. Feelings of shame, inadequacy, missing the mark, not measuring up, are some sources of guilt feelings. The answer to guilt is grace and the new birth. The new birth leads to the forgiveness of sin."

Forgiveness is hard for many to believe. Dr. Warren Wiersbe of Chicago calls forgiveness "the greatest miracle in the Bible."

I have a letter from a young man who said, "In 1971 I was a drug-dealing dropout from Northwestern University. During your Chicago crusade I came forward at the invitation and prayed for the Lord to save me, even though I personally didn't feel bad about my ungodly practices. I also asked that He forgive me my sins (I could intellectually conceive of them, but not personally feel them) and that He would make Himself known in a personal way.

"I was expecting a lightning bolt from heaven to knock me down, or for God to put me through a mental breakdown so He could straighten out my mind and use it for His glory. Needless to say, He didn't do that. I began to feel quite disappointed and also somewhat scared and thought this God thing might easily turn out to be a hoax after all. At that instant a middle-aged, short-haired, suit-wearing, Bible-carrying counselor came up to me and put a Jesus sticker on my shirt and shook my hand. 'God bless you, young man,' he said. Think of it! This establishment dude shaking my hand—me, a freaked-out hippie. The love of God coming through him showed me that Jesus loved me regardless of how I dressed or abused society. That simple act hit me and I suddenly realized the simplicity of God's salvation. He didn't want to put me through the pain of a mental breakdown—all He wanted me to do was to receive His Son as I had just done!"

When Conscience Fails

Sin not only affects the mind and the will, but also the conscience. A person becomes very slow to detect the approach of sin. It's like telling an untruth: The first time you tell a story it really bothers you; but with repetition your conscience is no longer your guide, and soon the lie is woven so strong that you are convinced it's the truth. You no longer have sensitivity to things you know are wrong.

One day Joe Medina, to whom I referred earlier in this chapter, called Ruth from a telephone booth and said, "Ruth, I'm not drunk, but I just wanted to tell you something."

Ruth asked him what he was doing in a phone booth. He explained that he was riding around with a buddy who had a fifth of whiskey with him. Joe explained that his friend didn't have a North Carolina driver's license and shouldn't drive the car, especially while drinking. So Joe said, with his typical logic, "Ruth, I felt it was my Christian duty to drink that fifth of whiskey for him."

The patience of my wife never ceases to amaze me. She said, "Joe, you drank that fifth of whiskey because you wanted to drink that fifth of whiskey."

There was a long pause. Then, "Ruth, you're exactly right."

Joe had been trained in calling badness "good." He knew how to lie, cheat, and rationalize out of any situation. But for the grace of God, he would still be that way today.

The results of the infection of no longer knowing the difference between good and evil are reflected in every part of the Scriptures. When David first looked at Bathsheba, a train of events began which led from adultery to deceit to murder. David was forgiven for his sins, but he had to pay the natural consequences. He reaped a bitter harvest and his reign was clouded with constant trouble.

In view of the way we allow our consciences to become dulled, it is amazing that God is so patient. The Bible says, "The Lord is not slack concerning his promise, as some men count slackness, but is longsuffering to us-ward, not willing that any should perish, but that all should come to repentance" (2 Pet. 3:9, KJV).

No matter how patient God is, He is also just. When man hardens his heart, God continues to speak. But man cannot hear. Genesis 6:3 says, "My Spirit shall not always strive with man" (KJV). Eventually, if God sees that man won't repent, "There is a sin unto death" (1 John 5:16, KJV). This refers to blasphemy against the Holy Spirit, which is final rejection of God's plan of salvation, and it is also described in Hebrews 6:4–6:

"For in the case of those who have once been enlightened and have tasted of the heavenly gift and have been made partakers of the Holy Spirit, and have tasted the good word of God and the powers of the age to come, and then have fallen away, it is impossible to renew them again to repentance, since they again crucify to themselves the Son of God and put Him to open shame."

When a man's conscience is gone he uses all kinds of excuses to justify his action. He blames his family, his business associates, his bad breaks, anything. He can cheat on his income tax because the laws are unjust. He can cheat on his wife (or a wife can be unfaithful to her husband) because the other one is cold—or thoughtless. The good and bad are gone, and life is lived in gray tones.

In Athens the columns and statues of the Parthenon have been eroding in recent years at an accelerated rate. It hasn't been storms or time which have caused the imminent destruction of these priceless ancient works of art, but the pollution of the wastes of modern society. In the same way, it's not the heavy storms of life that erode us, but the insidious, gradual pollution of sin which leads to our destruction.

SICK TO DEATH

Crime requires punishment, and sin has a penalty. Although this may be a subject we would like to ignore, it is an unavoidable fact. Not only does everyone suffer as a result of sin in this life, but everyone must face the judgment to come. "For the wages of sin is death" (Rom. 6:23).

First, there is *physical death*. The Bible says, "It is appointed for men to die once" (Heb. 9:27). Incidentally, this completely rules out the possibility of reincarnation.

Death is inevitable and unpredictable in many cases. For each of us there is a day, an hour, a minute, when physically we are no longer earth beings. If God had not given the judgment of physical death, the earth would soon become uninhabitable, because men would live forever in their sins.

Because life is brief, the Bible teaches that we must "prepare to meet [our] God" (Amos 4:12). In the course of my life I have known many people who are thoroughly prepared to meet God. There is a startling difference between them and people who have lived a life without God.

I will never forget the summer of 1973. That was the year that one of the greatest Christians I ever knew entered heaven. He was my father-in-law, Dr. L. Nelson Bell. Dr. Bell served Christ for years in China as a missionary surgeon. In 1972 he had been Moderator of the Presbyterian Church in the United States, the highest honor his denomination could bestow. The night before he died he spoke with the World Missions Conference in a larger auditorium in Montreat.

89

At the end of his talk he said, "Before I pray I have a few words today. After hearing that singing, no one can deny that our Presbyterian Church is waking up. Now in this place there are two groups of people. There are those who know they are saved and love the Lord Jesus Christ, and there are those here who as yet may not know Christ. My hope is that before you leave this place you will come to know Him as your personal Lord and Savior. The Lord said, 'Behold, I stand at the door and knock; if any man hears my voice, and opens the door, I will come in to him, and will sup with him and he with me.'"

Those were the last words that Dr. Bell said in public. That night he went to sleep and when he woke he was in the presence of his Lord. His life had come full circle. His favorite hymn was "All the Way My Savior Leads Me," and when I saw him that morning, it was a great comfort to see the face of one so peaceful.

He was prepared to meet our God.

I remember hearing of the last words said by Pearl Goode, a wonderful woman who through the years was one of our most faithful prayer supporters, often going into seclusion and praying night and day for the crusade team wherever they were. She walked in such close fellowship with God that when it was her time to go, she sat up in bed and said, "Well, there He is. There's Jesus!" She was prepared to meet God.

In the summer of 1976 there was a flash flood in Colorado that took the lives of a great many people. Among the victims were some young Christian girls who had been at a retreat in the mountains. The men who had the job of searching out the bodies of those who were killed reported later that most of the people had expressions of horror on their faces, but they were astounded to see that every one of the girls appeared to be at peace. They were prepared to meet their God.

Life is so short. The Bible says that we must be prepared to meet God at all times. We never know when we step into our car, walk out the door of our home, or just open our eyes to a new day, what lies ahead. "Since his days are determined, the number of his months is with You, and his limits you have set so that he cannot pass" (Job 14:5).

The second dimension of death is *spiritual death.* Millions of people on earth are walking around physically alive, but spiritually dead. When your eyes and ears become attuned to the cries of others, you hear those who say they are empty and lost. They are separated from the source of life and like a lamp which is unattached, they are dark and lifeless. The lamp may be very expensive, may have a beautiful shade which draws attention, but has no light without being plugged into the source of energy. Jesus said, "I am the life."

Newspapers and magazines throughout the world carried the story of the suicide of Freddie Prinze. At the age of twenty-two he had attained one of the highest status roles in show business. He was the darling of television and had just performed for an incoming president at the Inaugural gala in Washington. Yet something was terribly wrong in the life of this talented comedian. A close friend, comedian David Brenner, explained to *Time* magazine, "There was no transition in Freddie's life. It was an explosion. It's tough to walk off a subway at age 19 and then step out of a Rolls-Royce the next day." Producer Komack, also a close confidant, said, "Freddie saw nothing around that would satisfy him. He would ask me, 'Is this what it is? Is this what it's all about?'" Mr. Komack said, "His real despondency, whether he could articulate it or not, concerned the questions: 'Where do I fit in? Where is my happiness?' I would tell him, 'God, Freddie, your happiness is right here. You're a star.' He'd say, 'No. That's not happiness for me any more.'" As *Time* magazine commented at the end of the story, "For one of the most singular escape stories in ghetto history, escape was not enough."

We may be physically alive, but spiritually dead, like the woman who is described as "dead even while she lives" (1 Tim. 5:6).

The third dimension of death is *eternal death*. This may be a subject which most try to avoid. We hear a lot about "hell on earth," but there is another hell which is more real and certain, and that's the hell of eternal death. Jesus Himself spoke frequently about hell. He warned of a hell to come. The Scripture teaches us that we'll be in hell alone and bearing pain alone. There is no fellowship in hell except for fellowship with darkness. I have heard some people say, "If I thought my father [or some other loved one] were in hell, that's where I want to be, too!" What an illusion! Hell is the loneliest place imaginable.

Jesus warned men, "And these will go away into eternal punishment" (Matt. 25:46). He also said, "The Son of Man will send forth His angels, and they will gather out of His kingdom all stumbling blocks, and those who commit lawlessness, and will throw them into the furnace of fire; in that place there will be weeping and gnashing of teeth" (Matt. 13:41–42).

There is never such an urgency to talk about eternity as there is when physical death confronts us. A friend of mine told me that the day after her son was killed in an airplane accident, while their house was full of people offering love and consolation, something went wrong with the furnace. A repairman was called. After looking at the heater, he said, "Lady, if you had waited a little while longer to call me that furnace might have blown up." In the midst of her own grief she paused and looked the repairman squarely in the eyes. "There is only one thing that's important right now," she said. "If that furnace had exploded while you were working on it, do you know for sure where you would spend eternity?"

Before he left the house he learned how to have assurance of his eternal destiny.

TWO FACES OF MAN

Man has two faces. One shows his ingenuity, his capacity to create, to be kind, to honor truth. The other face reveals him using his ingenuity maliciously. We see him doing kind acts in a shrewd manner in order to forward a private desire. We see one side of him enjoying a sunset, but at the same time working in a job that fills the atmosphere with waste products that nearly obscure the sunset. His search for truth often degenerates into a rat race to discover a scientific fact so the credit will be his.

Man is both dignified and degraded.

The need for spiritual rebirth is evident to the most casual observer of human nature. Man is fallen and lost, alienated from God. From the very beginning, all attempts to recover man from his lostness have revealed one or the other of two ways.

PLAN A AND PLAN B

Remember Cain and Abel? The sons of Adam and Eve represent Plan A and Plan B of salvation. One of them, Cain, came his own way: he initiated Plan A; the other, Abel, was obedient and came God's way, Plan B.

Cain was the self-sufficient materialist and religious humanist. He brought to the altar an expression of his own labors; he became the prototype of all who dare approach God without the shedding of blood.

Cain's way didn't work for him. It has never worked for anyone, and it will not work today. Only God can properly diagnose our disease and provide the cure. God chose blood as the means of our redemption. The apostle John wrote that Jesus Christ "washed us from our sins in his own blood" (Rev. 1:5, KJV).

When Jesus Christ, the perfect God-man, shed His blood on the cross, He was surrendering His pure and spotless life to death as an eternal sacrifice for man's sin. Once and for all, God made complete provision for the cure of man's sins. Without the blood of Christ, it is a fatal disease.

Each of us makes his choice between the two ways—man's way or God's way. Which?

PART TWO

GOD'S ANSWER

7

THE MAN WHO IS GOD

It's just after Christmas as I write this chapter. The cards are still coming in each day, bulging the mailbox and dazzling the eye. Many of them have pictures of Jesus, some as a baby in a rough-hewn cradle, others as a shepherd, surrounded by His children. The world is fascinated with how He might look. From the magnificent cathedrals of Europe to Sunday school classrooms in the USA, we see pictures of artists' conceptions of Jesus. I was in Africa a few days before Christmas and saw Jesus depicted as a black baby. Last year we were in the Orient just before Christmas and saw Him depicted as an Oriental.

What is the image the world has of Jesus Christ? Some visualize him as a pale, blue-eyed man, smiling rather weakly beneath an ethereal halo. In America, the new popular Jesus is a handsome, virile type with robust charm and appeal. Probably Jesus looked Middle Eastern, with a swarthy-colored skin—we really don't know. And it's just as well that we don't know what He really looked like physically—because today He belongs to the world!

No matter how we imagine Him to be, Jesus Christ has no stronger portrait than the one in the Bible. It is a picture of the man who is God. The claim that Jesus Christ is deity is the focal point for all belief. It is the foundation of Christianity. Since the quickest way to destroy any edifice is to tear out or weaken its base, men have always tried to disprove, ignore, or scoff at the claims of Christ. However, our hope of redemption from sin is dependent upon the deity of Christ.

Who is He?

JESUS: UNIQUE IN ALL WAYS

We know that Jesus lived. He was a man in history, as well as a man for all times. Tacitus, perhaps the greatest Roman historian born in the first century, speaks of Jesus. Josephus, a Jewish historian born in A.D. 37, tells of the crucifixion of Jesus. A contemporary Bible scholar said that "the latest edition of the *Encyclopedia Britannica* uses 20,000 words in describing this person, Jesus. His description took more space than was given to Aristotle, Cicero, Alexander, Julius Caesar, Buddha, Confucius, Mohammed, or Napoleon Bonaparte."[1]

Rousseau said, "It would have been a greater miracle to invent such a life as Christ's than to be it."

Jesus lived, taught, and died on earth in a small area of the

Middle East, mostly in what is Israel today. That is a confirmed fact of history.

HIS INTELLECT

Many men in history have been admired and many have been given honors for their intellectual achievements, but no man has had the incisive intellect of Jesus. In all circumstances, whether tired from a long journey, or plagued by his enemies, Jesus was able to confound some of the greatest minds of His day.

He had three years of intellectual encounters with the religious leaders of His day. These men often tried to put Him on the spot by asking questions which were difficult to answer. On one occasion, when He was teaching in the temple, the chief priests and elders questioned Him belligerently. They asked, "By what authority are You doing these things, and who gave You this authority?" (Matt. 21:23).

Here were the men who had control of all the religious teaching, and this Jesus, a carpenter from Nazareth, who was not their pupil, was teaching in their territory. Can you imagine what would happen at one of our prestigious seminaries if the janitor suddenly stepped onto the platform and began to instruct the students?

Jesus answered the question of the religious authorities with another question. "I will ask you one thing too, which if you tell Me, I will also tell you by what authority I do these things. The baptism of John was from what source, from heaven or from men?"

Now, John the Baptist had not been ordained by them either, and he had urged his followers to obey Jesus. The religious leaders were thrown into confusion. They knew if they said, "From heaven," that Jesus would say, "Then why didn't you believe him?" On the other hand, if they answered, "From men," they feared the people would become irate, because they believed John was a prophet. So they simply said, "We don't know."

Jesus replied, "Neither will I tell you by what authority I do these things" (Matt. 21:27).

Jesus possessed a mental agility that has astounded scholars for two thousand years.

HIS FRANKNESS

No matter what the consequences, Jesus was very open and frank. The members of the religious establishment of His day were meticulously following certain rites for cleansing the dishes they ate from each day. Using this practice as an illustration, Jesus said, "Woe to you, scribes and Pharisees, hypocrites! For you clean the outside of the cup and of the dish, but inside they are full of robbery and self-indulgence. You blind Pharisee, first clean the inside of the cup and of the dish, so that the outside of it may become clean also" (Matt. 23:25–26).

The charge Jesus made is just as applicable today. True belief in God is inward and has to do with a personal commitment and attitude, rather than strict observance of rituals and rules. Most of us would be reticent to speak so frankly to church leaders of our time. Jesus, however, was a man who was frank, bold, and honest in every situation.

HIS OPENNESS

Jesus had the ability to understand all people, no matter what their position in society. On one occasion He was dining with a prominent religious leader named Simon. While they were eating, a repentant prostitute came into the hall where the meal was being served and began to wash the feet of Jesus with her tears and to dry them with her hair. The religious leader was shocked and began to look at Jesus with doubt. He thought, *If this man were a prophet He would know who and what sort of person this woman is who is touching Him. . . .*

Jesus, sensing his thoughts, told him this story: "A certain money-lender had two debtors; one owed five hundred denarii [a denarius was then a day's wage], and the other fifty. When they were unable to repay, he graciously forgave them both. Which of them therefore will love him more?"

Simon must have wondered, *What's the purpose of this story?* He probably shrugged as he answered, "I suppose the one to whom he forgave more."

Jesus told him that was the right answer. Then He reminded Simon that when He had come into his house as a guest, Simon had ignored all the normal courtesies of the day. "You gave Me no water for My feet, but she has wet My feet with tears, and wiped them with her hair. You gave Me no kiss; but she, since the time I came in, has not ceased to kiss My feet."

Then Jesus turned to the woman and reassured her that her sins had been forgiven.

The other guests at the dinner party were astounded. They asked, "Who is this man who even forgives sins?" (Luke 7).

We know that Jesus often dined with the social elite but defended the social outcasts.

His Forgiving Spirit

His opponents were powerful and persistent. They mocked Him, plotted against Him, and finally maneuvered the crowds to support His death by crucifixion.

As He was hanging on the cross, bleeding and suffering from the pain and the hot sun, many jeered at Him, saying, "Save Yourself, and come down from the cross!" (Mark 15:30).

Under such extreme circumstances, Jesus exhibited a trait that was beyond our comprehension. He spoke to God the Father and said, "Father, forgive them; for they do not know what they are doing" (Luke 23:34).

How many mere men could forgive their persecutors under such brutal circumstances?

His Moral Authority

The pictures of Jesus as a vague, colorless man do not fit the true account of His strength and moral authority. At the end of His life the establishment, both religious and political, had united together to end His work by sending officers to arrest Him. The burly henchmen approached Jesus, but stopped to listen to what He was saying. They returned to their superiors without Him.

"Why didn't you bring him?" they were asked.

The officers replied in astonishment, "Never has a man spoken the way this man speaks" (John 7:45–46). They were experiencing what the crowds of ordinary people already knew. "The crowds were amazed at His teaching," Matthew reported, "for He was teaching them as one having authority, and not as their scribes" (Matt. 7:28–29).

Jesus Christ lived the type of life He taught. There are many men we know who are noble, intelligent, frank, and open, and who speak with authority. But only in Jesus do we find the human characteristics which we would expect God to display if He were to become a man.

Jesus' claim to deity is fully supported by His character. He was unique in history.

MORE THAN JUST A MAN

If this were all we had to say about Jesus Christ, He would have very little more to offer than many great men of history. However, the uniqueness of Christ is that in His life on earth He displayed every known attribute or characteristic of deity.

What is an attribute? One Bible scholar offered this simple definition: "The attributes of God are those distinguishing characteristics of the nature of God which are inseparable from the idea of deity, and which constitute the basis and grounds for His various manifestations to His creatures."[2]

Jesus Christ was the supreme manifestation of God. "God was in Christ reconciling the world to Himself" (2 Cor. 5:19).

He was no ordinary man. Several hundred years before He was born, Isaiah, the prophet, said, "Behold, a virgin will be with child and bear a son" (Isa. 7:14). No other man in all history could say that his mother was a virgin. The Scriptures teach that He did not have a human father; if He had, He would have inherited the sins and infirmities that all men have, since "that which is born of the flesh is flesh" (John 3:6). Since He was conceived not by natural means, but by the Holy Spirit, He stands as the one man who came forth pure from the hand of God. He could stand before His fellow men and ask, "Which of you can truthfully accuse me of one single sin?" (John 8:46, *The Living Bible*). He was the only man since Adam who could say, "I am pure."

If we honestly probe our minds, we have to admit that there are mysteries about the incarnation that none of us can ever understand. In fact, Paul speaks of God, manifest in the flesh, as a "mystery" (1 Tim. 3:16).

Paul explained the Man who is God in another epistle: "Have this attitude in yourselves which was also in Christ Jesus, who, although He existed in the form of God, did not regard equality with God a thing to be grasped, but emptied Himself, taking the form of a bond-servant, and being made in the likeness of men" (Phil. 2:5–7).

First, *God is holy.* This is a characteristic possessed by Jesus Christ which is central to the entire Christian faith. What does *holiness* mean? It is a term used in reference to people, places, and sometimes circumstances. However, this very common word, often misused and misunderstood, means "self-affirming purity." No mere human being now or ever could possess pure holiness and moral perfection.

In the Old Testament, God is described as "righteous in all His ways" (Ps. 145:17) and the prophet Isaiah, in his vision of the Lord God, declares "Holy, holy, holy, is the LORD of hosts" (Isa. 6:3). In the New Testament this unique attribute is possessed by Jesus Christ, the holy child, the sinless man. Thus Jesus Christ had a characteristic that only God could possess.

Second, *God is also just.* In order to guard His holiness, God must exercise justice. Since all sin is an offense to God, the principle of God's justice is vital to an orderly universe, just as a nation must have certain laws and codes. But unlike human government, which uses justice in ways that are suitable to the rulers or heads of government, God's justice is pure; no mistake is ever made.

Jesus Christ was just. During His earthly career He exhibited this characteristic when He drove the racketeers out of the temple with a whip. He is also described as faithful and just in forgiving us our sins. When He died for our sins it was "the Just" dying for the unjust.

Third, *God is mercy.* This characteristic of deity was seen in the entire life of Jesus Christ. When the woman who was an adulteress was brought before the authorities and condemned to be stoned, Jesus defended her with the charge, "Let him who is without sin cast the first stone." Her accusers retreated in embarrassment. Jesus Christ, exhibiting God's mercy, told her to go and sin no more. The love, mercy, and compassion of Jesus comes out time after time throughout His public ministry. In the opening address that Jesus gave at His hometown of Nazareth, He quoted Isaiah the prophet, "The Spirit of the Lord is upon Me, because He anointed Me to preach the gospel to the poor. He has sent Me to proclaim release to the captives, and recovery of sight to the blind, to set free those who are oppressed, to proclaim the favorable year of the Lord" (Luke 4:18).

Fourth, *God is love*. The first songs children learn in Sunday school, when they are barely able to carry a tune, are about God's love. A child can understand God's love, but the depths are so infinite that an adult finds it difficult to fathom. God's love is the continuing result of His holiness, justice, and mercy.

As a holy God, He hates sin and can have no fellowship with sin. Because the Bible tells us that the soul that sins must surely die, we can see that separation from God is a result of sin. However, because God is also mercy, He longs to save the guilty sinner and must then provide a substitute in Jesus Christ. There is God's love: "For God so loved the world, that He gave His only begotten Son, that whoever believes in Him shall not perish, but have eternal life" (John 3:16).

GOD AND JESUS CHRIST THE SAME

Fifth, Jesus Christ possesses the three great "omnis" of God. This prefix means "completely or all" and when used within the word *omnipotent* it means that the possessor has all power. The dictionary has one word to describe the Omnipotent, and that is God.

While a man on earth, Jesus Christ performed many miracles. He raised people from the dead; He took a few loaves and fish and multiplied them to feed thousands; He cured the chronically sick and healed the crippled. But why should this be surprising? Jesus said, "All power is given unto me in heaven and in earth" (Matt.

28:18, KJV). That is a startling statement if it were made by any ordinary man. Only God could make such a claim.

Jesus Christ was also *omniscient*. This means that He knew all things, and He still knows all things. The Scriptures say, "Jesus knowing their thoughts" (Matt. 9:4); "He knew all men . . . He Himself knew what was in man" (John 2:24–25); "In whom are hidden all the treasures of wisdom and knowledge" (Col. 2:3).

Do you know anyone of your acquaintance or any person in history who knew everything? Have you ever heard of a person who could know, without a mistake, the minds of men? Only an all-powerful God knows everything, and Jesus Christ was omniscient.

Probably no idea is more difficult for man to comprehend than the thought of *omnipresence*. How can God be everywhere at once? From our viewpoint we are bound by time and space. We are physical creatures who can only be one place at a time. We frequently complain, "I can't be everyplace at once!" God transcends time and space, and so does Jesus Christ. He existed before time began. "Before Abraham was born, I am" (John 8:58). "He is before all things" (Col. 1:17).

Jesus is not earthbound. He said, "Wherever two or more of you are gathered together in My name there am I in the midst of you." He can be with a gathering of believers in a primitive hut in New Guinea or a businessman's luncheon in Dallas. He can be at the supper table of a family or in the banquet hall of royalty. Jesus Christ is omnipresent.

Jesus Christ claimed to be God. He said, "I and the Father are one" (John 10:30) and, "He who sees Me sees the One who sent

Me" (John 12:45). He made it very clear when He spoke to the religious leaders of his time who He was. "I am He who bears witness of Myself, and the Father who sent Me bears witness of Me." Members of the local church hierarchy said to Him, "Where is Your Father?" Jesus answered, "You know neither Me, nor My Father; if you knew Me, you would know My Father also."

Christ represents Himself as having been "sent from God" and being "not of this world." He declares that He is "the light of the world," "the way, the truth, and the life," and "the resurrection and the life." He promises eternal life to everyone who believes in Him as Lord and Savior.

Knowing the claims of Jesus Christ, you are faced with this vital decision—

WHAT WILL YOU DO WITH JESUS?

Question: Who do you think Jesus Christ is? If He is not who He claimed to be, He is a deceiver or an egomaniac. We cannot settle for a middle-of-the-road answer that He was "a good man," or the modern form of adulation as a "superstar." He Himself eliminates a neutral answer. Either we decide He is a liar or a lunatic, or we must declare Him to be Lord.

In light of the evidence of Scripture and the physical fact of the Resurrection, the only wise conclusion is that He is God, worthy of our worship and trust. When I decide to be a Christian, I am deciding who Jesus Christ is. Trust in Him makes me a believer in Him and leads to being truly alive!

Out of His Private Wilderness

We heard about a young couple who were separated during World War II. While the father was gone the mother gave birth to a baby girl. The months passed, and the mother kept a large picture of her husband on the desk so that the little girl would grow up knowing what her daddy looked like. She learned to say "Daddy" and associated the name with the picture on the desk. Finally the day came when her father returned home from the war. The whole family gathered to watch the little girl when she saw her father for the first time. Imagine their disappointment when she would have nothing whatever to do with him. Instead, she ran to the photograph on the desk, saying, "That's my daddy." Day after day the family had to blink back the tears as they saw the young father on his knees trying his best to get acquainted with his little daughter, explaining as simply as he could that he was her daddy. But each time she would shake her head, then run to the picture on the desk and exclaim, "That's my daddy." This went on for some time, but one day something happened. The little girl, having gone repeatedly to the picture on the desk, returned to her father and looked carefully into his face. Then she went back to the picture on the desk and studied it. The family held their breath. After several trips the little face lit up as the child exclaimed excitedly, "They're both the same daddy!"

C.S. Lewis describes his experience: "You must picture me alone in that room in Magdalen, night after night, feeling, whenever my mind lifted even for a second from my work, the steady unrelented approach of Him whom I so earnestly desired not to meet. That which I greatly feared had at last come upon me. In the Trinity Term of 1929 I gave in, and admitted that God was God, and knelt and prayed: perhaps, that night, the most dejected and reluctant convert in all England. I did not then see what is now the most shining and obvious thing; the Divine humility which will accept a convert even on such terms. The Prodigal Son at least walked home on his own feet. But who can duly adore that Love which will open the high gates to a prodigal who is brought in kicking, struggling, resentful, and darting his eyes in every direction for a chance of escape? The words *compelle intrare*, compel them to come in, have been so abused by wicked men that we shudder at them; but, properly understood, they plumb the depth of the Divine mercy. The hardness of God is kinder than the softness of men, and his compulsion is our liberation."[3]

A certain professor said that in over forty years on campus he had never been asked, "Are you a Christian?" When he was a student he had read books that explained away Christ's miracles; he considered himself well informed and sophisticated on the subject. As a result, on the one hand he disbelieved the deity of Jesus Christ while on the other hand he kept some vague belief in God.

In practice, however, he said, "I usually chose to ignore Him in my early post-college days. This started the path into my own personal wilderness. I tried to satisfy my inner needs by reading and studying literature and science. These studies often confirmed my opinion that I could leave Christ out of my life because He was just another prophet."

Then one day a student entered the professor's "private wilderness" to invite him to hear a campus talk on the deity of Christ.

The professor later recalled, "I was confronted with the positive side of Christ's deity for the first time since I was a child. I didn't expect to have my disbelief in the deity of Christ changed.

"As I listened that evening, partly in skepticism, partly in hope, I admit I also yearned to be convinced. The speaker had scarcely completed half of his remarks before I was convinced of the deity of Christ. A lifetime's assumption that Jesus was just another gifted teacher was destroyed. The turnabout in my convictions was simple."

I must agree with the professor. It is simple. Jesus is God. Our earthly lives and eternal destinies depend on our belief in that fact.

8

WHAT HAPPENED
AT THE CROSS

In jewelry stores from Fifth Avenue to the airport in Rome one piece of jewelry is universally displayed—the cross. Clerical robes have this emblem sewn on the front or back. Churches display the cross in wood, bronze, concrete, or brass. The last month of the year some office buildings light certain windows at night to form a cross which can be seen for miles.

What does the cross of Jesus mean? If we stopped people on the street and asked that question we might hear, "It's a symbol for Christianity, I guess." Or, "Jesus was a martyr and was nailed to the cross." Others might say it was a myth, or a history major might say it was an example of Roman justice.

Another answer to the question, "What does the cross mean?"

was given by the poet, Thomas Victoria. He tried to express how Jesus Himself might speak of the cross if we asked Him. The poet pictured Jesus on the cross, surrounded by men who were intent upon killing him.

Jesus looks at them and says:

> Oh, how sweet the wood of the cross,
> How sweet the nails,
> That I could die for you.

This deeply personal, intimate view of the cross is what the apostle Paul taught when he said, "In human experience it is a rare thing for one man to give his life for another, . . . though there have been a few who have had the courage to do it. Yet the proof of God's amazing love is this: that it was *while we were sinners* that Christ died for us" (Rom. 5:7–8, Phillips).

The focus of Paul's whole ministry to the great commercial city of Corinth was summed up when he said, "For I determined to know nothing among you except Jesus Christ, and Him crucified" (1 Cor. 2:2).

The average person in Corinth would have answered a question about the cross in the same way as the man on the street in the USA or any European, African, or Asian country. Corinthians lived in a city which was known for its depraved moral character. It was the kind of town in which we wouldn't want to raise our families. The Corinthians were a sophisticated, sexually dissolute bunch, who thought that the cross was ridiculous, foolish, and even idiotic. Commenting on this view, Paul said, "The foolishness of God is wiser than men, and the weakness of God is stronger than men" (1 Cor. 1:25).

In Corinth the preaching of the cross of Christ was a stumbling block to the Jews, and idiocy to the philosophic Greeks. The philosophers believed they could unravel divine mysteries because they were overconfident of their own mental capacities. However, Paul said that the natural man (meaning the man who does not have the Spirit of God indwelling him) cannot understand the things of God. He meant that sin has twisted our understanding of truth so that we cannot recognize the truth about God.

Before the teaching in the Bible about the cross can mean anything to us, the Spirit of God must open our minds. The Scriptures teach that a veil covers our minds as a result of our separation from God.

To an "outsider" the cross must appear to be ridiculous. But to those who have experienced its transforming power, it has become the only remedy for the ills of each person, and of the world.

In spite of this available power, the gospel about Christ who was crucified is still unimportant to millions. They reflect the failure Paul analyzed when he questioned, "What have the philosopher, the writer and the critic of this world to show for all their wisdom? Has not God made the wisdom of this world look foolish? For it was after the world in its wisdom had failed to know God, that he in his wisdom chose to save all who believe by the 'simpleminded-ness' of the gospel message" (1 Cor. 1:20–21, Phillips).

How can we brand the message of the cross as foolishness? Have we done so well with our private lives, with our families, and with our society that we can claim wisdom? It's time we abandoned the pretense of being intellectual and recognize that our best minds are baffled by life.

God successfully changes men and women by the message that centers in the cross. His approach recognizes our disease and presents the right medicine. He offers His wisdom as an alternative to our failures.

In our everyday life we profit from many helps that we can't understand. We go to the sink and turn on the water tap, never stopping to figure out the source of the water, or how it was carried through the pipes to us. What about a prescription from a doctor? We can't read it or analyze it. We pay a sum we may think is too much because we rely on the doctor's knowledge and authority to make us well.

In the same way we may not be able to fully comprehend the deep significance of the cross, but we can benefit from it because the Bible gives us the authoritative answer to the problem of sin.

WHAT HAPPENED AT THE CROSS?

The cross is the focal point in the life and ministry of Jesus Christ. Some think that God didn't want Christ to die, but was forced to adjust His plans to adapt to it. Scripture makes it very clear, however, that the cross was no afterthought with God. Christ was "delivered over by the predetermined plan and foreknowledge of God" (Acts 2:23).

God designed the cross to defeat Satan, who by deception had obtained squatters' rights to the title deed of the world. When Satan with all of his clever promises separated man from God in the Garden of Eden, he was more than the deceiver of Adam and Eve. In some mysterious manner he began to exert a kind of pseudosovereignty over man. In his arrogant violence, Satan unleashed his fiercest attack to stop Christ's ministry by seeing that He was murdered. But Satan was stopped by God and caught in his own trap. He hadn't realized that God loved the world so intensely that He could let His own Son be subjected to the worst Satan could do. Satan miscalculated. He didn't comprehend the greatness of God's love and the wisdom of His plan.

Satan's power was broken at the cross. "The Son of God appeared for this purpose, to destroy the works of the devil" (1 John 3:8).

What a blow was dealt to Satan! Although he is still a wily pretender, his destruction was made certain by the victory of Christ at the cross. "That through death He might render powerless him who had the power of death, that is, the devil" (Heb. 2:14). What seemed to be the biggest defeat of history turned into the greatest triumph.

Through the cross, God not only overpowered Satan but brought Himself and man together. Christ rescued the slaves that Satan held captive and reconciled them to Himself. The Bible describes this amazing divine plan in these words: "We speak God's wisdom in a mystery, the hidden wisdom which God predestined before the ages to our glory; the wisdom which none of the rulers of this age has understood; for if they had understood it they would not have crucified the Lord of glory" (1 Cor. 2:7–8).

The cross revealed an eternal secret. This was "the mystery

which has been kept secret for long ages past, but now is manifested" (Rom. 16:25–26).

If it were possible for one man, Adam, to lead mankind to ruin, why shouldn't it be possible for one man to redeem it? The Bible says, "For as in Adam all die, so also in Christ all will be made alive" (1 Cor. 15:22).

What Did the Cross Cost God?

As human beings filled with our own hurts and desires and emotions, we find it almost impossible to stretch our minds enough to conceive the cost to God in allowing His only Son to go to the cross. If He could have forgiven our sins by any other method, if the problems of the world could have been solved in any other way, God would not have allowed Jesus to die.

In the Garden of Gethsemane on the night before He was killed, Jesus prayed, "My Father, if it is possible, let this cup pass from Me" (Matt. 26:39), in other words, if there is any other way to redeem the human race, O God, find it! There was no other way. And then He prayed, "Not as I will, but as You will" (Matt. 26:39).

It's important to understand that when Jesus prayed that prayer, He was not just considering the simple act of dying. Just as His life was unique, so was His death. What happened to Him when He died never happened to any other person in the past and would never happen to anyone in the future. To be able to understand this we need to look into God's revelation before Christ's earthly ministry, back to the Old Testament.

The orthodox Jewish religion was founded on God's grace. God entered into a covenant relationship with Israel, declaring Himself to be their God and stating in a special way that they were to be His people (Deut. 7:6). With this type of relationship, how were they to express their love for Him? The answer was by doing His will as it was described in the Old Testament law. But the people could not keep the law perfectly, and when they broke it, they sinned. As the Bible says, "Sin is the transgression of the law" (1 John 3:4, KJV).

The sacrifices in the temple were meant by God to show graphically that a person's guilt and penalty for sin could be transferred from him to another. In the case of the Old Testament, a perfect animal symbolically bore the penalty and was killed.

Why did God give the law if He knew people couldn't possibly keep it? The Bible teaches that the law was given as a mirror. When we look into it, we see what true righteousness is. The Ten Commandments describe the life that pleases God. If we are separated from God by sin, the law exposes our sin and faces us with our true spiritual condition. The mirror does not reveal a very attractive image!

Sin had to be paid for, so in the beginning God instituted the sacrificial system by which we finally could be brought into a right relationship with God. In Old Testament times, those who had sinned brought sacrifices of animals and offered them to God. These sacrifices were shadows of the Great Sacrifice who was yet to come.

In Leviticus 4, Moses described a situation in which a leader needs to offer a sacrifice. We can think of it in seven steps:

1. "When a leader sins . . .
2. he shall bring for his offering a goat,
3. a male without defect.
4. He shall lay his hand on the head of the male goat
5. And slay it . . . ; it is a sin offering.
6. Then the priest is to take some of the blood of the sin offering . . . and put it on the horns of the altar . . .
7. Thus the priest shall make atonement for him in regard to his sin, and he will be forgiven" (vv. 22-26).

Notice the sequence. Man sinned and wants forgiveness of God. He brings an animal, a perfect specimen, to the priest and lays his hand on its head. Symbolically, at that point the guilt and punishment he bears because of his sin passes to the animal. He then kills it as a sin offering, and the priest places some of the blood on the altar.

What is the significance? It is an atonement for the man in regard to his sin. In place of a broken relationship between God and the sinner, "atonement" results and "he shall be forgiven" by God.

The sacrifices were visual aids to show sinners that there was hope because the punishment for sin could be transferred to another. However, they were only symbols, because "It is impossible for the blood of bulls and goats to take away sins" (Heb. 10:4). But God could forgive them in the light of what He would one day do at the cross. Jesus, "having offered one sacrifice for sins for all time, sat down at the right hand of God" (Heb. 10:12).

God did not initiate the sacrifices because He was bloodthirsty or unjust. He wanted us to zero in on two things: first, the loath-someness of sin, and second, the cross on which God Himself would satisfy forever the demands of His justice. "Not through the blood of goats and calves, but through His own blood, He [Jesus] entered the holy place once for all, having obtained eternal redemption" (Heb. 9:12).

When Christ atoned for sin, He stood in the place of guilty men and women. If God had forgiven sin by a divine decree, issuing some sort of a heavenly document written across the sky, without the atonement which involved the personal shame, agony, suffering, and death of Christ, then we might assume that God was indifferent to sin. Consequently we would all go on sinning, and the earth would become a living hell.

In the suffering of Jesus we have the participation of God in the act of atonement. Sin pierced God's heart. God felt every searing nail and spear. God felt the burning sun. God felt the scorn of His tormenters and the body blows. In the cross is the suffering love of God bearing the guilt of man's sin. This love alone is able to melt the sinner's heart and bring him to repentance for salvation. "He [God the Father] made Him who knew no sin [Jesus] to be sin on our behalf" (2 Cor. 5:21).

THE REASON FOR COMMUNION

Many people do not understand communion. For them, the communion service has no mystical meaning. And yet the cross is what communion is all about. In the Lord's Supper, Jesus likens Himself to the Lamb that was offered in the sacrifice or atonement and says to His disciples and to all who will believe in Him, "This is My body broken for you." This is symbolic of what He did on the cross. When the cup is offered the emphasis is upon the fact that His blood is shed for the remission of sins. The elements of bread and wine convey to us the reality of atonement and forgiveness. We can touch them, taste them, and see them. We have bread in our hands, but we have Christ in our hearts. We have the cup in our hand, but we have the benefits of forgiveness through His blood in our hearts.

One of the most famous Scottish theologians was John Duncan of New College in Edinburgh. As communion was being held in a Church of Scotland on one occasion, when the elements came to a little sixteen-year-old girl, she suddenly turned her head aside. She motioned for the elder to take the cup away—that she couldn't drink it. John Duncan reached his long arm over, touched her shoulder, and said tenderly, "Take it, lassie, it's for sinners!"

How Can I Understand All This?

There is a mystery to the death of Christ that is beyond our human understanding. The depths of God's love in sending His Son to pay such an awful price is beyond the measure of the mind of man. But we must accept it on faith or we will continually bear the burdens of guilt. We must accept the atonement that Christ has made and not try to make our own atonement, and this we can never do. Salvation is by Christ alone through faith alone, and for the glory of God alone.

Christ took the punishment which was due us.

My friend and associate, Cliff Barrows, told me this story about bearing punishment. He recalled the time when he took the punishment for his children when they had disobeyed. "They had done something I had forbidden them to do. I told them if they did the same thing again I would have to discipline them. When I returned from work and found that they hadn't minded me, the heart went out of me. I just couldn't discipline them."

Any loving father can understand Cliff's dilemma. Most of us have been in the same position. He continued with the story: "Bobby and Bettie Ruth were very small. I called them into my room, took off my belt and my shirt, and with a bare back, knelt down at the bed. I made them both strap me with the belt ten times each. You should have heard the crying! From them, I mean! They didn't want to do it. But I told them the penalty had to be paid and so through their sobs and tears they did what I told them."

Cliff smiled when he remembered the incident. "I must admit I wasn't much of a hero. It hurt. I haven't offered to do that again, but I never had to spank them again, either, because they got the point. We kissed each other when it was over and prayed together."

In that infinite way that staggers our hearts and minds, we know that Christ paid the penalty for our sins, past, present, and future.

That is why He died on the cross.

9

THE KING'S COURTROOM

The United States has a presidential election every four years. Changes are usually made in the White House, the Congress, and in many governors' mansions. When one elected leader is about to step down for his successor, he may grant some pardons to prisoners under his jurisdiction. It's always interesting to see who might benefit from these last-minute gestures.

If you or I were in prison and were told, "You're free. The president just granted you a pardon," we would certainly pack up and get out fast! That pardon would change our lives.

In the courtroom of the King of kings, a pardon means much more. At the cross, God not only delivered the believer in Christ from punishment, He also welcomed him with open arms into His family. He opens His home to us.

At the cross we have not only acquittal, but also justification (just-as-if-I'd-never-sinned); not only pardon, but also acceptance. We saw in the last chapter that God Himself bore the burden of our sin and suffered for us. Now we must see that the cross offers us more than a pardon.

The issue involved is not just in Jesus' blood, which cleanses us from sin, but also in His righteousness. The key is in the word *justified*. We are "justified as a gift by His grace through the redemption which is in Christ Jesus" (Rom. 3:24).

Several years ago I was to be interviewed at my home for a well-known television show and, knowing that it would appear on nationwide television, my wife took great pains to see that everything looked nice. She had vacuumed and dusted and tidied up the whole house but had gone over the living room with a fine-tooth comb since that was where the interview would be filmed. When the film crew arrived with all the lights and cameras, she felt that everything in that living room was spick-and-span. We were in place along with the interviewer when suddenly the television lights were turned on and we saw cobwebs and dust where we had never seen them before. In the words of my wife: "I mean, that room was festooned with dust and cobwebs which simply did not show up under ordinary light."

The point is, of course, that no matter how well we clean up our lives and think we have them all in order, when we see ourselves in the light of God's Word, in the light of God's holiness, all the cobwebs and all the dust do show up.

Picture a courtroom. God the Judge is seated in the judge's seat, robed in splendor. You are arraigned before Him. He looks at you in terms of His own righteous nature as it is expressed in the moral law. He speaks to you:

GOD: John (or) Mary, have you loved Me with all your heart?
JOHN/MARY: No, Your Honor.
GOD: Have you loved others as you have loved yourself?
JOHN/MARY: No, Your Honor.
GOD: Do you believe you are a sinner and that Jesus Christ died for your sins?
JOHN/MARY: Yes, Your Honor.
GOD: Then your penalty has been paid by Jesus Christ on the cross and you are pardoned.

I have my pardon, but there is much more. When the Bible says that the person who believes in Jesus is justified as a gift by His grace (see Romans 3:24), this sounds like more than a mere pardon. And it is. If I'm a criminal whom the president or the governor pardons, everyone knows I'm still guilty. I simply don't have to serve my sentence. But if I'm justified, it's *just-as-if-I'd* never sinned at all.

Both pardon and justification come to us when we believe in Jesus. On the one hand God pardons our sin because of the death of Christ. He paid our penalty. On the other hand God actually declares us "righteous" (a word which means the same as "just").

GOD: Because Christ is righteous, and you believe in Christ, I now declare you legally righteous.

How can God do that and remain "just" Himself—when He

attached the penalty of death to sin? The answer is in the righteousness of Jesus Christ. He lived an unblemished, perfect life. His character perfectly supported His claim to deity, as we saw in chapter 7, "The Man Who Is God." It's easy to see God the Father declaring Jesus just, because He was. But how does that help me, a sinner? Paul gives the answer in 2 Corinthians 5:21. To make it clear we'll substitute the words *God* and *Christ* where the words *He* and *Him* appear. "God made Christ who knew no sin to be sin on our behalf, that we might become the righteousness of God in Christ."

God put my sin on Christ, who had no sin; He punished Him in my place, as we have seen. But He did one other thing, according to this verse. By God's action the righteousness of Christ was put on us who believe, "that we might become the righteousness of God in Him."

The Judge, God, has transferred Christ's righteousness to your legal account if you have believed in Christ. Now He examines you according to the law. What does He see? All of your past evil deeds and thoughts? Your sinful actions of the present? No. He doesn't see your sin because that has been transferred to Christ when God made Christ to be sin. Rather He looks at you carefully and sees the righteousness of Christ.

But you may say, "Look, am I not still a sinful person?"

The answer is "yes and no." If you mean that you have the legal status of a sinner before God, the answer is "no." To Him, legally, you are just. You are in right standing before Him, and "standing" is the issue in the courtroom.

Do you still have the capacity to sin? The answer is "yes." Of course you are not perfect. You may still at times think and act in ways contrary to God's desires. But your character and mine aren't the issue here. Our legal standing is. And legally we are declared just.

AM I FREE TO SIN?

"Love God and live as you please!" Now are we free to sin without restraint? Can we run out of the courtroom, pardoned and justified, and do anything we want? Yes. But you are now "born again." You don't want to do the same old wrong things; your desires are changed.

If you have trusted Jesus and seen what depth of concern He had for you at the cross, you can say with the apostle Paul, "It is Christ's love that controls me" (2 Cor. 4:14, Goodspeed). The inner changes God begins to achieve in our character will be the subject of a later chapter. But they are all based on a change in status. We who were properly condemned are now properly declared just if we have trusted Christ.

Can you imagine what a newspaper man would do with this event?

SINNER PARDONED—GOES TO LIVE WITH JUDGE

It was a tense scene when John and Mary stood before the Judge and had the list of charges read against them. However, the Judge transferred all of the guilt to Jesus Christ, who died on a cross for John and Mary.

After John and Mary were pardoned the Judge invited them to come to live with Him forever.

The reporter on a story like that would never be able to understand the irony of such a scene, unless he had been introduced to the Judge beforehand and knew His character.

Pardon and Christ's righteousness come to us only when we totally trust ourselves to Jesus as our Lord and Savior. When we do this, God welcomes us into His intimate favor. Clothed in Christ's righteousness we can now enjoy God's fellowship and "come boldly unto the throne of grace, that we may obtain mercy, and find grace to help in time of need" (Heb. 4:16, KJV).

CONCLUSIONS FROM THE TESTIMONY

If I were a lawyer, I'm sure I would study the procedures of great trials of the past, the evidences presented, and the conclusions reached by the findings.

There are some vital conclusions we can draw from the death of Christ. First, at the cross we see the strongest evidence of the guilt of the world. Here sin reached its climax when its terrible display occurred. Sin was never blacker or more hideous than on the day Christ died.

People have said that man has improved and that if Christ returned today, He wouldn't be crucified but might be given a glorious reception. I am convinced that if Christ came today He might be tortured and put to death even more quickly than He was two thousand years ago, though perhaps in, more sophisticated ways. But sinful people would still shout, "Away with Him."

Human sinful nature has not changed. As we look at the cross we see clear proof that all men have "sinned and fallen short of the glory of God." This is God's inescapable verdict.

The second conclusion we see at the cross is that God hates sin and loves righteousness. He has told us repeatedly that the soul that sins shall die, and that He cannot forgive our sin unless our debt has been paid. The Scripture says, "Without the shedding of blood there is no forgiveness of sins" (Heb. 9:22, RSV).

God will not tolerate sin. As the moral judge of the entire universe, He cannot compromise if He is to remain just. His holiness and His justice demand the penalty for broken law. There are some schools of thought which feel that such a view of God is too severe. Sin, they say, has its psychological basis. Some time ago a young man was executed for killing two other young men. The newspapers were full of the legal arguments, the debates over the death penalty, and the frequent postponements of the execution date. Why did he do it? What events or people in his past influenced his twisted mind?

Many say they are not responsible for what they do. Poor parents, bad environment, the government are all blamed. But God says that we are responsible. When we look at the cross, we see how drastically God deals with sin. The Bible says, "He who did not spare His own Son, but delivered Him over for us all, how will He not also with Him freely give us all things?" (Rom. 8:32). "For our sake he [God] made him [Christ] to be sin who knew no sin" (2 Cor. 5:21, RSV).

If God had to send His only Son to the cross to pay the penalty for sin, then sin must be terrible indeed in His sight.

However, we see that God loves righteousness and clothes the believer in His righteousness because of the cross. It is amazing to think about! We are clothed, we are covered, protected, shielded. A wonderful old hymn says, "Jesus, thy blood and righteousness, My beauty are, my glorious dress."[1] This is not self-righteousness, but "the righteousness which comes from God on the basis of faith" (Phil. 3:9).

God is now at work through the Holy Spirit to make the believer righteous in his inner character. Peter shows how intimately this is based on the cross also when he says of Christ that "He Himself bore our sins in His body on the cross, so that we might die to sin and live to righteousness" (1 Pet. 2:24).

What other conclusion must we reach from the testimony of the cross? We see the greatest demonstration of God's love. "For God so loved the world, that He gave His only begotten Son, that whoever believes in Him shall not perish, but have eternal life" (John 3:16).

In our own weakness as humans, we tend to grade sins. Here's a little sin on our scale, but over here there's a very, very heavy sin. We may see God as able to forgive the small sin, but incapable of forgiving and accepting the gross sinner. I recall a story out of World War II that illustrates this graphically. Hitler and his Third Reich had gone down to defeat at the hands of the Allies. Many of the men who had been Nazi leaders in some of the most infamous crimes known to man were brought to trial in Nuremberg. The world watched as sentences of imprisonment and death were brought against these war criminals.

However, out of the Nuremberg trials came an amazing account by Chaplain Henry Gerecke. He was called upon to be prison chaplain to the former Nazi high command. He described himself as a humble preacher, a one-time Missouri farm boy, and then he was given this extremely difficult assignment.

Chaplain Gerecke recalls the sincere conversion to faith in Jesus Christ by some of these men who had committed despicable crimes. One of them was a former favorite general of Hitler. At first the chaplain was very leery of confessions of faith. He said the first time he saw this criminal reading his Bible he thought, *a phony*. However, as he spent time with him he wrote, "But the longer I listened, the more I felt he might be sincere. He said he had not been a good Christian. He insisted he was very glad that a nation which would probably put him to death thought enough of his eternal welfare to provide him with spiritual guidance." With this Bible in his hand he said, "I know from this book that God can love a sinner like me."[2]

What an amazing love God exhibited for us at the cross!

The fourth conclusion we can reach from the testimony at the cross is that it is the basis for true world brotherhood. There are many groups which espouse the brotherhood of man and make appeals in behalf of peace. Only when we are brought into the family of God through the fatherhood of God can there be any true brotherhood of man. God is not our Father automatically (except by creation) when we are born; He must become our Father spiritually.

The Bible teaches that we can experience glorious brotherhood and fatherhood through the cross. "For He Himself is our peace, who made both groups into one and broke down the barrier of the dividing wall, by abolishing in His flesh the enmity, which is the Law of commandments contained in ordinances, so that in Himself He might make the two into one new man, thus establishing peace" (Eph. 2:14–15).

Outside the work of the cross we see bitterness, intolerance, hatred, prejudice, lust, and greed. Within the powerful working of the cross grow love, new life, and new brotherhood. The only human hope for peace lies at the cross of Christ, where all men, no matter what their background of nationality or race, can become a new brotherhood.

You are probably familiar with the story of Hansei. Her book *Hansei* describes vividly her absolute dedication to Adolf Hitler and the Nazi movement as a member of the Hitler Youth; her subsequent disenchantment and disillusionment; then her conversion to Jesus Christ. My wife has a letter from Hansei telling of her first meeting with Corrie ten Boom, whose book *The Hiding Place* tells of the ten Boom family's experiences during World War II. The family was arrested and put in prison for hiding Jews, and Corrie's father and sister died there.

One day Hansei and Corrie were at a convention and were seated in the same building, autographing their books. Hansei waited as long as she could, then made her way to Corrie because she simply had to ask forgiveness for what she had done. Hansei pushed through those standing in line with their books for Corrie to sign, knelt in front of Corrie with tears streaming down her cheeks, and said, "Corrie, I'm Hansei." Corrie's reaction was not only absolute forgiveness, but love and acceptance. This could only happen between Christians and illustrates what the cross does.

Captain Mitsuo Fuchida was the Japanese naval air commander who led the bombing attack on Pearl Harbor. He relates that when the Japanese war prisoners were returning from America, he was curious as to what kind of treatment they had received. An ex-prisoner he questioned told him what made it possible for those in the camp to forget their hate and hostility toward their captors. One young girl had been extremely kind and helpful and had shown such love and tenderness for them that their hearts were touched. They wondered why she was so good to them and were amazed when she told them it was because her parents had been killed by the Japanese army! She explained that her parents had been Christian missionaries in the Philippines at the beginning of the war but when the Japanese landed they were forced to flee to the mountains. They were later found by the Japanese, accused of being spies, and put to death. But before they were killed they had asked for thirty minutes of time to pray, which was granted. The girl was convinced that her parents had spent that thirty minutes praying for forgiveness for their executioners, and because of this she was able to allow the Holy Spirit to remove the hate from her heart and replace it with love.

Captain Fuchida could not understand such love. Several months passed and one day in Tokyo he was given a leaflet as he left a railroad station. This told the story of Sergeant Jacob DeShazer who was captured by the Japanese, tortured, and held prisoner of war for forty months. While in prison camp he received Christ through reading the Bible. God's Word removed the bitter hatred for the Japanese from his heart and replaced it with such love that he was compelled to return to tell the Japanese people of this marvelous love of Christ.

Captain Fuchida bought a Bible and began to read. He faced the scene of the crucifixion of Christ and was struck by Jesus' words, "Father, forgive them; for they do not know what they are doing" (Luke 23:34). Jesus prayed for the very soldiers who were about to thrust the spear into His side. In his book *From Pearl Harbor to Golgotha*, Captain Fushida tells how he found the source of this miracle love that can forgive enemies, and how he could now understand the story of the American girl whose parents had been slain and the transformation in Jake DeShazer's life.

PERSONAL QUESTIONS THE CROSS ANSWERS

"Why can't I seem to solve my problems?" This question reminds me of a Peanuts cartoon. It pictures Lucy in her psychiatrist's booth giving counsel to Charlie Brown. Charlie has lost another ball game and feels depressed and defeated. Lucy, the psychiatrist, is explaining to him that life is made of ups and downs. Charlie goes away screaming, "But I hate downs, all I want is ups."

I'm afraid that often those of us who teach the Christian message give the impression that once we have accepted Jesus Christ we will never again have any problems. This isn't true, but we do have Someone to help us face our problems. I have a paraplegic friend who has been that way for over thirty years. In spite of overwhelming problems for which there is no solution, she has learned not only to live with her condition, but to be radiant and triumphant, blessing and winning others to Christ.

Paul Tournier, one of the great Swiss psychiatrists, has stated that in the Christian life we have to realize that each day will present new circumstances and there will always be adjustments that have to be made. If I drive my car into a city, I can't rigidly place my hands on the steering wheel and drive at a set rate of speed. I have to stop and start and turn to make adjustments. The same thing is true in daily living. There is always a price to being a person; part of that price is pain and problems, but we have the promise Christ made that He will always be with us.

In Psalm 34 there are three great statements about our problems:

"This poor man cried, and the LORD heard him and saved him out of all his troubles" (v. 6).

"The righteous cry, and the LORD hears and delivers them out of all their troubles" (v. 17).

"Many are the afflictions of the righteous, but the LORD delivers him out of them all" (v. 19).

The Christian life is not a way "out" but a way "through" life. The "out of" in these verses refers to deliverance not *from* but *through* difficulty. English scholar Dr. Arthur Way phrased it, "Deliverance out of, not from the crisis of trial. So that the sense appears to be, 'bring me safely out of the conflict'" and "not simply keep me from entering into it."

Another question: "I feel so guilty—how can I find relief?"

Guilt is a very debilitating feeling. It can destroy our attitude, our personal relationships, and our outreach. Sometimes we feel guilty because we've done things that are wrong for which we must accept the responsibility and also accept God's forgiveness.

I have been told by doctors that a large percentage of the patients in psychiatric hospitals could be released if only they could be assured of the fact that they had been forgiven.

It's so easy to blame someone or something else. Anna Russell, the British comedienne, has an interesting little poem about guilt:

I went to my psychiatrist to be psychoanalyzed.
To find out why I kicked the cat, and blacked my wife's eyes.
He laid me on this downy couch to see what he could find,
And this is what he dredged up from my subconscious mind.
When I was one my mama hid my dolly in a trunk,
And so it falls naturally that I am always drunk.
When I was two I suffered from ambivalence toward my brothers,
And so it falls naturally I poisoned all my lovers.
Now I am so glad that I have learned the lessons this has taught,
That everything I do that's wrong is someone else's fault.

For some people guilt is an exercise. They won't accept the forgiveness that is offered to them; it is so hard to believe. It seems too good to be true that God should let us go eternally scot-free from our sins—and yet that is the message that the Gospel brings to us. When we cling to our guilt we do not honor God and we handicap our own lives terribly.

Forgiveness is an opportunity that Christ extended to us on the cross. When we accept His forgiveness and are willing to forgive ourselves, then we find relief.

After the sewage plants of London have reclaimed all that is usable of sewage, sludge barges on the river Thames collect the residue and carry it out to sea a certain number of miles and dump it. Apparently it is only a matter of minutes before the sea water is as pure as it was before! This is a beautiful illustration of how He has buried our sins in the depths of the sea.

Corrie ten Boom tells a story of a little girl who broke one of her mother's treasured demitasse cups. The little girl came to her mother sobbing, "Oh, mama, I'm so sorry I broke your beautiful cup."

The mother replied, "I know you're sorry and I forgive you. Now don't cry anymore." The mother then swept up the pieces of the broken cup and placed them in the trash can. But the little girl enjoyed the guilty feeling. She went to the trash can, picked out pieces of the cup, brought them to her mother, and sobbed, "Mother, I'm so sorry that I broke your pretty cup."

This time her mother spoke firmly to her. "Take those pieces and put them back in the trash can and don't be silly enough to take them out again. I told you I forgave you so don't cry anymore, and don't pick up the broken pieces anymore."

Guilt is removed with confession and cleansing. "If we confess our sins, he is faithful and just to forgive us our sins, and to cleanse us from all unrighteousness" (1 John 1:9, KJV).

However, the story of David's sin (Ps. 51) shows that forgiveness does not preclude the natural consequences of our sin. Murder can be forgiven, but that does not bring the dead to life again.

There is a well-known story of some fishermen in Scotland

who had spent the day fishing. That evening they were having tea in a little inn. One of the fishermen, in a characteristic gesture to describe the size of the fish that got away, flung out his hands just as the little waitress was getting ready to set the cup of tea at his place. The hand and the teacup collided, dashing the tea against the whitewashed walls. Immediately an ugly brown stain began to spread over the wall. The man who did it was very embarrassed and apologized profusely, but one of the other guests jumped up and said, "Never mind." Pulling a pen from his pocket, he began to sketch around the ugly brown stain. Soon there emerged a picture of a magnificent royal stag with his antlers spread. That artist was Landseer, England's foremost painter of animals.

This story has always beautifully illustrated to me the fact that if we confess not only our sins but our mistakes to God, He can make out of them something for our good and for His glory. Somehow it's harder to commit our mistakes and stupidities to God than it is our sins. Mistakes and stupidities seem so dumb, whereas sin seems more or less to be an outcropping of our human nature. But Romans 8:28 tells us that if they are committed to God He can make them work together for our good and His glory.

When you bake a cake, you put in raw flour, baking powder, soda, bitter chocolate, shortening, etcetera, none of which taste very good in themselves, but which work together to make a delicious cake. And so with our sins and our mistakes—although they are not good in themselves—if we commit them in honest, simple faith to the Lord, He will work them out His own way and in His own time to make something of them for our good and His glory.

Question: "Do I have to understand all this about Christ's death?"

The depths of God's love in sending His Son to pay such an awful price is beyond the measure of the mind of man. We must accept it on faith or we will continually bear the burden of guilt. Salvation is by Christ alone, through faith alone, for the glory of God alone.

Jesus never said, "Only understand." He said, "Only believe."

10

JESUS CHRIST IS ALIVE

In a mausoleum in Moscow's Red Square lie the embalmed remains of Lenin. A crystal casket in that tomb has been viewed by millions of people. On the casket it says: "For he was the greatest leader of all people of all time. He was the lord of the new humanity; he was the savior of the world."

The tribute to Lenin is stated in past tense. What a startling contrast to the triumphant words of Christ. "I am the resurrection and the life; he who believes in Me will live even if he dies" (John 11:25).

The basis for our belief in Jesus Christ is in His resurrection. Karl Barth, the great Swiss theologian, said that without belief in the physical resurrection of Jesus Christ there is no salvation.

If Christ were entombed someplace in a grave near Jerusalem

where the millions who visit Israel each year could walk by a grave and worship Him, then Christianity would be a fable. The apostle Paul said, "If Christ has not been raised, then our preaching is in vain and your faith is in vain. . . . If Christ has not been raised, your faith is futile and you are still in your sins" (1 Cor. 15:14, 17, RSV).

We usually hear a sermon about the resurrection every Easter, and that's about all. But when the early apostles preached, the cross and resurrection were their constant themes. Without the resurrection, the cross is meaningless.

SHALL MAN LIVE AGAIN?

Some say we are nothing but bone, flesh, and blood. After we have died, nothing happens—we don't go anywhere. Or if we do go somewhere it is to a nebulous location, devised by the imagination to represent almost anything.

Does science help? I have questioned scientists concerning life after death and most of them say, "We just don't know." Science deals in formulas and test tubes; the spiritual world is beyond its reach.

Many who do not believe in life after death fill their writings with tragedy and pessimism. Gore Vidal, Truman Capote, Dalton Trumbo, and many others write with almost unrelieved pessimism. How different are the words of Jesus Christ, who said, "Because I live, you will live also" (John 14:19). We must base our hope of immortality on Christ alone—not on any longings, arguments, or instinctive feelings of immortality.

The Bible speaks of the resurrection of Jesus as something which could be examined by the physical sense. The disciples saw Him under many different conditions after He had been raised. A single disciple saw Him on one occasion, five hundred on another. Some saw Jesus separately, some together; some for a moment, some for a long time.

The disciples heard Him in conversation. They were told to touch Him to verify His physical reality. They touched Him, walked with Him, conversed with Him, ate with Him, and examined Him. This took the resurrection appearances of Jesus out of the realm of hallucination and put them into the realm of demonstrable physical fact.

Historical fact provides the basis for our belief in the bodily resurrection of Christ. We have more evidence for it than for any other event of that time, secular or religious.

WHAT ABOUT THE OTHER RELIGIONS?

Most of the world religions are based upon philosophical thought, except for Judaism, Buddhism, Islam, and Christianity. These four are based upon personalities. Only Christianity claims resurrection for its founder.

Abraham, the father of Judaism, died about nineteen centuries before Christ. There are no evidences for his resurrection.

Buddha lived about five centuries before Christ, and taught principles of brotherly love. It is believed that he died at the age of eighty. There are no evidences for his resurrection.

Muhammad died A.D. 632, and his tomb at Medina is visited

by thousands of devout Mohammedans. His birthplace at Mecca sees many pilgrims each year. However, there are no evidences for his resurrection.

EVIDENCES OF CHRIST'S RESURRECTION

There is something called "the swoon theory" which says that Jesus didn't actually die, but only fainted. Since there could be no resurrection without a death, this thought denies His resurrection. Yet the evidence for His death is strong.

The soldiers were positive Jesus was dead, so they didn't need to induce death by shock through breaking His legs, which they did to the two thieves beside Him. It was not the friends of Jesus, but His enemies who vouched for His death. Also, they made certain when they thrust a spear into His heart.

One of the wealthiest men in the world, Howard Hughes, died recently. The events and circumstances surrounding his death are still shrouded in mystery, and yet he had an entourage of men who followed and guarded him for years.

In a city in the Middle East, however, there is more historical evidence for the death of one man, alone on a cross between two thieves, than any other in history. The great Bible student Wilbur Smith said, "Let it simply be said that we know more about the details of the hours immediately before, and the actual death of Jesus, in and near Jerusalem, than we know about the death of any other one man in all the ancient world."[1]

Jesus was buried. We know more about the burial of Jesus than we know of the burial of any character in ancient history. His body was taken from the cross and wrapped in fine linen with spices. Joseph of Arimathea, a rich man and a secret disciple of Jesus, mustered up his courage and asked Pilate for the body of Jesus. When his request was granted, we are told, he took Him down from the cross and wrapped Him in a linen sheet (Matt. 27:59). We are told that Nicodemus (the same religious leader who had asked Jesus how to be born again) came and brought a very expensive mixture of myrrh and aloes to wrap in with the linens, as was the custom of Jewish burial.

The body of Jesus was placed in Joseph's own tomb, which was located in the garden. This burial procedure shows that it was the body of Jesus which was buried, not His spirit. Spirits are immaterial and cannot be buried.

After Jesus was buried, a huge stone was placed against the face of the tomb and a seal placed upon that. Anyone trying to move the stone from the entrance to the tomb would have had to break the Roman seal and face the consequences of the harsh Roman law.

To make sure that His disciples didn't steal His body, a Roman guard was then placed in front of the sealed stone. The enemies of Jesus didn't want to take any chances that the prophecy about His resurrection would take place.

What about the Roman guards? These men weren't cowards. Their discipline was so severe that the punishment for quitting their post, or even falling asleep on the job, was death.

Historians say there were probably four guards on watch at the tomb, all of them outfitted with strong weapons and shields. No chances were taken that this Jesus would be removed from the tomb.

The empty tomb. It was the third day, the day Jesus said He would arise. Around the tomb the earth began to shake, and along with it the armor of the Roman soldiers must have clattered wildly. And then an angel of the Lord came from heaven and easily rolled away the stone and sat on it. He didn't even have to say, "Hi, fellas!" The guards just looked at him and became like dead men. The angel spoke to Mary Magdalene and Mary, too, but the Bible says that they took action and ran to tell the disciples that He had risen.

When Peter and John came running to the tomb, John peeped in and saw the linen clothes Christ had been wrapped in lying there empty. Peter, who, true to his character, blundered right in, saw that Jesus' body was missing. He was gone.

The bodily resurrection was a fact attested to by hundreds of eye-witnesses. We have records of thirteen different appearances of Jesus under widely different circumstances. His body was both similar and dissimilar to the one nailed to the cross. It was so similar to an ordinary human body that Mary mistook Him for the caretaker of the garden by the tomb when He appeared to her. He could eat, speak to people, and occupy space.

However, His body was not like a normal body. He could pass through closed doors or vanish in a moment. Christ's body was physical, and also spiritual. Why should this be surprising? Paul said to King Agrippa, "Why should it be thought a thing incredible with you, that God should raise the dead?" (Acts 26:8, KJV).

Over and over again the Bible affirms the fact of the bodily resurrection of Christ. Luke says it very directly in the book of Acts. He reports that Jesus "presented Himself alive after His suffering, by many convincing proofs, appearing to them over a period of forty days" (Acts 1:3).

In speaking about those "convincing proofs," C.S. Lewis says, "The first fact in the history of Christendom is a number of people who say they have seen the Resurrection. If they had died without making anyone else believe this 'gospel' no gospels would ever have been written."[2]

THE RESURRECTION ESSENTIAL

There is a series of events that form links in a chain from eternity to eternity. These include the incarnation of Jesus, His crucifixion, resurrection, ascension, and return. Any missing link and the chain is destroyed.

All of Christianity as a system of truth collapses if the resurrection is rejected. As Paul said, "If Christ has not been raised, then our preaching is vain, your faith also is vain" (1 Cor. 15:14).

In addition to breaking the chain of redemptive events, if the resurrection were not essential, then the good news of salvation would be flat, lifeless, and negative. Resurrection is central to the gospel. Paul said: "Now I make known to you, brethren, the gospel which I preached to you, which also you received, in which also you stand, by which also you are saved, if you hold fast the word which I preached to you, unless you believed in vain. For I delivered to you as of first importance what I also received, that Christ died for our sins according to the Scriptures, and that He was buried, and that He was raised on the third day according to the Scriptures" (1 Cor. 15:1–4).

In my book *World Aflame*, I told the story about Auguste Comte, the French philosopher, and Thomas Carlyle, the Scottish essayist. Comte said he was going to start a new religion that would supplant the religion of Christ. It was to have no mysteries and was to be as plain as the multiplication table; its name was to be *positivism*. "Very good, Mr. Comte," Carlyle replied, "very good. All you will need to do will be to speak as never a man spake, and live as never a man lived, and be crucified, and rise again the third day, and get the world to believe that you are still alive. Then your religion will have a chance to get on."

Today many "new religions" are springing up, like toadstools after a summer rain. I wonder how many could meet the criteria that Carlyle told his friend?

We have been emphasizing throughout this book the experience of being born again. A personal salvation experience is directly related to belief in the resurrection. Paul gave the formula for saving faith and showed that it centered in this belief: "If you confess with your mouth Jesus as Lord, and believe in your heart that God raised him from the dead, you shall be saved; for with the heart man believes, resulting in righteousness, and with the mouth he confesses, resulting in salvation" (Rom. 10:9–10).

It couldn't be clearer in the Scriptures. Yet there are churches where ministers say they believe in the resurrection, but that this means Jesus immediately rose from death into spiritual life with God. They say they believe in a "spiritual" but not a "physical" resurrection. This is what some modern preachers proclaim on Easter morning—though I am thankful they are diminishing in number.

No wonder there are many who sit in some churches week after

week, year after year, without hearing the whole gospel and knowing what it is to be born again. They hear a gospel which is incom-
plete, and consequently not good news at all. The resurrection was
not disembodied; it was physical. Eyewitnesses said, "We saw His
glory;" "You will see Him;" "He appeared;" "I have seen Jesus the
Lord."

Within the short span of three days both events, the death and
resurrection, took place bodily and not symbolically—tangibly,
not spiritually—watched by men of flesh and blood, not fabri-
cated by hallucination.

The resurrection was also the pledge and the promise of our
own resurrection.

To understand this we need to see that, in the Bible, death
affects both personality and body. (Remember the three dimensions of death?) The body, too, has to be retrieved from condemnation. Only by resurrecting the body could God make a complete
conquest of death. He started with the body of Jesus, but He will
also work in a similar manner with the bodies of all who believe.
As the judgment of death was total, so salvation from its penalty
is total, involving the physical, spiritual, and eternal.

Obviously our resurrection bodies will be recognizable, but they
can't possibly be the exact bodies we have here. However, they
must be like Christ's resurrected body. He had the nail prints and
the wound in His side, and yet He could pass through closed doors.
When it was time for Him to go to heaven, He was able to ascend.

What a promise this is! "For if we believe that Jesus died and
rose again, even so God will bring with Him those who have
fallen asleep in Jesus" (1 Thess. 4:14).

Jesus staked everything upon His rising from the dead. By His resurrection He would be judged true or false.

WHAT DOES THE RESURRECTION MEAN TO US TODAY?

Christ lives with every person who puts his trust in Him. The resurrection means the presence of the living Christ. He said, "Lo, I am with you always, even unto the end of the world" (Matt. 28:20, KJV). This is Christ's own guarantee: Life has a new meaning. After the crucifixion, the disciples were in despair. They said, "We had hoped that he was the one to redeem Israel" (Luke 24:21, RSV). They were full of anguish because they thought of Christ's death as such a tragedy. Life had lost its meaning for them. But when He rose from the grave, they saw the living Christ, and life took on purpose once more.

We can also claim the prayers of the living Christ. The Bible says, "Christ Jesus is He who died, yes, rather who was raised, who is at the right hand of God, who also intercedes for us" (Rom. 8:34). We don't have to think that our prayers are bouncing off the ceiling. The living Christ is sitting at the right hand of God the Father. God the Son retains the same humanity He took to save us, and is now living in a body that still has nail prints in its hands. He is our great High Priest, interceding for us with God the Father.

The resurrection presence of Christ gives us power to live our lives day by day and to serve Him. "Truly, truly, I say to you, he who believes in Me, the works that I do, he will do also; and greater works than these he will do; because I go to the Father" (John 14:12).

The resurrected body of Jesus is the design for our bodies when we are raised from the dead also. No matter what afflictions, pain, or distortions we have in our earthly bodies, we will be given new bodies. What a glorious promise of things to come! "For our citizenship is in heaven, from which also we eagerly wait for a Savior, the Lord Jesus Christ; who will transform the body of our humble state into conformity with the body of His glory, by the exertion of the power that He has even to subject all things to Himself" (Phil. 3:20–21).

Thousands of people today are excited about Bible prophecy. The revelation of what the Bible says about events past, present, and future has become more prominent in the themes of books, sermons, and conferences. The Second Coming of Christ is becoming a closer and closer reality for those of us who study the Bible and the world scene.

The entire plan for the future has its key in the resurrection. Unless Christ was raised from the dead, there can be no kingdom and no returning King. When the disciples stood at the place Jesus left this earth, which is called the place of ascension, they were given assurance by angels that the Christ of resurrection would be the Christ of returning glory. "Men of Galilee, why do you stand looking into the sky? This Jesus, who has been taken up from you into heaven, will come in just the same way as you have watched Him go into heaven" (Acts 1:11).

The resurrection is an event which prepares us and confirms for us that future event when He will return again.

Yes, Jesus Christ is alive.

Obviously Christ's physical resurrection is an essential part of God's plan to save us. Have you given yourself to this living Christ?

A woman wrote us this: "Last evening I was alone and watching television. I had no *TV Guide*. Something urged me to turn the dial to the station where the gospel was being preached. I had been really wrestling with a great problem. I was and am facing death, and may or may not be helped through surgery. I had been putting off the operation because I was afraid I had been cut off from God.

"I began to really seek the Lord. The message I heard was God's way of speaking to me and answering my prayers. Now I feel entirely at peace in my soul."

If you trust the resurrected Christ as your Lord and Savior, He will be with you when you die, and will give you life with Him forever. Because of the resurrection, you can be "born again."

PART THREE

MAN'S RESPONSE

11

THE NEW BIRTH IS FOR NOW

The coffee seems bitter and the toast cold when the morning newspaper is finished. Another riot in Egypt. Africa torn apart by rival factions. The Middle East seemed quiet until another border incident set off new hostilities. Three coeds murdered on the campus of a prominent state university.

What can the average person do? He feels inadequate, powerless. All of the committees, the resolutions, the changes in governments don't seem to change society.

We see that if mankind is to be saved, something radical needs to be done quickly. The forces building up in our world are so overwhelming that men and women everywhere are beginning to cry out in desperation. They feel like the man John Bunyan describes in the beginning of *Pilgrim's Progress*: " . . . He was greatly distressed in his mind, he burst out, as he had done before, crying, 'What shall I do to be saved?'"

So much in our world seems to improve, but man doesn't. We can send a spaceship to the moon and take closeup pictures of Mars, but we can't walk safely on the streets at night. The subtle sins of selfishness and indifference are everywhere. Seemingly upright men and women admit to desires of the grossest sort. (And who is shocked anymore?) Human viciousness breaks out as people steal, cheat, lie, murder, and rape.

Someone in the movie industry said that all we would have to do is contrast the titles of some of the old movie classics with current movie offerings to see the change in morality during the past generation. It's a long way from *Indian Love Call* to *Deep Throat*.

Man has made many attempts to change himself. We have tried without success to achieve moral goals by improvement in our environment and many are disillusioned with the results.

How can we change human nature?

FROM THE OUTSIDE IN

Studies in anthropology, psychology, and sociology to discover the laws of human behavior are an important part of educational research. Too often, however, the researchers themselves ignore the fact of human sin and see a human being as proceeding from a combination of genes and chromosomes, and then shaped by his environment. At a meeting of the American Anthropological Association a new discipline was introduced to the academic community by a Harvard zoologist. He calls it "sociobiology," and it is described as "the study of the biological basis for social behavior in every species; its practitioners believe that some—and perhaps much—of human behavior is genetically determined."[1]

The sociobiologists imply that "a good deal more of mankind's morality may be genetically based."[2] They fail to give a proper place to the inborn twist toward selfishness, viciousness, and indifference to God, so many of their conclusions are only pseudoscientific.

If we are shaped by our genes, and molded by our environment, then all we need to do is develop a way to alter genetic bases in humans or cure man's environment in terms of bad housing, slums, poverty, unemployment, and racial discrimination.

A best-selling author said this: "Many ministers today 'keep their cool' about questions of the sin and repentance of individuals and have turned their attack on the sin of society, in an attempt to make society squirm. This 'attack' varies from a mild sociology lecture to an angry assault against social injustice. However, slums and ghettos and put-downs are not going to disappear in society unless slums and games disappear from the hearts of people."[3]

But as Christians we need to do something about social injustice, slums, and ghettos. We cannot sit back with the attitude that the problems are too overwhelming or insolvable. We need to get involved in helping to make this world a better place to live for the unfortunate whose standard of living is so low as to defy imagination, and for those who live under terrible political oppression. Ultimately, however, society is not going to be changed with coercion and force because when it is changed that way, man usually loses his freedom. It can be changed by a complete transformation of the human heart.

Man also attempts to change himself by *chemistry*. Scientists have developed methods to control behavior by drugs, which in some cases have been helpful. A great deal of research is being done that may benefit the mentally ill. The danger is that these same drugs in the hands of a world dictator could control an entire population of normal people. Stories from prisoners in oppressed countries verify how present-day mind manipulators misuse drugs to influence human actions.

One of them wrote: "I personally witnessed the treatment undergone by political prisoners in psychiatric hospitals when they tried to protest by refusing the food and the 'treatments' inflicted upon them. They were tied up, injected with paralyzing sulphur and force fed . . . [They] have invented a powerful means to get rid of those who do not think as they do. Not only do they not hesitate to confine them in hospital-prisons, but they also compound their crime by injecting prisoners with chemical substances in order to destroy their personality and intellect."[4]

Changes in our body chemistry may benefit us or damage us permanently. The determining question is, "Who administers the drugs and for what purpose?"

Experiments are being made to try to give one person the intellectual capacities of another by what the mind-manipulators call "artificial reincarnation." In a study that came out of Russia, it was reported that one of the country's top physicists had experimented with "tuning one mind to another telepathically." The scientist explained, "'When this happens, the teacher can teach a student beyond the normal capacity of his mind by broadcasting over the defense mechanism into the normally empty 90 percent of the brain.'" He continues to explain that he "reincarnated a European mathematical genius in a college math student."[5]

Another human attempt to solve man's problems concerns *microbiology*. The increasing success with organ transplants may in time lead to a vast movement to change people by replacing certain organs connected with thinking, conscience, and emotions. However, the gospel of microbiology, administered by scientists who themselves are sinners, and who have access only to the substance of a fallen world, must likewise fail.

Many writers of science fiction consider their *interplanetary speculations* as the only source for solving man's problems. But the fundamental difficulty is that sin is too deeply ingrained in human nature to be rooted out by such influences. When God is ignored, the problem-solvers themselves participate in the problems. The superpowers are now frantically preparing for a "space" war. As a newspaper editorial says, "Whoever wins this race could control the world."

Many people today are trying to find a solution to man's problems by turning to *the occult world*. They seek knowledge and power from sources the Bible says we should wholeheartedly resist. The apostle Paul says, "For our struggle is not against flesh and blood, but against the rulers, against the powers, against the world forces of this darkness, against the spiritual forces of wickedness in the heavenly places" (Eph. 6:12). The occult world is a source only of terror and destruction.

The methods men use to change themselves from the outside in are truly varied, and sometimes amazing.

FROM THE INSIDE OUT

Jesus said that God can change men and women from the inside out. It was a challenge—a command. He didn't say, "It might be nice if you were born again," or, "If it looks good to you, you might be born again." Jesus said, "You *must be* born again" (John 3:7).

It has always astounded me that He made this statement to a devout religious leader, Nicodemus, who must have been shocked by it. After all, Nicodemus was a good, moral, religious man. His neighbors probably said of him, "He's a wonderful man. You could trust him with your life. He's a great theologian." Nicodemus fasted two days a week; he spent two hours a day in prayer at the temple and tithed all his income. He was a professor of theology at the local seminary. If a pastor-seeking committee were looking for the best man they could get for their local church, they would seek a man like Nicodemus. But Jesus said all his piety and goodness weren't enough. He said, "You must be born again."

In spite of all of his education and professional standing, Nicodemus saw something very special in Jesus Christ—something he couldn't understand. He saw in Jesus a new quality of living. He was honestly seeking to find out what this dimension of life was.

When Jesus told him that unless one is born again he cannot see the kingdom of God, he was explaining to Nicodemus that he didn't have to improve his moral standards or increase his educational credits, he needed to receive a new quality of life—eternal life—that begins in this world and carries into the next world.

On returning home from a trip one day I found my desk, as usual, piled high with letters to be answered. In this particular pile there happened to be two from two separate mental hospitals in different states. A glance at the handwriting and a reading of the letters made it clear that the writers needed to be in a mental institution. Yet each spoke of the Lord Jesus and the comfort He was.

I could not help thinking how kind and understanding and compassionate God has been in choosing to reveal Himself to man through simple childlike faith rather than the intellect. There would otherwise be no change for little children or the mentally retarded or the brain damaged. And yet the brilliant scientist, the true intellectual, the genius, must all come the same way. As Jesus said in Matthew 18:3, "Unless you are converted and become like children, you will not enter the kingdom of heaven."

John Hunter, an English Bible scholar, tells the story about a young man who came up to him after he had been preaching on John 3. "He, like Nicodemus, was obviously well educated, and he said: 'What you have been saying has really challenged me; in fact, if I could fully understand what you have told us, I would become a real Christian.' He was quite sincere in what he said, so I questioned him and talked further with him. He was a graduate of a university, trained to think and evaluate facts.

"I asked, 'If you could really understand the full meaning of the gospel, you would become a Christian?'

"'Yes,' he replied, 'I would.'

"'Well, consider this,' I went on, 'I have a friend who is a missionary on the Congo. He works among the Pygmies, people with little capacity for understanding. If, in order to become a Christian, we had to understand the gospel message, how could these simple people ever be blessed?'

"His reply was quite honest: 'You know, I never thought of that!'

"'No,' I replied, 'but God did. The gospel message doesn't have to be understood by the seeking soul, only to be received in simple faith. It isn't fully understanding the gospel that gives me the blessing, but simply believing and receiving it.'

"Nicodemus began by 'knowing,' but he continued by believing and receiving."[6]

There are many people sitting in churches today who have never heard this message of the new birth. Some churches preach good works, social change, and government legislation, and neglect the one thing that will help solve the problems of our world—changed men and women. Man's basic problem is first spiritual, then social. He needs a complete change from the inside out.

Some time ago I attended a historic conference in Africa. Every country except one from the whole continent of Africa was represented by delegates. Never before had there been such a Christian gathering. Time after time I heard African leaders express appreciation for what Christian missions had done, especially in the fields of evangelism, medical aid, and education. One of the speakers said, "Eighty five percent of all education south of the Sahara has been done by Christian missions."

An Anglican bishop from England told us, "Every social agency in England from the Society for the Prevention of Cruelty to Animals, on up, was founded as a result of a conversion to Christ and a spiritual awakening." We must be careful not to put the cart before the horse.

The Bible refers many times to this change Jesus talked about.

Through the prophet Ezekiel, God said, "I will give you a new heart and put a new spirit within you" (Ezek. 36:26). In the book of Acts, Peter called it repenting and being converted. Paul speaks of it in Romans as being "alive from the dead" (Rom. 6:13). In Colossians Paul calls it "(a putting off of) the old self with its evil practices, and (a putting on of) the new self who is being renewed to a true knowledge according to the image of the One who created him" (Col. 3:9–10). In Titus he calls it "the washing of regeneration and renewing by the Holy Spirit" (Tit. 3:5). Peter said it was being "partakers of the divine nature" (2 Pet. 1:4). In the Church of England catechism it is called "a death unto sin and a new birth unto righteousness."

The context of John 3 teaches that the new birth is something that God does for man when man is willing to yield to God. We have seen that the Bible teaches that man is dead in trespasses and sins, and his great need is life. We do not have within ourselves the seed of the new life; this must come from God Himself.

One of the great Christian writers of the this century, Oswald Chambers, said, "Our part as workers for God is to open men's eyes that they may turn themselves from darkness to light; but that is not salvation, that is conversion—the effort of a roused human being. I do not think it is too sweeping to say that the majority of nominal Christians are of this order; their eyes are opened, but they have received nothing. . . . When a man is born again, he knows that it is because he has received something as a gift from Almighty God and not because of his own decision."[7]

Conversion means "turning." The Bible is full of this concept and God pleads with man to turn to Him. He spoke through the prophet Ezekiel, "Repent . . . and *turn* your faces away from all your abominations" (Ezek. 14:6, emphasis mine). Another prophet, Isaiah, spoke, "*Turn* to Me and be saved, all the ends of the earth; for I am God, and there is no other" (Isa. 45:22, emphasis mine).

The new birth is not just being reformed, it's being transformed. People are always making resolutions to do better, to change, and breaking those resolutions soon afterward. But the Bible teaches us that through the new birth we can enter a new world.

The contrasts used in the Bible to express the change which comes over us when we are born again are very graphic; from lust to holiness; from darkness to light; from death to resurrection; from stranger to the kingdom of God to now being its citizen. The Bible teaches that the person who is born again has a changed will, changed affections, changed objectives for living, changed disposition, new purpose. He receives a new nature and a new heart. He becomes a new creation.

BEFORE AND AFTER

The Bible is full of people from all walks of life who have been changed by an encounter with Jesus Christ. Christ met a woman in Samaria who was a prostitute and an outcast in her own town. To avoid meeting other women she went to a well during the heat of the day when she knew she wouldn't encounter other villagers. But there she met Christ. She was changed immediately into a new person. In fact, she became an instant missionary and rushed to her own city, where she was despised and scorned, to tell others about Jesus Christ. And we are told, "Many of the Samaritans believed in Him because of the word of the woman who testified, 'He told me all the things that I have done'" (John 4:39).

Andrew was an ordinary fellow. He didn't seem to be the big personality man, but he was very quick to respond to Christ; in fact, he was on fire from the moment he met Jesus. The first thing he did was to go and find his brother to tell him the wonderful news about the Messiah. He may not have been a flaming evangelist, but wherever he appears in the biblical account, he is fruitful.

In these days of high taxes, the yearly or quarterly tax reports are not exactly greeted with enthusiasm. It wasn't any different in Jesus' time. Zacchaeus, a tax collector, and not a very honest one at that, was skillful in defrauding people, but when he met Jesus all that changed. He repented and wanted to make amends for his deceitful acts. "Behold, Lord, half of my possessions I will give to the poor, and if I have defrauded anyone of anything, I will give back four times as much" (Luke 19:8).

A young intellectual named Saul was on a journey along the road to Damascus, persecuting Christians, when he met Jesus Christ. To this day we speak about "Damascus Road experiences," because Saul was never the same again. He became the great apostle Paul. Many times he referred to that encounter, even recalling the very day and moment when he met Christ.

On the day of Pentecost, a dramatic change occurred in three thousand people who were born again. In the morning they were lost, uncertain about the purpose of life, many of them guilty over the death of Christ. Others were afraid of either the secular or religious authorities. But at the end of the day they had been born into the kingdom of God. Each one had passed out of death into life. "'Truly, truly, I say to you, he who hears My word, and believes Him who sent Me, has eternal life, and does not come into judgment, but has passed out of death into life'" (John 5:24).

Any person who is willing to trust Jesus Christ as his personal Savior and Lord can receive the new birth now. It's not something to be received at death or after death; it is for now. "Now is the accepted time; behold, now is the day of salvation" (2 Cor. 6:2, KJV).

THE NEW BIRTH IS FOR NOW

The "before-and-after" advertisements for diet remedies or face-lifts cannot match the impact of the testimonies of those who have been born again. From corporate president to prison inmate, stories unfold of lives turned right side up.

A young woman wrote us: "Until last January I was a stranger to Jesus. I was a rebel, thief, a drunkard, a hard drug taker, an adulteress, a hippie, and a self-centered, confused young woman. Thinking I was going to stump everyone with my cynical questions, I went to a Bible study about a year ago out of curiosity. That night I became sincerely interested in the Bible. Finally, after searching and studying the Scriptures for months, John 3:16 spoke to my heart and I gave my life to Christ. I never knew that this kind of happiness could exist. God shows you how to love and what it feels like to be loved. He was what I had been looking for since my early teens. He was 'the bag' I hadn't found. It seemed to me that drugs, liquor, free love, and bumming around the country would make me free, but they were all traps. Sin was the trap that led me to confusion, unhappiness, guilt, and near-suicide. Christ has made me free. Being a Christian is exciting because there is always a new challenge, so much to learn. Now I wake up glad to see the day.

"He has made me new."

Johnny Cash says, "A few years ago I was hooked on drugs. I dreaded to wake up in the morning. There was no joy, peace, or happiness in my life. Then one day in my helplessness I turned my life completely over to God. Now I can't wait to get up in the morning to study my Bible. Sometimes the words out of the Scriptures leap into my heart. This does not mean that all my problems have been solved, or that I have reached any state of perfection. However, my life has been turned around. I have been born again!"

12

THE NEW BIRTH
IS NOT JUST A "FEELING"

A man who was persuaded to go to a large evangelistic meeting recalled the following events:

> "It was here, I believe for the first time in my life, that I heard the claims of Jesus Christ presented, simply and authoritatively.
>
> "At the end of his talk the speaker invited those who wished to know more to come to the front of the auditorium. I went and was introduced to the speaker and we talked for a while. There were other people who wanted to ask questions, so I made my way to the exit, very interested in what he had said, but still in a deep fog.
>
> "Just as I was about to go out the door I was confronted by a man who looked me in the eye and said:

"'Are you a Christian?'

"*Strange question*, I thought, putting on my best Sunday school smile and saying, 'Oh yes, I think so.'

"'Are you a Christian?' he insisted, a light in his eye.

"*Crank*, I thought, *humor him and then escape!*

"So I replied, 'Well, I'm trying to be.'

"'Ever try to be an elephant?'

"Grinning at my dumb astonishment, he took me by the arm, sat me down in a chair, and explained that no amount of trying could ever transform me into a Christian (any more than it could turn me into an elephant). Then he began to explain what New Testament Christianity was all about. That Jesus Christ had died in *my* place. That He had paid the full penalty which *my* sins demanded. As I was, I stood condemned before a holy God; I needed a Savior. Jesus alone could save me. Forgiveness for the past was possible in Him. Moreover, in His resurrection, He was offering me power to live the sort of life I had hitherto considered hopelessly out of reach.

"What a stupendous offer! If the living God were really asking to come into my wretched, tarnished life, to take over what I was only wasting and spoiling—how dare I refuse Him! He was promising, 'Behold I stand at the door and knock.'

"I flung open the door. He was as good as His word."

This man was born again. He had a turnabout. He thought he was a Christian, but he had never personally made a commitment to Jesus Christ.

Jesus made everything so simple and we have made it so complicated. He spoke to the people in short sentences and everyday words, illustrating His messages with parables and stories.

Paul told the Philippian jailer who asked what he must do to be saved, "Believe in the Lord Jesus, and you will be saved" (Acts 16:31).

It's so simple that it's often overlooked. Although the gospel message is heard—especially in America—on radio stations, presented on television, sung on street corners, presented from pulpits, and tracts, millions overlook it. All you have to do to be born again is to repent of your sins and believe in the Lord Jesus as your personal Lord and Savior. You don't clean up, give up, or turn around yourself; you just come as you are. This is why we sing the hymn "Just As I Am" at our crusades.

KEY WORD: REPENTANCE

In the New Testament Peter says, "Repent ye therefore, and be *converted*, that your sins may be blotted out, [so that] the times of refreshing shall come from the presence of the Lord" (Acts 3:19, KJV, emphasis mine).

A person cannot turn to God to repent, or even to believe, without God's help. God must do the turning. Many times the Bible tells how men and women did that very thing, "Turn thou me, and I shall be turned; for thou art the LORD my God" (Jer. 31:18, KJV).

To many the word *repentance* is old-fashioned. It doesn't seem to have a proper place in a twentieth-century vocabulary. But repentance is one of the two vital elements in conversion and simply means recognition of what we are, and a willingness to change our minds toward sin, self, and God.

Repentance involves first of all an acknowledgement of our sin. When we repent we are saying we recognize we are sinners and that our sin involves us in personal guilt before God. This type of guilt does not mean incriminating self-contempt; it means seeing ourselves as God sees us, and saying, "God be merciful to me a sinner" (Luke 18:13, KJV). It is not just the corporate guilt of society we are acknowledging—it's so easy to blame the government, the school system, the church, the home, for our own personal guilt. The Bible teaches that when we reach the age of accountability—usually somewhere around ten or eleven years of age—God looks upon us as full-grown adults, making moral and spiritual choices for which we will be held accountable at the judgment. Each of us has an individual guilt before God. From the moment we are conceived we have the tendency toward sin; then we become sinners by choice and, ultimately, sinners by practice. That is why the Bible says we have all sinned and come short of the glory of God.

Every person through the world, of whatever race, color, language, or culture, needs to be born again. We are guilty of "sin" (singular) which is expressed in "sins" (plural). We break God's laws and rebel against Him because we are sinners by nature. It is this disease of sin (singular) that Christ dealt with on the cross.

We have heard so much about "roots." The roots of man's individual and corporate problems lie deep in his own heart. We are a diseased human race. This disease can only be dealt with by the blood of Christ, just as in the Old Testament blood was shed on hundreds of altars, looking forward to the day when Jesus Christ would come and be "the Lamb of God who takes away the sin of the world" (John 1:29). He became the cosmic scapegoat for the entire world. All of our sins were laid on Him. This is why God can now forgive us. This is why He can infuse new life into us—which is called regeneration, or the new birth.

When we look at the attributes of God and realize how far short we fall of His perfection, there is no alternative to the recognition of our sinful nature. The apostle Peter had been involved in sinful acts and harbored sinful thoughts, but far deeper than the physical or mental admission of wrongdoing, Peter realized that he had a twisted nature. He said, "Go away from me Lord, for I am a sinful man!" (Luke 5:8). Notice that he didn't say, "I sin," but "I am a sinful man."

Job saw how corrupt he was in relation to God's perfection, and said, "I have heard of thee by the hearing of the ear: but now mine eyes seeth thee. Wherefore I abhor myself, and repent in dust and ashes" (Job 42:5–6, KJV). Job compared himself with God and repented; he recognized what he was before God.

Repentance also involves a genuine *sorrow* for sin. Sorrow is an emotion, and we are creatures who vary greatly in the degree of sorrow we may experience. Repentance without sorrow is hollow, however. The apostle Paul said, "I now rejoice, not that you were made sorrowful, but that you were made sorrowful to the point of repentance; for you were made sorrowful according to the will of God, so that you might not suffer loss in anything through us" (2 Cor. 7:9).

With repentance comes a change of purpose, a willing turn-around from sin. If we had to repent without God's help, then we would be almost helpless. The Scripture teaches that we are dead in trespasses and in sins. A dead man can do nothing; therefore we need God's help even in our repenting. Sometimes this involves "restitution." If we have stolen, lied, or cheated to the hurt of other people, we must go and make this right if at all possible.

I've had hundreds of letters from people who have told me that they have had money returned to them that had been stolen by people who claimed to be "born again." Many people, before their conversion, have been shoplifters. Many have felt that they must go back to the store, discuss their wrongdoing with the manager, and make retribution.

When my wife was counseling with Joe Medina after he was tempted and helped a friend rob a filling station, she told him that his repentance would never be real unless he confessed his crime. He did. He earned the money that summer and returned it in full. The filling-station owner forgave him. Today that young man has finished four years at a Bible college and is now a minister.

When Jim Vaus, the underworld figure, came to Christ in 1949, he spent many weeks looking up people whom he had offended, injured, and stolen from. He returned everything he possibly could and apologized to all those whom he had offended.

This type of restitution is rare today, but it is most certainly taught in the Scriptures. It helps complete our repentance. It shows to those whom we have offended, and to the world, that we mean business with God.

When emotions are contrary to our willingness to turn from sin, hypocrisy enters the life of a believer, and doubts begin to grow. There are so many things in the Bible that seem so difficult to believe. When we become a new creature in Christ, we are pro-pelled into an exhilarating, joyful, exciting experience which car-ries us emotionally for a time. Then doubts may enter our lives, quietly at first, but then more boldly as the questions begin to crowd out the trust. "How can I be willing to turn over my life to God when He might make me do something I don't want to do?"

When a wealthy, beautiful woman who was a leader in her community was converted, one of the first persons she told, a friend of many years, said, "Well, Dorothy, what are you going to do now—go to Africa as a missionary?"

Dorothy struggled with her emotions, but answered with her surrendered will, "If that's where God wants me, I'll go."

But it's not that easy for most to be willing to turn over the action and direction to God.

A wonderful old woman who wrote one of the classics in Christian books told a story about a young man of great intelli-gence who was having tremendous difficulties in his new Christian experience with this matter of will. He was a great doubter, and emotionally nothing seemed real to him. He was given this piece of advice: "'A man's will is really the man's self; . . . what his will does, he does. Your part then is simply to put your will . . . over on God's side, making up your mind that you will believe what He says [in the Bible], because He says it, and that you will not pay any regard to the feelings that make it seem so unreal. God will not fail to respond, sooner or later, with His revelation to such a faith.'

"The young man paused a moment, and then said solemnly, 'I understand, and will do what you say. I cannot control my emo-tions, but I can control my will; and the new life begins to look possible to me, if it is only my will that needs to be set straight in the matter. I can give my will to God, and I do.'"[1]

Biblical repentance is the fuel which is used to propel our life with God at the controls. Until we utilize that fuel, we are earthbound, tied down by our ego, our pride, our troubles, and our guilt. Young people are often chained in a prison of purposelessness, uncertainty, and even guilt. Many an older person faces old age and death with dread and fear. True repentance can release those chains.

Thus, repentance is *first,* and absolutely necessary, if we are to be born again. It involves simple recognition of what we are before God—sinners who fall short of His glory; *second,* it involves genuine sorrow for sin; *third,* it means our willingness to turn from sin.

KEY WORD: *FAITH*

In considering the conversion we have seen that it has a "turning-from" side called repentance. It also has a "turning-to" side called faith.

Faith is first of all belief—belief that Christ was who He said He was. Second, faith is belief that He can do what He claimed He could do—He can forgive me, and come into my life. Third, faith is trust, an act of commitment, in which I open the door of my heart to Him. In the New Testament the words *faith, belief,* and *believe* are translations of similar Greek words, so they are interchangeable.

Placing your faith in Christ means that first you must make a choice. The Scripture says, "Whoever believes in him [Jesus] is not condemned, but whoever does not believe stands condemned already because he has not believed in the name of God's one and only Son" (John 3:18, NIV). The person who believes is not condemned; the person who has not believed is condemned. In order not to be condemned you must make a choice—you must choose to believe.

So we can see how important belief is. The Bible says that without faith it is impossible to please God. But what does it mean to believe? It means to "commit" yourself to Christ, to "surrender" to Him. Believing is your response to God's offer of mercy, love, and forgiveness. God took the initiative and did everything that was needed to make the offer of salvation possible. When Christ bowed His head on the cross and said, "It is finished," He meant just that (John 19:30). God's plan for our reconciliation and redemption was complete in His Son. But only by believing in Jesus—committing yourself to Him, surrendering to Him—are you saved.

Belief is not just a feeling; it is the assurance of salvation. You may look at yourself in the mirror and say, "But I don't feel saved—I don't feel forgiven." But don't depend on feelings for your assurance. Christ has promised, and He cannot lie. Belief is a deliberate act of committing one's self to the person of Jesus Christ. It's not a "hanging on" to some vague idea. It is an act of trust in the God-Man, Jesus Christ.

The New Testament never used the words *belief* and *faith* in the plural. Christian faith does not mean accepting a long list of dos and don'ts. It means a single, individual relinquishment of mind and heart toward the one person, Jesus Christ. It does not mean believing everything or just anything. It is belief in a person, and that person is the Christ described in Scripture.

Faith is not anti-intellectual. Faith involves a very logical premise—that is, trusting that God's superior ability is able to save us.

Francis Schaeffer, a brilliant Christian living in Switzerland, explains that faith is not only logical, but that lack of faith is illogical. He writes: "Man is made in the image of God; therefore, on the side of the fact that God is a personal God the chasm stands not between God and man, but between man and all else. But on the side of God's infinity, man is as separated from God as the atom or any other finite [object] of the universe. So we have the answer to man's being finite and yet personal.

"It is not that this is the best answer to existence; it is the *only* answer. That is why we may hold our Christianity with intellectual integrity. The only answer for what exists is that he, the infinite-personal God, really is there."[2]

Faith in Christ is also voluntary. A person cannot be coerced, bribed, or tricked into trusting Jesus. God will not force His way into your life. The Holy Spirit will do everything possible to disturb you, draw you, love you—but finally it is your personal decision. God not only gave His Son on the cross where the plan of redemption was finished: He gave the law as expressed in the Ten Commandments and the Sermon on the Mount to show you your need of forgiveness; He gave the Holy Spirit to convict you of your need. He gives the Holy Spirit to draw you to the cross, but even after all of this, it is your decision whether to accept God's free pardon or to continue in your lost condition.

Faith also involves the whole person. In his book *Knowing God*,

J. I. Packer says, "Knowing God is a matter of *personal involvement*, in mind, will, and feeling. It would not, indeed, be a fully personal relationship otherwise."[3]

So faith is not just an emotional reaction, an intellectual realization, or a willful decision; faith is all-inclusive. It involves the intellect, the emotion, and the will.

STEPS LEADING TO CONVERSION

We have seen that conversion occurs when we repent and place our faith in Christ. But what is the process like as we approach the point of conversion? How long will it take? Will it be emotional or dramatic? My answer is, I don't know. If everyone had the same reaction we could apply a neat little chemical formula with predetermined results. The key word is *variety*.

We can see this clearly if we stop for a moment to reflect on God. First, the point we are heading for is a point where God Himself is going to do something; He is the one who converts us when we repent and believe in Christ. "Salvation is of the Lord." Second, His help starts coming long before that point. As we have already seen, during the time before conversion He is preparing us for repentance by the conviction of the Holy Spirit and by making us want to turn from our sins. Also He is preparing us for faith by showing us how forgiving and majestic Christ is.

Questions about length of time and amount of emotion in the conversion process, consequently, are very personal. God looks at each of us differently, because each of us is different. He will relate to you just as you are. He will relate to me just as I am. Of course, in His concern His goal for each of us will be the same—our new birth. But to help us to that point He will be just as personal as a shepherd who knows each of his sheep by name.

We could go to the experiences of people we know, or to your own experience. If you have not been born again, the very fact that you are reading this book right now may be the process God is using in your life to lead you toward a decision.

God knows the needs of your heart. When we look at the process He used with different people in the Bible prior to their conversion, we see that He understands their individuality. In John 1, for instance, He talked to several men who had not yet been converted. On being approached by Andrew and a friend, Jesus asked a question, "What do you seek?" (John 1:38) and then invited them to spend the day with Him where He was staying. Quiet conversation was Andrew's need if he was to gain a sense of his sin and a trust in Jesus.

Andrew brought along his erratic brother, Simon. Christ acted very differently toward him. Regarding him seriously, Jesus said, "You are Simon the son of John; you shall be called 'Cephas' (which translated means Peter)," the word for *rock*. Jesus revealed a flash of His majesty by telling this volatile young man that in trusting Him his character would be changed to a rocklike steadiness (John 1:42). To be converted Peter needed to see his sin of relying on himself, which made him such a changeable personality, and he needed to trust Christ as the one who had the power and concern to change him.

The next day Jesus found Philip and treated him in still another way. He simply said, "Follow Me" (John 1:43). Unlike Andrew or

Peter, Philip needed a straightforward command. Philip then brought Nathanael, a very religious man of prayer who was seeking an experience with God. Jesus adapted to his special needs in John 1:51, saying, "Truly, truly, I say to you, you will see the heavens opened, and the angels of God ascending and descending upon the Son of Man."

Andrew, Peter, Philip, and Nathanael were all different. So Jesus treated them all differently. They all needed a personal relationship with Christ. This is essentially what the new birth is. To some of them the realization of what was happening came slowly. It took months of training by Jesus Himself. This is why I urge new converts to take plenty of time in Bible study and prayer before getting on a public platform to testify. The Scripture warns against "a novice." We have often unwittingly been guilty of this in our crusades—putting up to give a testimony young converts who had really not grown in the grace and knowledge of Christ enough. Through long years of experience we have become far more careful.

After the conversion of the apostle Paul he took three years of study in Arabia. It took God forty years to train Moses on the back side of a desert before he made his public appearance. In these days we often hear of a person who is in jail one day, and a few weeks later is on a public platform testifying concerning his conversion before a large crowd. Sometimes this is followed by a great tragedy—the so-called new convert had really not been born again; he had only professed Christ but had not been willing to pay the price of following Christ.

I know a young man who seemed to be gloriously converted in

one of our crusades, and I believe he was. He did have a rather long period of getting over his drug habit and growing in the knowledge of the Scriptures. We urged him to attend a Bible school, which he did for a year. His testimony was so thrilling that the invitations began to pour in from across America for him to give his witness. It wasn't long before this attention had caused him to backslide terribly, to the point of even leaving his wife and family. I am glad to report that he has been restored to fellowship with God, realizes his sins and mistakes, and is now going back to finish his studies.

What can we expect the process to be like as we approach the new birth? It will be tailored to our own environment, temperament, secret needs, and hopes. That is the way God works.

HOW LONG ARE THE STEPS?

The length of time and degree of emotion involved in the process which leads to our conversion is also varied. Some, but not all, will face an emotional crisis with symptoms similar to those accompanying mental conflict. They may experience deep feelings and even tears of repentance. The Holy Spirit is convicting them of sin. This is their way of responding to Him. Each of us may have a different emotional experience. The night I came to Christ there were several people around me weeping. I had no tears at all and wondered if my act of commitment was genuine.

I have learned since that many have had a much quieter conversion, with a shorter time in the process. Perhaps one person, reading the Scripture or singing a hymn, comes upon a simple statement and applies it to himself then and there. Another person hears a sermon and with no stress or conflict receives its message and believes in Christ. Conversion is no less real to these quiet people than to the more expressive or dramatic ones.

Acts 16 records two conversions which were striking contrasts. Lydia was a businesswoman in the city of Philippi. She had shown enough interest in God to be spending time in prayer by the side of a river, where she heard Paul preach. The Lord opened her heart to respond to the gospel message, and she was converted without fanfare or a strong emotional display.

Then there was the jailer in the city of Philippi where Paul was imprisoned. An earthquake came and the jailer panicked as he realized his prisoners could escape. He thought the only way out of his crisis was to kill himself. Just as he was drawing his sword he heard the apostle Paul say, "Do not harm yourself, for we are all here!" (Acts 16:28).

The jailer couldn't believe what he heard! Why hadn't the prisoners escaped? He was shaking from head to foot, and called for a light. He took one look at Paul and Silas, his prisoners, and fell down at their feet, crying, "What must I do to be saved?" Paul told him to believe in the Lord Jesus Christ and he would be saved, and he was converted right there, in the rubble of the prison.

Jesus described the conversion experience like the movement of the wind. "The wind blows where it wishes and you hear the sound of it, but do not know where it comes from and where it is going; so is everyone who is born of the Spirit" (John 3:8).

Wind can be quiet and gentle, or it can reach cyclone proportions. So it is with conversion, sometimes easy and tender, and other times a tornado which alters the entire landscape.

Is there one definite point in time, one hour of one day of one year when a person can say, "That was when I was born again"? I know many people who can point to that time and say with assurance, "That was my spiritual birthday." However, I know there are people who today are walking in fellowship with Jesus Christ, but have no memory of an exact time when they deliberately committed themselves to Him, and cannot remember when they did not love and trust Him. My wife is one of those great Christians in this category. However, it is my opinion that they may be the exception rather than the rule. Scripture teaches that belief is an act of the will, so whether they can remember the time or not, there was a moment when they crossed over the line from death to life.

Nevertheless, the issue for a person now is not so much "when" as "whether." When we were saved is not so important as whether we are now saved. We often cannot tell the exact moment when night becomes day, but we know when it is daylight. So the great question for a person to answer who has never by a conscious act of will committed himself to Christ as his Lord and Savior is this: "Are you now living in the day, in touch with Christ?"

HOW TO RECEIVE CHRIST

Just after I received Christ someone gave me a little tract entitled "Four Things God Wants You to Know," by an English writer. I often used those four points in my earlier preaching, and they were excellent. Years later, Bill Bright of Campus Crusade developed "The Four Spiritual Laws," which have been widely used throughout the world in helping people to understand how to be born again. Our own organization developed what we called "Four Steps to Peace with God," taken largely from one of my earlier books, *Peace with God*. I do not believe, however, that there is a tidy little formula, or a recipe which has the Good Housekeeping Seal of approval. However, I do believe these have provided little handles which help people to understand how to receive Christ.

Here are some guidelines from the Bible which will help you accept Christ as your Lord and Savior. You have seen the need, the direction, and the steps in previous chapters, and you may already have reached your own conclusions. Just the same let me summarize what you must do.

First, you must recognize what God did: that He loved you so much He gave His Son to die on the cross. Substitute your own name for "the world" and "whoever" in this familiar verse: "For God so loved the world, that He gave His only begotten Son, that whoever believes in Him should not perish, but have eternal life" (John 3:16). "The Son of God . . . loved me and gave Himself up for me" (Gal. 2:20).

Second, you must repent of your sins. Jesus said, "Unless you repent, you will . . . perish" (Luke 13:3). He said, "Repent and believe" (Mark 1:15). It's not enough to be sorry; repentance is that turnabout from sin that is emphasized.

Third, you must receive Jesus Christ as Savior and Lord. "But as many as received Him, to them He gave the right to become children of God, even to those who believe in His name" (John 1:12). This means that you cease trying to save yourself and accept Christ as your only Lord and your only Savior. Trust Him completely, without reservation.

Fourth, you must confess Christ publicly. This confession is a sign that you have been converted. Jesus said, "Every one who confesses Me before men, I will also confess him before My Father who is in heaven" (Matt. 10:32). It is extremely important that when you receive Christ you tell someone else about it just as soon as possible. This gives you strength and courage to witness.

Make it happen *now.* "Now is the accepted time . . . now is the day of salvation" (2 Cor. 6:2, KJV). If you are willing to repent of your sins and to receive Jesus Christ as your Lord and Savior, you can do it now. At this moment you can either bow your head or get on your knees and say this little prayer which I have used with thousands of persons on every continent:

O God, I acknowledge that I have sinned against you. I am sorry for my sins. I am willing to turn from my sins. I openly receive and acknowledge Jesus Christ as my Savior. I confess Him as Lord. From this moment on I want to live for Him and serve Him. In Jesus' name. Amen.

These are the steps and the prayer which many years ago, in a book I wrote, were read by people just like yourself who responded and wrote of their changed lives.

If you are willing to make this decision and have received Jesus Christ as your own Lord and Savior, then you have become a child of God in whom Jesus Christ dwells. You do not need to measure the certainty of your salvation by your feelings. Believe God. He keeps His word. You are born again. You are alive!

If you would like more help and literature, please feel free to contact the Billy Graham Evangelistic association:

1 Billy Graham Parkway
Charlotte, NC 28201
Phone: (704) 401-2432 or
toll free at (877) 247-2426

13

ALIVE AND GROWING

After thinking about it for three days, I realized I needed Jesus Christ, and I accepted Him. Now that my life has been turned over to Jesus Christ, I can function with an extra power bestowed by God."

Who made a statement like that? Someone down on the bottom of life's heap, struggling for worth and identity? No. A handsome young University of Southern California athlete, John Naber, who gained international attention by earning four gold medals with his swimming achievements in the 1976 Olympics. Naber said he was searching for something meaningful in his life and after attending one of our meetings he began to wake up to the realization of Jesus Christ. He was born again.

More and more celebrities, especially in the sports,

entertainment, and political worlds, are telling of their new experiences of being made alive in Christ. While it is thrilling to hear about it, there are also dangers (as I have already expressed) in a "novice" who has very little grounding in the Word of God. Yet I cannot help rejoicing in every one of them and believe that God has been moving mightily in reaching out for people of extraordinary gifts and talents all over the world. Many of them He is greatly using to win others to Christ. A newspaper feature said that "Evidence of a current religious revival is everywhere," and then related how famous personalities were "pinpointing the exact moment of spiritual turn-around" with their "often unbelievable accounts of being born again. Some say they have met Jesus Christ. Others experience a sensation similar to an electric shock. In all cases the new believers experience overwhelming feelings of love and joy."

Dean Jones, a Walt Disney film veteran, relates, "I was performing in summer stock at a New Jersey lodge and had gone to my room to be alone. Nothing was satisfying me. I looked out that window and felt fear and confusion. Impulsively, I knelt by the bed and spelled out my doubts to God; I don't know why I was moved to do this. I said to God, 'If You bring meaning to my life, I'll serve You.'"

There is nothing more exciting than a personal testimony from a person who has experienced a spiritual rebirth. This is more than an interesting story or fascinating experience. A newborn man or woman has been given so many riches by God. We will outline them and then discuss how to draw from that wealthy potential.

FORGIVEN!

"Your sins have been forgiven you for His name's sake" (1 John 2:12). What a stupendous promise! Throughout the New Testament we learn that the one who receives Christ as Lord and Savior also receives, immediately, the gift of forgiveness. The Bible says, "As far as the east is from the west, so far has He removed our transgressions from us" (Ps. 103:12).

"Forgive me." "I'm sorry." "I didn't mean it." How often we use those words and they echo back with a hollow sound. But God's forgiveness is not just a casual statement; it is the complete blotting out of all the dirt and degradation of our past, present, and future. The only reason our sins can be forgiven is because Jesus Christ paid their full penalty on the cross.

Guilt feelings provide the basis for many dramatic plots. Shakespeare's line from *Macbeth* is famous: "Out, damned spot! Out!" Guilt feelings are the focal point of much psychiatric counseling. Many feel like Judas, who, after he betrayed Christ, said, "I have betrayed innocent blood." So tremendous is the weight of our guilt that the great and glorious concept of forgiveness should be shouted by every believer in Jesus Christ.

God's goodness in forgiving us goes even farther when we realize that when we are converted we are also declared just—which means that in God's sight we are without guilt, clothed forever with Christ's righteousness.

As we saw in "The King's Courtroom," forgiveness and justification are God's free gifts.

ADOPTED BY THE KING

When you were converted, God adopted you as His son or daughter. As an adopted child each of us can claim to be a joint heir with Jesus Christ. "God sent forth His Son . . . that He might redeem those who were under the Law, that we might receive the adoption as sons" (Gal. 4:4–5).

I know a lawyer and his wife who have two adopted children, a boy and a girl. The little girl looks very much like her mother, and the young man could easily be the natural son of his father. The fact that they were chosen by their parents has given them a great sense of security and love.

To be the son or daughter of the Lord of the universe is a powerful realization.

THE INDWELLING HOLY SPIRIT

When you were converted, the Spirit of God immediately came to live in you. Before He ascended into heaven, Jesus Christ said, "I will ask the Father, and He will give you another Helper, that He may be with you forever; that is the Spirit of truth . . . you know Him because He abides with you and will be in you (John 14:16–17).

When Christ lived on this earth, He could be with only a small group of people at any one time. Now Christ dwells through the Holy Spirit in the hearts of all those who have received Him as Lord and Savior. Lloyd Ogilvie, pastor of the First Presbyterian Church in Hollywood, refers to the Holy Spirit as "the contemporary Christ." Paul wrote to the Romans, "He [God] will also give life to your mortal bodies through His Spirit who dwells in you" (Rom. 8:11).

At the historic Congress on World Evangelization in Switzerland in 1974, the Holy Spirit was the subject of many addresses and discussions. The Reverend Gottfried Osei-Mensah of Nairobi, Kenya, said, "The Spirit is our Master. It is the work of the Holy Spirit, living in us, to free us from the rule of sin in our daily lives, and to help us live the new life we share with Christ."

How long does the Holy Spirit live in the heart of a believer? Forever. God does not give a gift as powerful as the Holy Spirit and then take it back. By faith you accept God's statements that you are indwelt by the Spirit of God, but you can watch Him at work, too. The Holy Spirit can rejuvenate a tired Christian, captivate an indifferent believer, and empower a dry church.

A clergyman from Buenos Aires, Argentina, said, "The Holy Spirit today is renewing the fruit of the Spirit—love, joy, peace. All those things are going to be the elements that show the world that we are His people."

The Holy Spirit is there to give you special power to work for Christ. He is there to give you strength in the moment of temptation.

Jesus promised that we would receive power from the Holy Spirit (Acts 1:8). Perhaps you have heard the story of the woodpecker who was pecking with his beak against the trunk of a tree. At that very moment, the lightning struck the tree, splitting it from top to bottom. When he'd recovered from the shock, the woodpecker flew away exclaiming, "I didn't know there was so much power in my beak!" I don't ask you, have you the Holy Spirit, but does the Holy Spirit have you?

VICTORY OVER TEMPTATION

The Bible teaches that the new believer in Jesus Christ—the converted person—is to "abhor what is evil" (Rom. 12:9). Here is another strong admonishment, "in reference to your former manner of life, you lay aside the old self, which is being corrupted in accordance with the lusts of deceit" (Eph. 4:22).

Now wait a minute. How are we supposed to be able to stop doing some of the sinful things we have done for years, or get rid of some of the negative, suspicious, hateful, greedy attitudes which are ingrained in our personality? "I just can't do it myself," you might say.

You're right. However, the capacity to resist sin and obey God comes from the Holy Spirit, who lives in every true believer. It's not up to us to struggle against temptation alone. God lives in our hearts to help us resist sin. It is His job to work and our job to yield.

What about the old bugaboo of temptation? The Bible doesn't say we won't be tempted; that would be foolish. We know that we live in a world full of temptations, most of them tied up in very attractive packages and offered as something we must try or buy— just once! But the converted man or woman has the offer of victory over temptation. "No temptation has overtaken you but such as is common to man; and God is faithful, who will not allow you to be tempted beyond what you are able, but with the temptation will provide the way of escape also, so that you will be able to endure it" (1 Cor. 10:13).

To be tempted is not a sin; as a believer in Jesus Christ you do not need to blame yourself for an increase in the temptations that surround you. The indwelling Holy Spirit gives us strength to resist temptation.

Temptation is very powerful and will become even more so after you have been born again. The Scriptures tell us that we are in a spiritual warfare and that our enemies have more power and skill to tempt us than we have ever encountered before. Here is where many new believers make a big mistake. They think that when they are converted they will become perfect right away, that they will live on a continual high. Then they find themselves being tempted, in conflict, and even at times yielding to temptation. The new believer takes a look at himself and doesn't like what he sees. He is filled with discouragement and frustration. This is normal. The devil tempts you and God tests you. Often they are two sides to the same coin—God allows the devil to tempt you, and He uses it as a test, or as an experience to help deepen your faith and let you see how fragile you really are if you depend on yourself. He wants you to depend totally and completely on Him.

An old allegory illustrates this well: "Satan called together a council of his servants to consult how they might make a good man sin. One evil spirit started up and said, 'I will make him sin.'—'How will you do it?' asked Satan. 'I will set before him the pleasures of sin,' was the reply; 'I will tell him of its delights, and the rich rewards it brings.'—'Ah,' said Satan, 'that will not do; he has tried it, and knows better than that.' Then another imp started up and said, 'I will make him sin.'—'What will you do?' asked Satan. 'I will tell him of the pains and sorrows of virtue. I will show him that virtue has no delights, and brings no rewards.'—'Ah, no!' exclaimed Satan, 'that will not do at all; for he has tried it, and knows that "Wisdom's ways *are* ways of pleasantness, and all her paths are peace."'—'Well,' said another imp, starting up, 'I will undertake to make him sin.'—'And what will you do?' asked Satan, again. 'I will discourage his soul,' was the short reply. 'Ah, that will do!' cried Satan; 'That will do! We shall conquer him now.'"[1]

Spiritual conflict is at work in the heart of every believer. It is true that the Christian possesses a new nature, but the old sin nature is still there. It is now up to us, day by day, to yield to the new nature which Christ dominates.

There is the story of a housewife who found a mouse in her kitchen and took a broom to it. The mouse didn't waste its time contemplating either the housewife or the broom, but got busy looking for the hole. And so it is with us when we are caught by temptation. We don't spend time contemplating the temptation but get busy looking for a way out. The Scripture says, "God . . . will not allow you to be tempted beyond what you are able, but with the temptation will provide the way of escape also" (1 Cor. 10:13).

When the Christian sins he is miserable. Sometimes he avoids other Christians, stops going to church, believes that he is misunderstood. However, every Christian has access to God through prayer, and when he confesses his sin, God restores fellowship with him. This is the difference between the believer and the unbeliever. The unbeliever makes sin a practice; the believer does not.

A word about how believers should treat a "fallen" brother:

Some years ago we knew a young college student recently converted from a life of drugs. Shortly after his conversion he agreed to turn informer for a narcotics agent in order to try to catch the pushers in that area. Fellow Christians warned him against doing this, but he had already committed himself and the inevitable happened. He blew his Christian witness when he had to pretend to be a drug user himself in order to convince the pusher that he was for real, at one point having to take two shots of heroin. (Incidentally, the shots had an effect on him opposite to that before his conversion—instead of getting high he had violent withdrawals.) The Sunday before he left the school to return to his home, he stood up before the Sunday school class to tell them what had happened. The pusher had been caught, and although this young man had blown his Christian witness, he wanted the students to know that he was still a believer and a follower of the Lord. He stood up before the class, holding two fingers together to explain, "Me and Jesus are just like this." This gave the teacher an opportunity to talk to the students on how a brother should be treated when he has apparently fallen. During the time when he was trying to assist the narcotics agent, all the Christians on campus thought he had backslidden and gave him the cold shoulder. Actually, when we see a brother fall (or one whom we think has fallen), we should, like the Good Samaritan, get down and help him up again and do what we can to encourage him, pray for him, and let him know that we love him and believe in him.

The believer hates sin and wants to abide by God's commands. Paul says believers "do not walk according to the flesh but according to the Spirit" (Rom. 8:4). The Holy Spirit who indwells us convicts us in various ways. A believer will begin to realize that the dirty jokes which were once a part of his office repertoire are sticking in his throat. The cocktail parties which were once so interesting and funny have become dull and boring. Ruth and I have sometimes gone to cocktail parties in various parts of the world. Always we have taken a soft drink and tried to be a witness. The first convert of the New York crusade was a direct result of my going to a cocktail party like this on board a ship coming from Japan in the early 1950s. Such occasions may afford a great opportunity for Christian witness. We have often had a whole group of people gather around us and ask spiritual questions. In this same way Jesus talked with publicans and sinners, and for a clear purpose. On the other hand, going to cocktail parties just to be one of the gang not only often becomes boring, but carries the painful risk of hearing someone swear and take the name of the Lord in vain.

The choices of a new believer are made from a new perspective. He may hand himself over to sin (and feel miserable in it) or give himself over to God. Paul's advice is excellent: "I urge you, brethren, by the mercies of God, to present your bodies a living and holy sacrifice, acceptable to God, which is your spiritual service of worship. And do not be conformed to this world, but be transformed by the renewing of your mind, so that you may prove what the will of God is, that which is good and acceptable and perfect" (Rom. 12:1–2).

The transformation by the "renewing of your mind" may happen quickly and dramatically, as the addict who experiences instant withdrawal, or it may permeate into your lifestyle more gradually.

GROWING SLOWLY,
ALMOST IMPERCEPTIBLY—BUT GROWING!

Many people grow into Christian maturity very rapidly; others much more slowly, almost imperceptibly. I once saw a picture on television of flowers growing, budding, and opening. This was done by slow-motion photography over a long period of time. If you had watched the same process with your naked eye in your garden it would have taken days. In the same way, we watch our lives from day to day and often get discouraged at the slow growth. But if you wait for a year or two and then look back over your life you will see how much you have grown. You've become kinder, more gracious, more loving. You love the Scriptures more. You love to pray more. You are a more faithful witness. You never will reach that point of full maturity in Christ until you see Him face to face in heaven.

Abrupt or gradual, the changes in a converted person are a part of his growth. He is not reborn full-grown; rather he is reborn with the energies of a new life that will mature him as time passes. This growth is spiritual and moral. It's just like a baby learning to crawl, then toddle, then walk, then run. It takes time, study, patience, and discipline.

A person can attempt to imitate Christian growth by religious effort, but the result is like a plaster of Paris model of Michelangelo's David. It's phony and easily broken.

A Christian grows as the life of God exerts its new power from deep in the center of his personality. The unconverted person cannot duplicate that life, no matter how religious he tries to act. He lacks the sources for growth because he has not been reborn.

A group of students at Harvard once tried to fool the famous professor of zoology Agassiz. They took parts from a number of different bugs and with great skill attached them together to make a creation they were sure would baffle their teacher. On the chosen day they brought it to him and asked that he identify it. As he inspected it with great care, the students grew more and more sure they had tricked this genius.

Finally, Professor Agassiz straightened up and said, "I have identified it." Scarcely able to control their amusement, they asked its name. Agassiz replied, "It is a humbug."

A person with genuine life from God will detect the counterfeit and think, *Humbug*.

The new convert is a babe in Christ. A babe must be nourished in order to grow. He must be protected because he has been born into a world of many enemies. His primary battle will be with "the world," "the flesh," and "the devil." This is why he needs the encouragement of his family, Christian friends, and especially the Church. At the time of birth the child of God is born into great riches, and has a marvelous inheritance, but it takes some time to find out about all his wealth.

The most important thing in the beginning of new life is to be nourished and strengthened. Here are the important nutrients to use.

GET A BIBLE

If you have a Bible, fine. If the Scriptures are a whole new world to you, however, I would advise that you get one of the newer translations which may be easier for you to understand. It is important for you to begin reading the New Testament, and the Gospel of John is a good place to start.

Saturate yourself in the Word of God. Don't worry about understanding everything you read, because you won't. Pray before you read and ask the Holy Spirit to clarify what you are reading. The Scriptures are the greatest source of hope you will find in this hopeless world. "For whatever was written in earlier times was written for our instruction, so that through perseverance and the encouragement of the Scriptures we might have hope" (Rom. 15:4).

Memorize portions of the Word of God. "Thy word have I hid in mine heart, that I might not sin against thee" (Ps. 119:11, KJV). Try taking a Bible verse that speaks to your needs and typing it on a file card. Put it in your pocket or purse and refer to it frequently. Review it daily, and by the end of the week you will have a verse memorized.

Satan is the great discourager. He doesn't want you to read the Bible or memorize Scripture. In the past you may not have been attacked by Satan, but now you've done something which makes him very angry. You've left his camp and joined the army of God. You're a Christian soldier and Satan will unleash all of his secret weapons. From now on it's upstream all the way against the current of the evils of this world.

But you can overcome everything he hurls at you with the weapon God has provided—"the sword of the Spirit, which is the word of God" (Eph. 6:17). Not only is the Word of God a sword to be used in offense, but you also have a shield to be used in defense. You have "the shield of faith, wherewith ye shall be able to quench all the fiery darts of the wicked" (Eph. 6:16, KJV).

When Christ was in the wilderness He was tempted by Satan, and every time he met temptation with Scripture, saying, "It is written" (Matt. 4).

Christ needed this mighty weapon and so do we.

LEARN TO PRAY

There are complete books written about prayer, seminars held which deal in prayer, and hundreds of sermons on the power of prayer. The new believer is sometimes baffled by what and how to pray.

The Bible says, "Men ought always to pray" (Luke 18:1, KJV). The apostle Paul said, "Pray without ceasing" (1 Thess. 5:17).

A prayer does not have to be eloquent or contain the language and terms of a theologian. When you made your decision for Christ, you were given the privilege of addressing God as Father. You pray to Him as a child talking to his loving and gracious father. In the beginning you may not be fluent, but it's important to begin. My wife has a notebook she has kept of our children as they were beginning to talk with us. She treasures these first attempts, mistakes and all. She said, "I wouldn't take anything for that book."

When Paul said we should pray without "ceasing," he chose a term used in his day to describe a persistent cough. Off and on, throughout our day we should be turning quickly to God to praise and thank Him, and to ask for His help. Prayers should be specific. God is interested in everything you do and nothing is too great or too insignificant to share with Him.

FIND CHRISTIAN FELLOWSHIP

God doesn't intend for you to live the Christian life alone. This is why He has brought other believers together to form fellowships. A church where the Bible is taught and believed is the first place a reborn man or woman must seek. I do not advise that just any church will do. Is the pastor teaching the Word of God or expounding his own or some other philosophy of living? You'll know. Does the church have Bible classes for all ages?

Without the fellowship of believers, a newly born Christian has a tendency to wither. The writer of the book of Hebrews says, "Let us consider how to stimulate one another to love and good deeds, not forsaking our own assembling together, as is the habit of some, but encouraging one another" (Heb. 10:24–25).

Perhaps there's a Bible class or prayer group in your community. It's exciting to find a whole new set of friends, people who are in various stages of their own Christian growth, to share with and strengthen your faith.

One of my daughters lives in a high middle-class neighborhood. Some of the social leaders of the city are her neighbors. After a great deal of prayer she decided that she would go to her neighbors' houses and ask them if they would like to have a Bible study. She knocked on the door of house after house, and in almost every instance the women not only said "yes," but some of them burst into tears and said, "I've been waiting for someone to ask me to a

Bible class so I could learn the Bible." Today, my daughter teaches a weekly Bible class of three hundred women, with many on the waiting list to get in. If there's not a Bible class in your community, perhaps you could start one. You will find your neighbors "hungrier" and "thirstier" than you had ever dreamed. They are just waiting for someone to take the initiative. At first it may be that only two or three of you will meet, read a passage in the Bible, discuss it, and have prayer over a cup of coffee. There are tens of thousands of such Bible classes springing up throughout the world in homes, in offices, in professional football teams. Even the touring golf professionals have a weekly Bible class that attracts anywhere from ten to fifty of the golfers and their wives.

You are no longer alone. The fatherhood of God forms the true brotherhood of man, an ideal which the philosophers and moralists have sought from the beginning of time. This brotherhood erases barriers of language, cultural background, and race. One of the greatest joys a Christian experiences is that of meeting a fellow believer in an unexpected place. The waitress in the restaurant finds a common bond with her customer. The passenger on an airplane discovers that the stewardess is a believer. You are in a foreign country and immediately feel at home when you encounter another Christian. No lengthy introductions are necessary. You share the greatest bond on earth. There is no fellowship on earth to compare with it.

At the beginning of this book I said that I believed the most important subject in the entire world is that of the new birth. It is the most important event which can happen to any man, woman, or child.

ALIVE AND GROWING

It is only when you are born again that you can experience all the riches God has in store for you. You are not just a living person, you are truly ALIVE!

NOTES

PREFACE

1. Corrie ten Boom, *In My Father's House* (Old Tappan, N.J.: Fleming Revell Publishing Co., 1976), p. 24.
2. *Los Angeles Times*, September 23, 1976, pp. 3, 30.
3. *Time*, September 27, 1976, p. 86.

CHAPTER ONE

1. Charles Colson, *Born Again* (Old Tappan, N.J.: Chosen Books, 1976), p. 110.
2. Bertrand Russell, *Power: A New Social Analysis* (New York: Norton, 1938), p. 11.
3. H. R. Rookmaaker, *Modern Art and the Death of a Culture* (London: Inter-Varsity Press, 1970), p. 196.
4. Ibid., p. 202.
5. Os Guinness, *Dust of Death* (Downers Grove, Ill.: Inter-Varsity Press, 1973), p. 233.
6. Hal Lindsey, *The Terminal Generation* (Old Tappan, N.J.: Fleming H. Revell Co., 1976), p. 83.
7. Rookmaaker, *Modern Art*, p. 233.
8. Guinness, *Dust of Death*, p. 392.

CHAPTER THREE

1. Josh McDowell, *Evidence That Demands a Verdict* (Campus Crusade for Christ, 1972), p. 17ff.

CHAPTER FOUR

1. Sir James Frazer, *The Golden Bough* (New York: Macmillan Co., 1960), p. 194.
2. Ibid., p. 196.
3. Walter Kaufmann, *Critique of Religion and Philosophy* (New York: Harper and Row, 1958), p. 74.
4. Ibid., p. 88.
5. T.W. Doane, *Bible Myths* (New York: University Books, 1971), p. 252.
6. *Time*, December 30, 1974, p. 38.
7. Ibid., p. 40.

CHAPTER FIVE

1. *Time*, June 30, 1975, p. 10.
2. *Time*, February 2, 1976, p. 62.
3. William Barclay, *Letters to Timothy* (Philadelphia: Westminster Press, 1960), p. 44.

CHAPTER SIX

1. *Time*, February 7, 1977, p. 37.

CHAPTER SEVEN

1. Josh McDowell, *Evidence That Demands a Verdict* (Campus Crusade for Christ, 1972), p. 89.
2. Harry Rimmer, *The Magnificence of Jesus Christ* (Grand Rapids, Mich.: Wm. B. Eerdmans Publishing Co., 1943), p. 112.
3. C. S. Lewis, *Surprised by Joy* (New York: Harcourt, Brace & World, 1955), pp. 228ff.

CHAPTER NINE

1. Nicolaus von Zinzendorf, 1739, tr. John Wesley, 1940.
2. *Saturday Evening Post*, September 1, 1951, p. 19.

CHAPTER TEN

1. Josh McDowell, *Evidence That Demands a Verdict* (Campus Crusade for Christ, 1972), p. 193.
2. Ibid., p. 233.

CHAPTER ELEVEN

1. *Time*, December 13, 1976, p. 93.
2. Ibid., E-3, p. 94.
3. Thomas Harris, *I'm OK—You're OK* (New York: Harper & Row, 1967), p. 229.
4. Sergiu Grossu, *The Church in Today's Catacombs* (New Rochelle, N.Y.: Arlington House Publishers, 1975), p. 43.
5. Ostrander and Schroeder, *Psychic Discoveries Behind the Iron Curtain* (Englewood Cliffs, N.J.: Prentice-Hall, 1970), pp. 151ff.
6. John Hunter, *Impact* (Glendale, Calif.: Regal Books, 1966), pp. 45, 46.
7. Oswald Chambers, *My Utmost for His Highest* (New York: Dodd Mead & Company, 1946), p. 10.

CHAPTER TWELVE

1. Hannah Whitall Smith, *The Christian's Secret of a Happy Life* (London: Nisbet and Co., Ltd., 1945), p. 88.
2. Francis A. Schaeffer, *He Is There and He Is Not Silent*, (Wheaton, Ill.: Tyndale House, 1972), p. 15.
3. J. I. Packer, *Knowing God* (Downers Grove, Ill.: Inter-Varsity Press, 1973), p. 35.

CHAPTER THIRTEEN

1. Hannah Whitall Smith, *The Christian's Secret of a Happy Life*, p. 133.

HOW TO USE THIS BOOK

The questions and exercises in this study guide are designed for individual study which will in turn lead to group interaction. Thus, they may be used either as a guide for individual meditation or group discussion. During your first group meeting we suggest that you set aside a few minutes at the outset in which individual group members introduce themselves and share a little about their personal pilgrimage of faith.

If possible, it is a good idea to rotate leadership responsibility among the group members. However, if one individual is particularly gifted as a discussion leader, elect or appoint that person to guide the discussions each week. Remember, the leader's responsibility is simply to guide the discussion and stimulate interaction. He or she should never dominate the proceedings. Rather, the leader should encourage all members of the group to participate, expressing their individual views. He or she should seek to keep the discussion on track, but encourage lively discussion.

If one of the purposes of your group meeting is to create a caring community, it is a good idea to set aside some time for sharing individual concerns and prayer for one another. This can take the form of both silent and spoken petitions and praise.

1. WHY AM I SO EMPTY?

1. Do you agree with Mr. Graham's statement, "Today . . . much of the world in search of knowledge and fulfillment ignores God" (p. 4)?
2. What had become meaningless in Tom Phillips's life (p. 8)?
3. What did he discover was missing?
4. Discuss the questions listed in the second paragraph of p. 9.
5. Do you agree that man is desperately seeking for "peace" (p. 10)?
6. What is peace? Define and discuss.
7. Can you think of anything more important?

2. CAN ANYONE TELL ME WHERE TO FIND GOD?

1. Do you think the religion of "nationalism" is as prevalent as Mr. Graham suggests on p. 19?
2. Discuss the statement from Blaise Pascal on p. 20. Put it in your own words.

3. On p. 21 Mr. Graham says, "Faith is the link between God and man." Discuss the implications of that statement.
4. Using a concordance or topical Bible, explore the various facets of God's love.
5. In what ways are you aware of God's love right now?

3. DOES GOD REALLY SPEAK TO US?

1. Discuss the concept of "spiritual blindness" (pp. 27–28).
2. What are some of the ways in which it manifests itself?
3. What, for you, is the most compelling evidence of God's existence (see p. 30ff.)?
4. In what ways does God speak to you?
5. Which way is the most common?
6. What is your favorite Bible verse?

4. BUT I'M NOT RELIGIOUS!

1. Contrast the sacrifices of Cain and Abel (pp. 47–48).
2. Why was Abel's sacrifice accepted by God and not Cain's?
3. If Christianity is not a religion, what is it?
4. Answer the question on p. 52, "Can we really lump Christianity with every 'religion' of the world?" Discuss your answers.
5. Someone has said, "Everyone has a God-shaped vacuum in his life." Discuss in the light of Mr. Graham's comments on p. 52ff. under "Without Excuse."
6. Discuss "The Deceivers" listed on p. 58ff.

5. WHAT IS THIS THING CALLED SIN?

1. Where did sin originate?
2. Discuss our "terrible freedom" (p. 67).
3. Discuss the similarity between "sin" and the skater's fall on p. 69.
4. Read the letter from the girl that appears on p. 71. What does it reveal about her?
5. Reread the "X-rays" on pp. 72–75. Have you broken any of these "rules for living"—or all of them?

6. DOES GOD HAVE A CURE FOR SPIRITUAL DISEASE?

1. "Sin is like cancer" (p. 78). Discuss.
2. Read and discuss the first paragraph on p. 79.
3. Discuss our similarity to babies as we begin the Christian life.
4. Reread Dr. Wilson's statement on p. 85: "One of the greatest causes of mental illness is unresolved guilt. Feelings of shame, inadequacy, missing the mark, not measuring up, are some sources of guilt feelings. The answer to guilt is grace and new birth. The new birth leads to the forgiveness of sin." Discuss and apply.
5. Discuss Mr. Graham's statement on p. 88: " . . . it's not the heavy storms of life that erode us, but the insidious, gradual pollution of sin which leads to our destruction."
6. What are the three dimensions of death (pp. 89–93)?

7. THE MAN WHO IS GOD

1. "Jesus possessed a mental agility that has astounded scholars for two thousand years" (p. 100). Think about and discuss this aspect of Jesus' personality. What about His physical attributes in comparison to those around Him?
2. Read Matthew 23:25–26 in a more modern translation or paraphrase. Do you think Jesus was too frank in His appraisal? Where does frankness end and rudeness begin?
3. Have you ever had to forgive someone who had wronged you?
4. Do you need to extend forgiveness to someone even now?
5. Review and discuss the four attributes of God listed on pp. 104 through 106.
6. Review and discuss the three great "omnis" of Jesus (and God) listed on pp. 106 through 108.
7. Discuss the concluding statement in this chapter (p. 111): "It is simple. Jesus is God. Our earthly lives and eternal destinies depend on our belief in that fact."

8. WHAT HAPPENED AT THE CROSS

1. What does the cross of Jesus mean (p. 113)?
2. Reread the third paragraph on p. 115: "To an outsider the cross must appear . . . ridiculous. But to those who have experienced its transforming power, it has become the only remedy for the ills of each person, and of the world." In what ways is the cross "the only remedy"?

3. What happened at the cross?
4. What did the cross cost God?
5. Discuss the significance of and the reason for communion (p. 121).

9. THE KING'S COURTROOM

1. In the light of God's forgiveness to those who sin, how should we then live?
2. Are we really free to go on sinning?
3. Review and discuss the concept of "responsibility" Mr. Graham offers on p. 131.
4. Review and discuss the four conclusions Mr. Graham draws from his contemplation of the death of Christ beginning on p. 130.
5. Discuss the three questions at the end of this chapter:
   "Why can't I seem to solve my problems?"
   "I feel so guilty—how can I find relief?"
   "Do I have to understand all this about Christ's death?"
   Have you ever asked yourself these questions?

10. JESUS CHRIST IS ALIVE

1. What is the basis of our belief in Jesus Christ (p. 143)?
2. What are the implications of Wilbur Smith's statement at the bottom of p. 146: "Let it simply be said that we know more about the details of the hours immediately before, and the actual death of Jesus, in and near Jerusalem, than

we know about the death of any other man in all the ancient world"?

3. Review the three points Mr. Graham makes on pp. 146–148: Jesus was buried . . . the empty tomb . . . the bodily resurrection. What more do we need to know?

4. What does the Resurrection mean to us today?

11. The New Birth Is for Now

1. How can we change human nature?

2. Ultimately, how can we bring about change in society (p. 159)?

3. Evaluate John Hunter's statement on p. 164: "Nicodemus began by 'knowing,' but he continued by believing and receiving."

4. Mr. Graham says on p. 166: "The new birth is not just being reformed, it's being transformed." What does he mean by that? Put the concept in your own words.

5. On p. 169 the writer of the letter said: "He has made me new." Explore the implications of that statement.

12. The New Birth Is Not Just a Feeling

1. Read the "elephant" story on pp. 171 and 172. Do you think many people make the same mistake about the Christian life that this man did?

2. Define "repentance." Do you think many people today take this step in our modern fast-paced world?

3. Mr. Graham says that Jesus became "the cosmic scapegoat for the entire world" (p. 175). Explore the meaning of this definition.

4. What is the connection between "repentance" and "restitution"?

5. "Faith is first of all belief (in) Christ (p. 178) . . . faith in Christ is also voluntary" (p. 180). Explore the meaning of these definitions.

6. Faith is also experiential. Discuss that aspect.

7. Review the four steps on pp. 187 and 188.

13. ALIVE AND GROWING

1. Using a topical Bible or concordance, explore the various facets of forgiveness.

2. Discuss the "adoption" process as a picture of what happens when we join God's family.

3. How long does the Holy Spirit live in the heart of a believer? When does He start doing so?

4. What role does the Holy Spirit play in helping the believer overcome temptation?

5. What three vital steps does Mr. Graham recommend for "growing" Christians on p. 202ff.?